MW00761917

# ADVENTURE HOLIDAYS 1986

# ADVENTURE HOLIDAYS 1986

by
Simon Calder

Published by Vacation-Work
9 Park End Street, Oxford

First, second, third and eighth editions by David Stevens
published by Vacation-Work in 1978, 1979, 1980 and 1985
Fourth and seventh editions by Susan Griffith 1981 and 1984
Fifth and sixth editions by Gillian Nineham 1982 and 1983
Ninth edition 1986


ADVENTURE HOLIDAYS 1986
Copyright © 1986

No part of this publication may be reproduced or transmitted in any form
without the prior written permission of the publisher

ISBN 0 907638 50 3 (softback)
ISBN 0 907638 51 1 (hardback)
ISSN 0143-389 X


Distributed in the U.S.A. by
WRITER'S DIGEST BOOKS
9933 Alliance Road, Cincinnati, Ohio 45242


Distributed in Canada by
HENRY FLETCHER SERVICES LTD.
304 Taylor Road, West Hill, Ontario M1C 2R6


Cover photograph supplied by Exodus Expeditions


Printed by **Gibbons Barford Print,** Wolverhampton, England

# Contents

**Telephones.** Numbers in the United Kingdom — England, Scotland, Wales and Northern Ireland — are shown in the form (0123) 456789. The first part is the area or city code and the second part is the subscriber's number. When calling from outside the UK, dial the appropriate international access code — 011 from the USA and Canada — followed by the UK country code, 44, then the area code without the initial zero, and finally the subscriber's number. So to call the above number from the USA or Canada, dial 011 44 123 456789.

Numbers outside the UK are shown in the internationally accepted form (+123) 45-67890; the + represents the international access code (010 from Britain), 123 is the country code, 45 the area code and 67890 the subscriber's number. Note that if you are calling from within the same country, you should omit the country code and usually add a zero before the area code.

Linkline numbers (prefix 0345) can be dialled for the price of a local call from anywhere in the UK. Toll-free numbers (prefix 1-800) can be dialled free of charge from most places within the USA.

# Preface

The golden age of cheap travel which we are currently enjoying means that a fortnight on a Mediterranean beach is only a couple of hours and a few hundred pounds away. But as the amount of leisure time available to us increases, more and more holiday-makers are demanding something more interesting and challenging than the usual routine of beaches, beer and boogying — at least for part of their free time each year. While many still subscribe to the idea that the best form of relaxation is to do nothing for a fortnight, the more imaginative are deciding that a change is as good as a rest and are choosing a holiday-with-a-difference. You may not end up with such a deep suntan, but your muscles will be in better shape and you'll come back with a wealth of experience and memories.

This book is for anyone considering taking the plunge (often literally) and embarking on an adventure holiday. It is also for the cognoscenti who — having sampled canoeing in Cumbria — are ready for rafting the Colorado; for windsurfers who learnt on an inland reservoir and want to try out their skills on the Med; for hikers who want to swap the Pennine Way for Nepal. Hang-gliders, riders, divers and trekkers can take advantage of low air fares to fly off and enjoy their chosen pursuit almost anywhere in the world. **Adventure Holidays 1986** tells you what is available: when, where and how much. The choice is yours.

Simon Calder

Abbreviations for national and international Authorities, Associations, Clubs and Societies.

| | |
|---|---|
| ABRS | Association of British Riding Schools |
| ABTA | Association of British Travel Agents |
| AOPA | Aircraft Owners and Pilots Association |
| ASTA | American Society of Travel Agents |
| ATOL | Air Tour Operator's Licence |
| BAPC | British Association of Parachute Clubs |
| BCU | British Canoe Union |
| BGA | British Gliding Association |
| BHGA | British Hang Gliding Association |
| BHS | British Horse Society |
| BOF | British Orienteering Federation |
| BPA | British Parachute Association |
| BS-AC | British Sub Aqua Club |
| BSF | British Ski Federation |
| BTA | British Tourist Authority |
| ETB | English Tourist Board |
| FIYTO | Federation of International Youth Travel Organisations |
| IATA | International Air Traffic Association |
| IWS | International Windsurfer Schools |
| NFSS | National Federation of Sailing Schools |
| NSFGB | National Ski Federation of Great Britain |
| POB | Ponies of Britain |
| RYA | Royal Yachting Association |
| SAGTA | School and Group Travel Association |
| SSC | Scottish Sports Council |

Prices and other details in this book are as accurate as we have been able to determine but inevitably minor changes will occur.

# Multi Activity Holidays

The natural way to begin a directory of adventure holiday opportunities is by dealing with organisations which offer a variety of activities. These multi activity centres provide the chance to sample a very wide range of pursuits, and enable you to choose which to follow up at a later date.

Multi activity centres are a growth industry in Britain and abroad. Many are specifically arranged for young people of school age. The North American idea of sending youngsters off to a summer camp is catching on fast, and it seems likely that an annual visit to an activity centre will soon become the rule rather than the exception. See *Young People's Holidays* for the opportunities available.

Whether young or old, you can choose a multi activity centre which offers canoeing and climbing, windsurfing and waterskiing, and much more. Prices normally include all meals and accommodation, so the only extra expenses are for transport, pocket money and postcards. But most visitors are far too busy — or exhausted — to write home.

# England

**ACTIVITY CENTRE — SWANAGE**
**1 Harrow House, Harrow Drive, Swanage, Dorset BH19 1PE. Tel: (0929) 424421.**
Directors: C J B Hadingham, R a'Barrow. Residential accommodation with full board for groups of all ages and of all interests throughout the year. Sports facilities include five all weather tennis courts, tennis practice wall, tennis trainer, heated swimming pool, gymnasium, dance hall, darts/pool clubhouse, multi purpose sports dome and playing fields. Professional coaching available for most sports.

**ADVENTURE DAYS**
**The Waterfront Centre, Higher Wharf, Bude, Cornwall. Tel: (0288) 2493/2662.**
Partners: Paddy Frost, Keith Marshall.
Recognised by BCU, ETB, RYA.
Multi activity holidays throughout the year. Archery, abseiling, canoeing, climbing, BMX, cycling, surfing, sailing, land yachting, surf skiing and many more activities. Prices from around £91 per week all inclusive.
Hire of equipment and tuition also available on day-by-day basis.
"A stimulating package of outdoor pursuits conducted within a framework of safety."
Minimum age: 8 years.
Unaccompanied children: 12 years.

**BIRCHFIELD LODGE RESIDENTIAL CENTRE**
**Hope, near Sheffield S30 2RA. Tel: (0433) 20346.**
Operated by the Greater Manchester Youth Association, St Thomas Centre, Ardwick Green North, Manchester M12 6FZ. Tel: 061-273 7264.
Established 1908.
A variety of activity courses, intended mainly for groups of young people, but some also open to individuals and families. Monday-Friday and weekend courses throughout the week. Activities include climbing, caving, orienteering, walking and cross-country skiing (winter only). Prices: weekend £19-£36, five days £48-£90 inclusive.
Handicapped visitors catered for.
Minimum age: 8 years.
Book through: GMYA, St Thomas Centre.

**BOWLES OUTDOORS PURSUITS CENTRE (4)**
**Eridge Green, Tunbridge Wells TN3 9LW. Tel: (089 26) 4127.**

Educational Charitable Trust.
Owned by Bowles Rocks Trust Ltd.
Patron: HRH The Duke of Edinburgh.
In business since 1961.
Holidays for 2,600 arranged annually.
Adventure holidays including skiing, rock climbing, camping, orienteering, pony trekking and canoeing. Prices for weekend from £32, 7 days from £92 (plus VAT); full board and accommodation included. All equipment is provided. Specialist courses are also offered in each of the activities (see individual activity entries).
No experience needed.
Disabled students catered for.
Ages: 10-65 years.
Unaccompanied children welcome.

**CALSHOT ACTIVITIES CENTRE**
**Calshot Road, Calshot, Southampton SO4 1BR. Tel: (0703) 892077/891380.**
Administered by Hampshire County Council.
In business since 1966.
Recognised by: RYA, BCU, the Sports Council.

A SMALL, CARING, PROFESSIONAL CENTRE

* ROCK CLIMBING    * SKI-ING
* CANOEING    * SAILING
* PONY TREKKING    * CAMPING

Adventure holiday age range 10-16.
Specialist courses for adults also.
Full time staff. High standards of safety and instruction.
Special group rates available.
**Prices from £92 + VAT per week.**
including accommodation and instruction.
**BOWLES OUTDOOR CENTRE (4)**
**Eridge Green, Tunbridge Wells TN3 9LW**
**Crowborough (08926) 4127**

CALSHOT
ACTIVITIES CENTRE
Calshot Spit, Fawley, Southampton, SO4 1BR
Telephone: Fawley (0703) 892077

A Hampshire Education Committee Establishment

*Holiday Adventure and Watersports Courses*
Speciality Courses — Sailing, Canoeing and Windsurfing
*Week and Weekends*
Prices include Food, Accommodation, Instruction and Equipment
**Children from £80.00 per week**
*Courses For Young People From 10 Years.*
Special Group Rates
*Send For Your Brochure Today!*
**The Solent's Major Watersports Centre**

Holidays for 12,000 arranged annually. Sailing, canoeing, windsurfing, climbing, cycling, skiing, orienteering and riding courses for individuals and groups of 8-100. Weekends and weeks all year round. Price from around £80 for a child/teenager for a five day course including accommodation, food, use of equipment and instruction. Handicapped people catered for. No experience needed. Minimum age: 10 years. Unaccompanied children accepted.

## THE CALVERT TRUST ADVENTURE CENTRE FOR DISABLED PEOPLE
**Little Crosthwaite, Underskiddaw, Keswick, Cumbria CA12 4QD. Tel: (0596) 72254.**
In operation since 1978. Recognised by ETB, the Sports Council. Courses for over 1,000 arranged annually. Outdoor pursuits courses in sailing, canoeing, birdwatching, riding, climbing, fell-walking and wildlife in the Lake District National Park near Keswick. Weekend and weekly courses February-November. Accommodation in specially converted farmhouse with all possible facilities for disabled children and adults. Price of one week course is £121.90. Minimum age: 12 years. "This Centre gives disabled people an opportunity to discover, in safety, what they can do, and will help them to get as nearly as possible into the mainstream of life."

## CASTLE LEISURE PARK
**Sleaford Road, Tattershall, Lincs LN4 4LR. Tel: (0526) 43193.**
Directors: R F Dickinson, P M Larke, J G Larke. In business since 1981. Canoeing, sailing, windsurfing, waterskiing, riding and racquet sports available throughout the year for periods of one day or more. Individuals and groups catered for. Accommodation is on the adjacent caravan park or camp site (tents not provided). Prices by agreement.

## CHURCHTOWN FARM FIELD CENTRE
**Lanlivery, Bodmin, Cornwall PL30 5BT.**

**Tel: (0208) 872148.**
Owned by the Spastics Society. Principal: J M Overton, MSc, MIBiol, FLS. In operation since 1975. Adventure and education holidays for the disabled, regardless of degree or type of disability. Weekly prices range from £72 (child, November-March) to £130 (adult, March-November). Accompanying helpers: £64 winter, £75 summer. Full board included. "We provide the facilities, time and staff to enable disabled people to enjoy outdoor holidays normally available only to able-bodied people." No age limits; no experience necessary.

## CONSTANCE ALLSTARS
**Grosvenor Hall, Bolnore Road, Haywards Heath, West Sussex RH16 4BX. Tel: (0444) 458011.**
Director: D M Constance. In business since 1980. Multi-sport and specialist sports coaching holidays for adults in Bournemouth, July and August. Specialist courses in cricket, dance, golf, squash, and lawn or table tennis; multi-sports holidays involve choosing four from the above list or archery, badminton, bridge, canoeing, fencing and swimming. Expert coaching by sports personalities plus video analysis and individual assessment reports. Prices around £175 per week fully inclusive; reductions for second weeks and non-residents.

## CONSTANCE HOLIDAYS FOR THE DISABLED
**Grosvenor Hall, Bolnore Road, Haywards Heath, West Sussex RH16 4BX. Tel: (0444) 458011.**
Proprietor: D F Constance. In business since 1984. Multi activity holidays for the disabled at Ullenwood Manor, near Cheltenham, each summer. Participants can select activities including archery, basketball, canoeing, golf and swimming. Prices around £175 per week, including accommodation in specially adapted rooms, all meals, tuition, equipment and medical supervision. Minimum age: 8 years.

**COURTLANDS CENTRE**
**Kingsbridge, South Devon TQ7 4BN. Tel: (0548) 550227.**
Owned by Peralta Estates Ltd.
Director: I Garland.
In business since 1975.
Recognised by: BCU, RYA.
Holidays for 2,700 arranged annually.
Canoeing, sailing, waterskiing, fishing, riding, archery, climbing, abseiling, caving, assault course and field study holidays and courses for individuals and groups of up to 70. Centre based at a 13th century manor farm. Weekends and one or two weeks throughout the year. Prices from £45 for weekend and £77-£155 for one week, including instruction, equipment, accommodation and meals. Facilities include: gym, sauna, laboratory, sports fields and licenced bar. Accommodation in single bunk cabins, dormitories or twin-bedded rooms.
No experience needed.
Unaccompanied children: 9 years+.
Handicapped catered for by arrangement.

**CRAG HOUSE FARM VENTURE CENTRE**
**Crag House, Falstone, Hexham, Northumberland. Tel: (0660) 40259.**
Proprietors: Donald and Rosemary Macleod.
In business since 1968.
Holidays for 500-600 arranged annually.
Riding instruction and opportunities for groups or individuals. Sailing, canoeing, orienteering and camping holidays in the fells of Northumberland and in the Kielder Border Forest Park. Weekly April-October. Self-catering, full board or dormitory accommodation provided. Groups and individuals welcome. Prices from £96.
Minimum age: 8 years.

**THE DALES CENTRE**
**Grassington, Skipton, North Yorkshire. Tel: (0756) 752757.**
Director: T. M. Parker.
Multi activity holidays in the Yorkshire Dales for young adults. A wide range of activities including climbing, caving, mountain walking, bivouacing, cycling and skiing. Based at Kettlewell hostel with an extensive social programme. Price £120 for 7 day or 9 day holidays.
No experience needed.
Ages: 17-25 years.

**DERBYSHIRE ACTION HOLIDAYS**
**Kirby House, Main Street, Winster, Matlock, Derbyshire DE4 2DH. Tel: (062988) 716.**
Proprietor: Geoff William.
In business since 1982.
Holidays for 500 arranged annually.
Walking, cycling, canoeing, orienteering, climbing, caving, skiing, riding and conservation holidays in the Peak District for individuals and groups of up to 15. Open throughout the year. Holidays arranged as an organised programme to suit individual requirements. Special rates available in the winter and for youth groups and outdoor activity club members. Camping, hostel or hotel accommodation arranged. In winter cross country skiing is available, weather permitting.
Ages: 7-70 years.
Unaccompanied children: 8 years.

# Eurosports Village

**Eurosports Village, an International Residential Sports and Leisure Centre East Anglia**

*Why not join us for a sporting break with your group or school for professional coaching or just for fun? (Families welcome in the high season).*

*Eurosports coaching weekends and holidays can be designed for your needs.*

★ Accommodation for over 400
★ First class football and hockey pitches
★ Three sports halls
★ Plus a wide range of other sporting activities

For further details please contact Sales and Marketing Manager Eurosports Village, Shotley Gate, Suffolk IP9 1QJ
Telephone: Shotley 8181
Telex: 988739

**EUROSPORTS VILLAGE LTD.** Shotley Gate, Ipswich, Suffolk IP9 1QJ. Tel: (0473) 348181.
Administrator: R I Hayhoe. In business since 1980. Recognised by the Sports Council, All England Women's Hockey Association, Badminton Association of England. Sports holidays for teams, clubs, etc. in groups of up to 400+. Prices from £12.20 (plus VAT) full board. The centre specialises in catering for individual group needs. No experience needed. Minimum age: 7 years. Unaccompanied children accepted in groups. For further details contact the Sales and Marketing Manager.

**FOLKESTONE ACTIVITY HOLIDAY CENTRE**
Marine Crescent, Folkestone, Kent CT20 1PS. Tel: (0303) 55651.
Proprietor: Ed Mackenzie.
In business since 1973.
Recognised by ETB, BCU.
Multi activity holidays including adventure rambling, riding, cycling, waterskiing, seafishing, windsurfing, canoeing, surfing, parascending, power boating, snorkelling and sailing. Courses for individuals and groups of up to 100, situated on the Folkestone sea front. Open throughout the year; special weekly courses for young people during school holidays March-September. Prices from £84 per week including full social programme, all meals and accommodation, all activity equipment and instruction.
No experience needed.
All ages.
Unaccompanied children: 8 years +.
Bookings through: Folkestone Activity Holiday Centre and travel agents.

**HF HOLIDAYS**
Dept 43, 142 Great North Way, London NW4 1EG. Tel: 01-203 3381.
President: Peter Boulter.
In business since 1913.
Watersports holidays in Devon, Dorset and the Lake District based at HF holiday centres. Canoeing, cruising, sailing, waterskiing and windsurfing available in various combinations. Prices from around £180 for one week. Reduced rate rail travel available.

**HYDE HOUSE ACTIVITY HOLIDAY CENTRE**
Hyde, near Wareham, Dorset. Tel: (0929 471) 847.
Director: Christopher Reynard.
In business since 1980.
Multi activity holidays including windsurfing, waterskiing, canoeing, climbing, abseiling and sailing.
Holidays of two, four or five days, March-November. Prices around £45, £67 and £98 respectively, plus VAT. Dormitory accommodation, all meals, equipment and instruction provided. Horse riding is available as an option for around £3 per hour.
Age limits: 8-65 years.
Minimum age for parascending: 18 years.
Book through head office at 6 Kew Green, Richmond, Surrey TW9 3BH. Tel: 01-940 7782.

**KIELDER ADVENTURE CENTRE**
Kielder Water, Hexham, Northumberland.
Northumbria Calvert Trust; registered charity no. 511851.
In operation since 1982.
Member of ETB, the Sports Council.
Holidays for 1,500 arranged annually.
Mixed activity holidays for the disabled and their families throughout the year. Price of £147 per week includes equipment, instruction, all meals and purpose-built accommodation for the disabled and family.

**LAKELAND EXPERIENCE ADVENTURE HOLIDAYS**
Brook House, Boot, Eskdale, Cumbria CA19 1TG. Tel: (09403) 288.
Proprietor: Paul van Casteren.
In business since 1981.
Multi activity holidays in the Lakeland Fells. Rock climbing, mountaineering, canoeing, windsurfing and orienteering, pony trekking available as an optional extra.
Holidays of one day (£25 for adults/£18 for children), weekend (£50/£35), and one week (£140/£90). Accommodation in hotel/guest house and all meals included. Reductions for groups and day visitors.
Age limits: 4-100 years.
Minimum age (unaccompanied): 12 years.

## LANDS END VENTURE

Skewjack Surf Village, Porthcurno, Penzance, Cornwall TR19 6NB. Tel: Sennen (073687) 498.

Directors: A D Hemley, C D South.

Multi activity courses including rock climbing, surf skiing, surfing, sea angling, windsurfing, riding and coastal walking. One or more weeks March-October. Prices from £43 per week self catering. Courses can be specifically tailored to the individual needs of schools and colleges.

Ability to swim 50 metres required.

## LEISURE LEARNING LTD.

107 Station St, Burton on Trent, Staffs DE14 1BZ. Tel: (0283) 66587.

Directors: C Bond, D Herbert, D Neep.

In business since 1975.

Recognised by BTA.

Special interest weekends in 17 different subjects at various locations in England and Wales. Prices from £75-£105 including full board in good hotels.

Minimum age: 18 years.

## LOWTHER OUTDOOR ACTIVITIES CENTRE at ASKHAM near PENRITH in CUMBRIA

offers Self-Catering accommodation in a 250 year old modernised farmhouse. Bookings for weeks in AUGUST 1986/7. Very suitable for family parties or Youth groups.

Askham is in a very beautiful part of the Lake District National Park and the Centre is managed by the Earl of Lonsdale's Estates. There is an open-air swimming pool close at hand and car parking free in the Centre car park. Assistance and advice available in the organisation of holiday activities.

Maximum size of group 30 plus camping for an additional ten. Annexe in the Warden's house for additional six.

Party rate for the Centre around £125 per week Additional charge for camping and Annexe.

Recognised by the English Tourist Board.

*Full Information and Enquiries:*
**Please address to The Warden
Forge Cottage, Askham
Penrith, Cumbria CA10 2PF
Telephone: Hackthorpe 400**

## LOWTHER OUTDOOR ACTIVITIES CENTRE AND COUNTRY BASE

The Earl of Lonsdale's Estates, Robin Cottage, Askham, Penrith, Cumbria CA10 2PF. Tel: (093 12) 400.

Warden: F J Taylor Page, MBE, BSc.

Recognised by ETB.

Self-catering, self organising activity, holidays for 1,000 arranged annually, under guidance from the Warden.

Art, birdwatching, climbing, fishing, orienteering, pony trekking, wildlife interests and country pursuits arranged in the Lake District for families and groups of up to 30. Additional camping area with indoor wet weather accommodation. Mainly in August, but all months possible. Prices from around £125 per week for party booking of Robin Cottage and Annexe (self catering). Equipment including minibuses can be hired locally in advance. Associated with the Centre is a Lake District Interpretative Museum and a library of books for assistance in identification of species. Warm outdoor swimming pool next door.

All ages (Suitable for large family parties or youth organisations).

Bookings through: The Warden, Forge Cottage, Askham, Penrith, Cumbria.

## MOTHERBY HOUSE

Motherby, Penrith, Cumbria, CA11 0RJ. Tel: (08533) 368.

Proprietors: C Belton, D Freeborn, J Freeborn.

Recognised by ETB.

Multi activity holidays for around 300 people arranged annually.

Sailing, canoeing, fell walking, rock climbing and pony trekking in the Lake District for individuals and groups of up to 16, April-October. Bird watching weekends can also be arranged. Accommodation and full board are provided in a traditional Lakeland house and cottage (around £140 per week) or at local youth hostel (from £128 per week). Weekend or midweek courses in canoeing and rock-climbing from £70. All equipment provided.

No experience needed.

Minimum age: 12 years.

Unaccompanied children accepted.

## NOTTINGHAMSHIRE COUNTY COUNCIL
**Leisure Services Department, Trent Bridge House, Fox Road, West Bridgford, Nottingham. Tel: (0602) 824824.**
Sport activity weeks at Stanford Hall near Loughborough, July-August. Prices around £180 (adult) or £140 (under 15s) include full board, instruction, equipment and full social programme.
Handicapped people catered for.

## OUTDOOR ADVENTURE
**Atlantic Court, Widemouth Bay, Nr. Bude, Cornwall EX23 0DF. Tel: (028885) 312.**
Partners: Jeff, Richard and Teresa Gill.
In business since 1982.
Recognised by RYA, BCU, BSA.
Holidays for 400-600 arranged annually.
Canoeing, windsurfing, surfing, ski surfing, walking and climbing holidays for individuals and groups. One week April-October. Price £115 self catering and £157 including accommodation and meals. Prices include all equipment, instruction and local transport. Multi activity and specialist group training weeks with camping, self-catering or shared room accommodation prices £75-£155. Specialist courses are available October-March.
No experience needed.
Minimum age: 16 years.

## OUTWARD BOUND TRUST
**Chestnut Field, Regent Place, Rugby CV21 2PJ. Tel: (0788) 60423.**
Chairman: H. Roff.
In business since 1945.
Courses for 10,000 arranged annually.
Outward Bound Courses for adults including climbing, canoeing, hiking, sailing and orienteering. 7, 12 or 21 days at centres in Wales, the Lake District and Scotland. Inclusive prices from £140 per week. Some special weekend courses also available.
No experience needed.

## PARK HOUSE OUTDOOR CENTRE
**Ingleby Cross, Northallerton, North Yorks. DL6 3PE. Tel: (060982) 571.**
Director: Ewen Bennett.
Recognised by BCU, BMC, ETB.
In business since 1978.

Activity holidays tailored to suit individuals or groups. Canoeing, rock climbing, caving, hill walking, camping, orienteering, pony trekking and cycling. Traditional stone built farm house in the North York Moors National Park. Full board catering for a maximum of 24 guests. Courses for 1986 feature 6 day (7 night) multi activity weeks. Specialist canoeing, climbing, caving courses and "a mobile camping course across the moors using canoes, ponies, bikes and feet." Weekends and 5 day holidays also available. Prices in range £30-£80, fully inclusive.
No equipment necessary.
Minimum age (unaccompanied): 12 years.

## PGL YOUNG ADVENTURE LTD.
**110 Station Street, Ross-on-Wye, Herefordshire HR9 7AH. Tel: (0989) 64211 or 63511.**
Directors: P G Lawrence, R Lawrence, P J Churchus, P Craig, G Greer.
In business since 1957.

# PGL–Outstandingly different holidays for everyone

*PGL, the leaders in Adventure Holidays, have something for everyone. A massive choice of activities for unaccompanied youngsters, families and groups. Last year we welcomed over 60,000 guests to our residential and day Adventure Centres in some of the U.K.'s most beautiful locations.*

- ● SAILING
- ● CANOEING
- ● COMPUTING
- ● ABSEILING
- ● RIDING
- ● RIFLESHOOTING
- ● GO-KARTING
- ● ARCHERY
- ● SOCCER
- ● WINDSURFING

and lots more

I am interested in an outstandingly different holiday. Please send me a brochure.

☐ Residential Holidays 6-18
☐ Day Camps 3-15
☐ Family Holidays

Name_____
Address_____
_____
_____ Postcode_____
Age of Children_____

PGL Young Adventure Ltd,
127 Station Street, ROSS ON WYE,
Herefordshire, HR9 7AH.
Tel 0989 64211 or 63511

Holidays for around 60,000 arranged annually.
Member of ABTA.
Canoeing, abseiling, archery and other activities at over 40 centres throughout the UK. All equipment and specialist clothing provided. Specialised holidays in canoeing, pony trekking or sailing are also available. No experience needed.
All ages.

## PEAK NATIONAL PARK STUDY CENTRE
**Losehill Hall, Castleton, Derbyshire S30 2WB. Tel: (0433) 20373.**
Administered by Peak Park Joint Planning Board.
Principal: Peter Townsend.
Wildlife, rambling, cycling and activity (sailing, pony trekking, caving etc.) holidays for individuals, families and groups, July-September. Price from £123 per week including accommodation, full board and instruction. Evening talks and activities.
Minimum age: 8 years.
Unaccompanied young people 16 years+.

## STAFFORDSHIRE MOORLANDS DISTRICT COUNCIL
**New Stockwell House, Stockwell St, Leek, Staffs ST13 6HQ. Tel: (0538) 385181.**
Senior Tourist Officer: Ruth English.
Activity weekends involving a combination of cycling, pony trekking and walking in the southern Peak District and Churnet Valley. April-June and September-early December. Options in 1986 to visit the Garden Festival in the Potteries. Accommodation in local hotel; additional fee for guide and hire of equipment. "An area of spectacular scenery, off the beaten track."

## SUTHERLAND LODGE ACTIVITY CENTRES LTD.
**Cropton, Pickering, North Yorkshire YO18 8ET. Tel: (07515) 228.**
Directors: D Miller, A Clarke, J Thomas, B and B J Deniel, S H and H M Morley.
In operation since 1970.
Recognised by ETB, POB.
Year-round outdoor pursuits including canoeing, climbing, cycling, orienteering, pony trekking, walking.

Holidays for individuals or groups of up to 70 arranged for any period in one or many activities. Accommodation in family rooms or dormitories. Visitors make their own beds and set and clear tables for meals.
Minimum age: 6 years.
Unaccompanied children from 8 years accepted for certain holidays.

## WELLINGTON WATERSPORTS
**Reeds, Three Stiles Road, Farnham, Surrey GU9 7DE. Tel: (0252) 724433 or (0734) 884438.**
Directors: R Reed, H Reed, P Wicks.
In business since 1982.
Recognised by RYA, BCU.
Windsurfing, dinghy sailing and canoeing at Wellington Country Park near Reading. Three and five day 'multi activity fun' courses from April to October.
Minimum age: 8 years.
Participants must be able to swim.

## WHITE HALL CENTRE FOR OPEN COUNTRY PURSUITS
**Long Hill, Buxton, Derbyshire SK17 6SX.**

# Sutherland Lodge Activity Centre

## YOU MAKE THE CHOICE!
Choose from our wide range of outdoor pursuits in the moors and forest of North Yorkshire

● Camping ● Climbing ● Cycling
● Field Courses ● Orienteering
● Pony Trekking ● Wildlife . . .

Sutherland Lodge
Cropton
N. Yorks
YO18 8ET
(07515) 228

**Tel: (0298) 3260.**
Administered by Derbyshire Education Committee.
Caving, canoeing, climbing, backpacking and sailing courses for individuals and groups in the Peak District, Lake District and North Wales. 1 week or weekends throughout the year. Accommodation in White Hall or camping. Prices on application.
No experience needed.
Minimum age: 15 years.

**WORLD'S END LODGE**
**Staunton-on-Wye, Hereford HR4 7NF. Tel: (09817) 308.**
Owned by X-Persei Ltd.
Directors: K Charters, C Charters.
In business since 1983.
Holidays for 1,000 arranged annually.
Canoeing, pony trekking, orienteering, climbing, caving and cycling in and around the Brecon Beacons for individuals and groups of up to 60. One week April-October. Specialist programmes in all activities available. Price £135 for multi activity week including instruction, equipment, transportation, dormitory accommodation and all meals. School and youth group holidays arranged.
No experience needed except ability to swim for canoeing.
Minimum age: 18 years for individuals, all ages for group bookings.

**YMCA HIGH PLAINS LODGE**
**Alston, Cumbria. Tel: (0498) 81886.**
Recognised by: Sports Council.
Holidays for 5,000 arranged annually.
Fell walking, grass and snow skiing, climbing, canoeing, trekking and underground exploration in the North Pennines. Individuals and groups of up to 50. Open throughout the year. Prices from around £10 per day including equipment, bunk house accommodation and meals.
No experience needed.
Minimum age: 8 years.
Unaccompanied children accepted.
Bookings through: YMCA Office, Herrington Burn, Houghton-le-Spring, Tyne and Wear. Tel: (0385) 852822/ 853085.

# Scotland

**ABERNETHY OUTDOOR CENTRE**
**Nethy Bridge, Inverness-shire PH25 3ED. Tel: (047 982) 279.**
Centre Director: Richard Yarrow.
In business since 1972.
Holidays for 4,000 arranged annually.
Canoeing, cycling, hill walking and sailing for beginners at a Christian Centre, June-September. Accommodation, meals and all equipment are provided. From £92 per week.
No experience needed.
All ages.
Unaccompanied children: 12 years +.

**ACHNANELLAN STUDY AND ACTIVITY CENTRE**
**Achnanellan, Acharacle, Argyll PH36 4JA. Tel: (096 785) 265.**
Proprietor: Gerry Smith.
In business since 1981.
Holidays for 300 arranged annually.
Sailing, canoeing and mountain walking holidays combined with activities such as botany and painting in a remote part of western Scotland. Full board price £125 per week, self-catering £47 per week, including instruction and use of craft. Reductions for groups of 12-30.
"A unique wilderness environment. No road — access is by water."

**ARDEONAIG OUTDOOR CENTRE**
**near Killin, Perthshire FK21 8SY. Tel: (05672) 523.**
Centre Director: Philip Simpson.
In business since 1983.
Recognised by BCU.
Canoeing, mountaincraft, orienteering, rock climbing, gorge exploring, archery, cross-country skiing, Canadian canoeing and camping expeditions around Loch Tay. Weekends and one week April-October. Price for one week £95 (plus VAT) including accommodation and meals.
Minimum age: 12 years.

## BRIGHOUSE BAY HOLIDAY PARK
**Borgue, Kirkcudbright, Dumfries & Galloway DG6 4TS. Tel: (055 77) 267.**
Proprietors: T & J Gillespie.
In business since 1970.
Multi activity centre on Solway coast in Scotland offering opportunities for sailing, windsurfing, water skiing, jet skiing, parascending, cycling, canoeing, scuba diving, land yachting, pony trekking, hacking and fishing for individuals and groups of up to 8. Accommodation in self-catering cottages, caravans or camping site with all facilities for own caravan or tent. Water Sports School with tuition and hire. Price from £46 per week to hire accommodation, £3.50 per night with own. Activities paid for on an ad-hoc basis.

## CAIRDSPORT SKI SCHOOLS LTD.
**Aviemore Centre, Inverness-shire PH22 1PL. Tel: (0479) 810310.**
Directors: A Caird, D Brightman.
In business since 1967.
Member of: Association of Ski Schools in Great Britain.
Sailing, canoeing, windsurfing, dry slope skiing, pony trekking and hill walking in the Cairngorms. Five days May-October. Accommodation can be arranged in local hotels, self-catering units or youth hostels. Cost from £60-£70 for instruction in small groups. Life jackets, wet suits and other necessary equipment can be hired.
No experience needed.
Minimum age: 10 years.
Unaccompanied young people: 16 years +.

## CARNOCH OUTDOOR CENTRE
**Carnoch House, Glencoe, Argyll PA39 4HS. Tel: (08552) 350/374.**
Canoeing, sailing and hill walking holidays in and around Glencoe for individuals and groups of up to 36. Holidays of 2, 5 or 7 days from May to October. Bunk bed accommodation at the Centre. Price from around £83 per week including full board and accommodation, instruction and use of equipment. Some abseiling and rock climbing is included. Orienteering, windsurfing and camping can be arranged as a supplement. The Centre is also available for groups who wish to arrange

their own activities.
Handicapped people catered for.
Minimum age: 10 years.

## COMPASS SKI CLUB LTD.
**Glenshee Lodge, by Blairgowrie, Perthshire PH10 7QD. Tel: (025 085) 209.**
Directors: S N Anderson, W G Shannon, N J Pickering, A Grassick, J M Leiper, C Mackel, E Thomson.
In business since 1978.
Holidays for 3,000 arranged annually.
Backpacking, orienteering and pony trekking holidays in the Glen of Peace for individuals and groups of up to 46 for five or more days June-August. Prices from around £70. Dormitory accommodation; meals including packed lunch provided. Fishing, archery and hang gliding can be arranged. The Centre is run as a Christian home and short morning and evening prayers are held daily. Backpacking courses available in the summer and ski packages in the winter.
No experience needed.

## CRAIGOWER LODGE
**Golf Course Road, Newtonmore, Inverness-shire PH20 1AT. Tel: (05403) 319.**
Proprietors: Chris and Anne Monckton.
In business since 1982.
Holidays for 1,200 arranged each year.
Activity holidays in the Highlands. Pony trekking, rambling, hillwalking, climbing, cycling, canoeing and skiing. Holidays of 2, 5 or 7 days throughout the year. All activities paid for individually. Bed and breakfast £8 per night, half board £10.50. Minimum age: 17 years (Young People's Holiday also offered — see separate entry).

## CROFT NA CABER WATERSPORTS CENTRE
**Kenmore on Loch Tay, Perthshire PH15 2HW. Tel: (08873) 236.**
Partners: Mr and Mrs A C Barratt, Miss P Barratt, Mrs V Pritchard.
In business since 1981.
Recognised by RYA, NFSS.
Holidays for 1,000 each year.
Multi watersports holidays from May to September. Canoeing, dinghy sailing and windsurfing available; all equipment and

instruction provided. Most holidays are for five days (around £80) but shorter periods can be arranged. Accommodation not included, but chalets, hotels camping and bed and breakfast are available locally. Minimum age: 8 years. Unaccompanied children accepted. Participants must be capable of swimming 50m in light clothing.

## GLENMORE LODGE NATIONAL OUTDOOR TRAINING CENTRE
**Glenmore Lodge, Aviemore, Inverness-shire PH22 1QU. Tel: (047 986) 256.**
Operated by the SSC, 1 St. Colme St., Edinburgh EH3 6AA. Tel: 031-225-8411.
Principal: Fred Harper.
Canoeing, kayaking, climbing, hill walking, skiing and adventure courses in the Cairngorms. Weekly courses at all standards throughout the year. Sampling and young people's courses available in the summer. Prices from around £180 including equipment, instruction, accommodation and all meals. Courses are heavily subsidised by the SSC; visitors from overseas must pay a premium of 50%. All courses supported by a comprehensive evening programme of lectures, talks and seminars.
Minimum ages: 14 years.

## HIGHLAND ADVENTURE
**Knockshannoch Lodge, Glenisla, by Alyth, Perthshire PH11 8PE. Tel: (057 582) 238/207.**
Directors: M Bramley, E Bramley, A Main, B Main, B Russell, A Russell.
In business since 1983.
Holidays for 2,000 arranged annually.
Cycling, roller-skiing, abseiling, archery, hiking, windsurfing, sailing, canoeing and pony trekking holidays based at a Highland lodge for individuals and groups. Daily or weekly April-October. Weekly price from £120 including all activities, bunk room accommodation and meals. Nordic and Alpine instruction available in the winter.
No experience needed.
Minimum age: 5 years.
Unaccompanied children: 10 years+ during July and August.
Handicapped catered for by arrangement.

## HIGHLAND GUIDES (VW)
**Inverdruie, Aviemore, Inverness-shire PH22 1QH. Tel: (0479) 810729.**
Proprietor: Iain C Hudson.
In business since 1969.
Recognised by Scottish Tourist Board SSC.
Holidays for 3,000 arranged annually.
Canoeing, sailing, windsurfing, cross country skiing, hiking, pony trekking, cycling, hill craft and wildlife holidays in the Spey Valley and Cairngorm mountains near Aviemore. Families and groups of up to 60. 1 week May-October. Various types of accommodation can be arranged locally. Price from around £65-£165 (summer) and £85-£105 (winter) depending upon number of activities chosen, including all equipment and instruction.
No experience needed.
Age limits: 6-70 years.
Unaccompanied young people: 14+.

## JURA HOTEL
**Isle of Jura, Argyll. Tel: (049 682) 243.**
Proprietor: F A Riley Smith.
In business since 1960.
Opportunities to go birdwatching, hiking, sailing, canoeing and riding while staying at the Jura Hotel, open year round. Specialist weeks also arranged during the summer under direction of visiting experts. 1 or more weeks April-August. Price about £164 inclusive per week.

## LOCH INSH WATERSPORTS AND SKIING CENTRE
**Insh Hall, Kincraig, by Kingussie, Inverness-shire, PH21 1NU. Tel: (054 04) 272.**
Director: C Freshwater.
In business since 1970.
Recognised by RYA, BCU.
Holidays for 8,000 arranged annually.
Introductory canoeing, sailing and windsurfing courses or daily hire 'Sport-a-Day' holidays with cycling and walking. (Skiing from December to May). Situated on the shores of Loch Insh with hostel accommodation for 46 in rooms of 4 or 5. Full board or self catering. Shower and drying facilities.
No experience needed.
Minimum age: 12 years.

## RU'A FIOLA ISLAND EXPLORATION CENTRE
**Cullipool, Oban, Argyll.**
Resident Director: T Johnson-Ferguson.
In business since 1975.
Holidays for 500 arranged annually.
Canoeing, climbing, sea fishing, hiking and survival training based on several uninhabited islands in the Inner Hebrides. Individuals and groups of up to 30. One or more weeks throughout the year. Prices from £145 per week including timber cabin accommodation and meals. Watch wild stags, otters, baby seals and seabirds. Fish for prawns, mackerel, small sharks and lobsters. All transport in the Centre's unsinkable jet launch and inflatable assault boats.
No experience needed.
Minimum age: 8 years.
Book through Ru'a Fiola Island Exploration Centre, or Woodside, Solwaybank, Canonbie, Dumfriesshire. Tel: (05414) 240.

## SCOTTISH YOUTH HOSTELS ASSOCIATION
**7 Glebe Crescent, Stirling FK8 2JA. Tel: (0786) 72821.**
General Secretary: James Martin.
In business since 1930.
Holidays for 2,000 arranged annually.
"Try-an-Action Sport" holidays at Loch Morlich, Loch Ard and Rowardennan hostels include windsurfing, hill walking, grass skiing and canoeing. One week May-September. Hostel accommodation and meals. Price from £88.
Minimum age: 12 years.

# Wales

## HOLIDAYS PLUS
**2, Rhianfa, Corris Uchaf, Nr. Machynlleth, Powys. Tel: (065 473) 283.**
Proprietors: Dave and Ruth Sweeney.
In business since 1978.
Multi-activity holidays including sailing, canoeing, rock climbing, rambling, pony trekking and windsurfing; weekly for individuals during the summer and for groups of up to 19 throughout the year. Price £105 per week including accommodation and all activities.
Group reductions available.
All ages for group bookings.
Minimum age for individuals: 18 years.

## MOUNT SEVERN ACTIVITY HOLIDAY HOTEL
**Mount Severn Hotel, Llanidloes, Powys SY18 6PP. Tel: (05512) 2344.**
Archery, canoeing, walking, orienteering, pony trekking and assault course holidays for individuals and groups of up to 33. One week throughout the year. Prices £110-£140 depending on season, accommodation and all meals included.
Specialist one-sport holidays also available.
No experience needed.
All ages including unaccompanied children.

## PLAS Y BRENIN
**The National Centre for Mountain Activities, Capel Curig, Betws-y-Coed, Gwynedd. Tel: (069 04) 280.**

Enjoy freedom, fun and adventure on a S.Y.H.A. Breakaway Holiday — all at a price you can afford!

Please send me a copy of the Breakaway Holidays '86 Brochure.

Name ...............................................

Address.............................................

...............................................(AH)

Scottish Youth Hostels Association, 7 Glebe Crescent, Stirling FK8 2JA.

Owned and administered by the Sports Council, 16 Upper Woburn Place, London WC1H 0QP.
Centre Director: D Alcock.
Canoeing, rock climbing, hiking, orienteering and skiing courses in Snowdonia for individuals and groups. Weekly throughout the year; some specialist courses for young people July-August. Board and accommodation provided, with training and instruction from skilled and enthusiastic staff. All courses are graded and include evening programmes of technical lectures and slide/film shows. Minimum age: 16 years (14 years for young people's course).

## PLAS YR ANTUR OUTDOOR EDUCATION CENTRE
**Waverley Road, Fairbourne, Gwynedd. Tel: (0341) 250 282.**
Canoeing, mountain camping and walking, rock climbing, sailing, pony trekking and field and environmental studies for groups only of 20-43, 2, 5 or 7 days throughout the year. Permanent resident instructors for beginners or advanced students. Meals and dormitory accommodation provided, plus equipment and full activity programme. Tarriff on application.
No experience needed.

## TOWERS ADVENTURE CENTRE AND HOLIDAY APARTMENTS
**The Promenade, Llanfairfechan, North Wales. Tel: (0248) 680012.**
Proprietors: L C and S Goodey.
Holidays for 500 arranged annually.
Canoeing, orienteering, windsurfing, skiing, rock climbing, caving and mountain walking holidays on the north west coast and in Snowdonia for individuals and groups of up to 16 people. Weekly throughout the year. Accommodation from £10 per day in apartments or 2-4 bedded rooms, meals included; £40 per week in self-catering. All activities are optional, prices from £6 to £10 per day.
Also 5- or 7-day multi-activity courses for all age groups, especially 10-13 years (5 days, £70) and 50-75 years (1 week, £100-£120).
No experience needed.
Handicapped people catered for.

# Ireland

## ASSOCIATION FOR ADVENTURE SPORTS
**Tiglin Adventure Centre, Ashford, Co. Wicklow, Ireland. Tel: (+353) 404-4169.**
Voluntary organisation.
In business since 1969.
Holidays for 3,000 arranged annually.
Adventure Sport Weeks based south of Dublin and 8 miles from the sea. Water sports available such as canoeing and snorkelling, with rock climbing and orienteering also available. The AFAS is the Irish National Adventure Sports body and runs courses "to encourage activity and foster higher standards in the range of adventure sports for which it has a national responsibility. All courses are designed to present participants with controlled challenge and adventure." Hostel accommodation in Tiglin Centre and bed and breakfast also available. Prices about IR£120 (under £100 Sterling).
Minimum age: 16 years.
Some facilities for disabled participants.

## CRAIGAVON WATER SPORTS CENTRE
Operated by Craigavon Borough Council Recreation Department, Civic Centre, P.O. Box 66, Lakeview Road, Craigavon BT64 1AL. Tel: (0762) 41199.
In business since 1977.
Member of RYA, BSAC, Northern Ireland Sports Council.
Holidays (non-residential) for 12,000 arranged annually.
Multi activity holidays April-September including water-skiing, parascending, artificial snow skiing, windsurfing, canoeing and sailing for individuals and groups of up to 30. In winter, canoeing, orienteering, parascending and sailing are available.
No experience needed.
All ages.
Unaccompanied children: 14 years +.
Facilities for disabled participants.
Bookings through: Mr Averley, Recreation Officer, at the above address.

**SHARE CENTRE**
**Smith's Strand, Lisnaskea, Co Fermanagh, Northern Ireland. Tel: (0365) 22122.**
Director: Dawn Latimer.
Registered Charity.
In operation since 1981.
Recognised by BCU, RYA.
Mixed ability holidays including sailing, canoeing, fishing, hillwalking, boardsailing and waterskiing. Monday-Friday and Friday-Sunday courses in March-May and September-October (from £25 all inclusive); one week courses in July and August (from £98 inclusive).
"The aim is for the integration of able-bodied and disabled people; all facilities are adapted for the disabled."
Minimum age (unaccompanied): 14 years.

# Europe

**AQUA VIVA ADVENTURE CLUB**
**Carsac, 24200 Sarlat, France. Tel: (+33) 53-592109.**
Proprietor: Jan Wester.
In business since 1970.
Holidays for 360 arranged annually.
Canoeing and trail hiking expeditions through the Dordogne Valley accompanied by guide/instructor and cook. Two weeks mid-June to mid-September. Camping accommodation and meals, with participants helping with chores. Opportunities to visit castles, caves and cave paintings. All equipment supplied. English speaking staff. Price from Fr. 2,800 (about £240) excluding travel to and from centre.
No experience needed.
Minimum age: 17 years.

**CLUB MEDITERRANEE**
**UK Office: 106-108 Brompton Road, London SW3 1JJ. Tel: 01-581 1161.**
Directors: M Boeuf, J Giraud, O Michel, G Trigano.
In business since 1955 (in the UK since 1965).
Holidays for one million arranged annually.
Multi Activity Holiday Villages located in all parts of the world from Mexico to Bulgaria and Senegal to Polynesia. 1-2 weeks departing from Paris (or occasionally London) throughout the year. Accommodation varies among Club Med "villages" from straw huts with no electricity or running water to luxury hotels. Most water sports available at sea-based centres and mountain activities organised at other centres. Instruction is available in surfing, scuba-diving, sailing, riding, tennis and many other sports. Almost all villages are equipped with a library of taped music, facilities for aerobics, a discotheque and other modern amenities. Special courses and tours also arranged.
Children are accepted on most holidays and children's activities are available.

**THE DALES CENTRE**
**Grassington, Skipton, N. Yorkshire. Tel: (0756) 752757.**
Multi activity holidays in the French Alps for young adults. A wide range of activities including climbing, caving, mountain walking, bivouacing, cycling and skiing. Based at Monzine hostel. Price £250 for 7 day or 9 day holidays.
No experience needed.
Ages: 16-25 years.

**DFDS SEAWAYS**
**Scandinavia House, Parkeston Quay, Harwich, Essex CO12 4QG. Tel: (0255) 554681.**
Directors: J Atkinson, K Bech-Nielsen, J Coombes, J Davis, L Juul-Jørgensen, E Pedersen.
In business since 1867.
Camping and self-catering holidays in Sweden with riding, canoeing, cycling and sailing. 1 week May-September at outdoor pursuits centres located in various parts of southern Sweden. Prices £100-£185 for camping and £95-£250 for self catering, including North Sea ferry crossing.
All ages.
Book through DFDS or ABTA agents.

**LENZERHEIDE — VALBELLA**
**Tourist Office, 7078 Lenzerheide, Switzerland. Tel: (+41) 81-34 16 89 or 34 19 59.**
Director: Willy Ziltener.

In operation since 1882.
The *Dolce far Sport* programme offers 25 activities, from Alpine walks and orienteering to windsurfing and water bicycling. The scheme operates from late May to mid October. Participants are given tuition in their chosen activities and are awarded performance badges. Accommodation is at hotels and apartments in the twin villages of Lenzerheide and Valbella. A special children's programme is also available: see *Young People's Holidays — Europe*.

**PGL YOUNG ADVENTURE LTD.**
**128 Station Street, Ross-on-Wye, Herefordshire HR9 7AH. Tel: (0989) 64211.**
Canoeing, windsurfing and sailing holidays in the South of France. 8, 10, or 15 days April-September. Windsurfing and sailing on the Mediterranean and canoeing on the River Ardeche in the Massif Central. All instruction and specialist equipment provided.
Ages: from 12 years and families.

**THOMAS COOK HOLIDAYS —**
**MARLBORO ADVENTURE TRAVEL**
**Thorpe Wood, PO Box 36, Peterborough, Cambs PE3 8LB. Tel: (0733) 63200.**
Directors: A G Kennedy, B R Norman.
In operation since 1841.
Windsurfing, sailing, whitewater canoeing, caving and many other activities at two centres in the south of France, the Carinthian Bay in Greece, Carinthia in Austria, and Llafranc and La Manga in Spain. 7 and 14 days June-September. Campsite or hotel accommodation. Price from £215 per fortnight, including coach or air travel and all meals.
Minimum age: 17 years.

# Israel

**TWICKENHAM TRAVEL**
**33 Notting Hill Gate, London W11 3JQ. Tel: 01-894 5500.**

Directors: C Maclean, N Scott, R Allard.
In business since 1975.
Member of ABTA; ATOL no. 334B.
Holidays for 25,000 arranged annually.
Camel riding, diving, jeep safaris, parascending, sailing, snorkelling, waterskiing and windsurfing available as options on holidays to Israel. One or two weeks, October-May. Prices from under £250.
Book direct or through ABTA agents.

# Americas

**CHEWONKI FOUNDATION**
**RFD 3, Wiscasset, ME 04578, USA. Tel: (+1) 207-882 7323.**
Executive Director: Tim Ellis.
Wilderness trips including backpacking, canoeing, sea kayaking, sailing and natural history workshops on the rivers, coast and in the mountains of Maine and Canada for individuals and groups of up to 10. 7-10 days in June and August. Camping and cabin accommodation with hearty outdoor meals. Price around $40 per day all inclusive.
Experience needed on some trips.
Minimum age: 7 years.

**LONE MOUNTAIN RANCH**
**PO Box 145, Big Sky, Montana 59716, USA. Tel: (+1) 406-995 4644.**
Proprietors: Robert & Vivian Schaap.
In business since 1976.
Ranch holidays with opportunities for riding, walking, fishing, whitewater rafting and observing wildlife in and around the ranch and in Yellowstone National Park for individuals and groups. 1-4 weeks from June to October. Special children's programmes also available.
Cross country skiing holidays. 1 or 2 weeks December-April. Accommodation in log cabins with all meals provided. Price $410-$788 per week all inclusive; special children's prices.
Handicapped people catered for.
No experience needed.
All ages.

**RAINBOW ADVENTURE
TOURS LTD.**
3089-3rd Avenue, Whitehorse, Yukon Y1A
5BB, Canada. Tel: (+1) 403-668 5599.
Directors: D H W & E B Howe.
In business since 1981.
Recognised by Canadian Government
Office of Tourism.
Holidays for 1,200 arranged annually.
Multi activity holidays including canoeing,
hiking and fishing in Alaska, Yukon and
British Columbia for individuals and groups
of 10-14. 12-21 days from May to
September. Camping and hotel
accommodation with all meals provided.
Price $800-$1,100 all inclusive. Also do-it-
yourself river holidays. Prices from $145
per week for two persons.
No experience needed.
Ages: 15-60 years.
Bookings through: Twickenham Travel.

# Africa

**ABERCROMBIE & KENT TRAVEL**
Sloane Square House, Holbein Place,
London SW1W 8NS. Tel: 01-730 9600.
Directors: G Kent, J Butler Kent, T D H
Roddam, Mrs P Stubbs, M C Thompson.
In business since 1961 (since 1971 under
present name).
Holidays for 2,000 arranged annually.
Game viewing, trekking, safaris and hot air
balloon trips in Kenya. Accommodation in
Kichwa Tembo luxury tented camp in
Masai Mara Game Reserve.
North American headquarters: 1000 Oak
Brook Road, Oak Brook, Illinois 60521,
U.S.A.

**EXPLORE WORLDWIDE LTD.**
7 High Street, Aldershot, Hampshire GU11
1BH. Tel: (0252) 319448/9.
Directors: T Cox, D Cook, P Newsom, D
Moore.

African expeditions include game viewing,
trekking, desert safaris and sailing in
Morocco, Algeria, Egypt, Kenya, Tanzania,
Ruanda, Senegal, Gambia and/or Zaire.
Camping and hotel accommodation. Small
groups of average 16 people.
No experience needed, but participants
should be reasonably fit.
Minimum age: 18 years.

# Asia

**EXPLORE WORLDWIDE LTD.**
7 High Street, Aldershot, Hampshire GU11
1BH. Tel: (0252) 319448/9.
Trekking, rafting, wildlife viewing and camel
safaris in India, Nepal, Thailand, Sri Lanka,
Malaysia, Pakistan and Burma. Summer
and winter departures. Accommodation
varies with area and activities, but includes
small hotels, tribal huts and camping. All
equipment provided except sleeping bags.
No experience needed.
Minimum age: 18 years.

**RAMBLERS HOLIDAYS**
Longcroft House, Fretherne Road, Welwyn
Garden City, Herts AL8 6PQ. Tel: (0707)
331133.
Established 1946.
Member of ABTA.
Holidays for 5,000 arranged annually.
Trekking, rafting and wildlife holidays in
Nepal. 22 days December-January.
Camping and jungle hut accommodation.
10 day trek in the Helambu region north
east of Kathmandu. 4-7 hours of walking
per day along the banks of the Indravati and
to the final camp at Shivapuri (2,715 m.).
Join rafting crew west of Kathmandu.
Travelling in 6 man,15 ft. rubber inflatables
along fast-moving waters. Destination is
Gaida Wildlife Camp in Chitwan National
Park, to observe jungle wildlife by elephant
and to go birdwatching by dugout canoe on
the Rapti River.
Hiking experience recommended; no
canoeing experience needed.

# Young People's Holidays

**AM HOLIDAYS**
**5 Eastfield, North Muskham, Newark, Notts NG23 6HE. Tel: (0636) 72488.**
Proprietor: A Myatt BA.
In business since 1981.
Multi-activity holidays for unaccompanied children in the Peak District and Pembrokeshire (Tenby). Individuals and groups of up to 20. Hill walking (optional map and compass work), cycling, pony trekking, caving, canoeing, archery, climbing, swimming, treasure hunt, craft work, trips, visits, disco, films, games, competitions. Certificates awarded. 7 nights from £99 inclusive. Accommodation: adventure centre and hotel.
"Emphasis on personal attention as we only cater for small groups."
Ages: 10-16 years.

**ARDMORE ADVENTURE**
**23 Ramillies Place, London W1. Tel: 01-439 4461.**
Camp Consultant: John Craven.
Day and residential adventure and specialist holidays at Easter and in the summer at centres in Buckinghamshire, Dorset and Spain, and year-round in Wales. Activities include pony riding, video filming, computing, tennis, sailing, break dancing and BMX. Residential prices from £128 (plus VAT) including all facilities and accommodation.
No experience needed.
Ages: 7-16 years.

**DOLPHIN ACTIVITY LTD.**
**Grosvenor Hall, Bolnore Road, Haywards Heath, West Sussex RH16 4BX. Tel: (0444) 458177.**
Directors: P Hopkins, A Colin, N Goddard, E Webb, L Smith, A Williams.
In business since 1981.
Holidays for over 20,000 arranged annually. Sports, camping and fantasy holidays. For unaccompanied children, both day and residential. Centres throughout the UK plus two in France. One week holidays at Easter and during summer vacation. Day camp from £65 to £85 per week (including all activities and lunch); residential from £135 to £235 including all meals and dormitory accommodation. Handicapped children catered for at Cheltenham Centre.
"The experience of mixing and maturing alongside children of the same age from all over the world."
Age limits: 3-17 years.
Book through above address or agents. North American agent: Dolphin/Campers Holidays USA, 242 Bellevue Avenue, Upper Montclair, NJ 07043, USA. Tel: (201) 744-8724.

**HF HOLIDAYS**
**Dept 43, 142 Great North Way, London NW4 1EG. Tel: 01-203 3381.**
In business since 1915.
Member of ABTA, SAGTA.
Canoeing, pony trekking, abseiling, archery, windsurfing, sailing, orienteering, assault course and BMX holidays and courses for groups. One or more weeks March-October at centres in the Lake District and Yorkshire Dales. Prices from £70 per week including instruction, round the clock supervision, accommodation and meals. Barbecues, discos and mini-Olympics each evening.

No experience needed.
Ages: 8-15 years.

## OUTWARD BOUND TRUST
Chestnut Field, Regent Place, Rugby CV21 2PJ. Tel: (0788) 60423.
Canoeing, climbing, hiking, orienteering and group problem solving. 2 or 3 weeks throughout the year. There are 5 schools in Britain situated in wild mountain settings: Eskdale and Ullswater in the Lakes, Aberdovey and Rhowniar in Wales and Loch Eil near Fort William in Scotland. Expert instruction in all activities. Price from £140 per week.
No experience needed.
Ages: 14-16 years and 16-20 years.

## PGL YOUNG ADVENTURE LTD.
128 Station Street, Ross-on-Wye, Herefordshire HR9 7AH. Tel: (0989) 64211.
Adventure holidays at over 50 residential centres in Britain, with a choice from over 40 activities including canoeing, trekking, abseiling and archery. All equipment and specialist clothing provided.
No experience needed.
Unaccompanied children: 6-18 years.
Ages: 4-15 years for day camps.

## YHA TRAVEL
Youth Hostels Association
14 Southampton Street, London WC2E 7HY. Tel: 01-240 5236.
In operation for over 30 years.
Holidays for 2,000 arranged annually.
YHA Travel organises sports, special interest, adventure and multi activity holidays throughout Britain. Hostel accommodation, board and equipment are included in the price where indicated in their entries throughout the book. Activities include watersports, skisports, pony trekking, cycling, walking and climbing.

# England

## ACTION YOUTH
PO Box 221, Stoke-on-Trent, Staffordshire ST1 6SR. Tel: (0782) 262032.
Partners: John Close and Eddie Robinson.
In operation since 1975.
Holidays for 3,000 arranged annually.
Sports and educational holidays at the University of Keele. Weekends and weekly July-August. Prices from £35 for weekend and from £145 for one week includes equipment, accommodation and meals. Computer studies and English as a foreign language available. "The holidays give young people the opportunity to meet others from all over the world."
No experience needed.
Ages: 8-17 years.

## BASE CAMP ADVENTURE HOLIDAYS
2 Daisy Hill, Addingham, Ilkley, West Yorkshire LS29 0PN. Tel: (0943) 830446.
Principal: Andrew Parker.
In business since 1984.
Sponsored by the Skipton Building Society. Multi activity holidays featuring rock climbing and abseiling, caving, fell walking and excursions to local places of interest. Pony trekking and canoeing available as options at additional cost. Holidays operational from Easter to autumn. £99 (plus VAT) per week all inclusive. Minibreaks also available.
"Each child is one of a closely knit team and yet each is kept as an individual."
Age limits: 7-16 years.
Marketed in Europe and North America by BTA.

## CASTLE HEAD FIELD CENTRE
Grange-over-Sands, Cumbria LA11 6QT. Tel: (04484) 4300.
Directors: F and J Dawson, G M Campbell, R J Cope.
In business since 1979.
Holidays for 300 arranged annually.
Wildlife observation, rock climbing and abseiling, map and compass navigation, rafting and riding instruction in Lakeland. 7 days July-August. Accommodation and meals in field centre. Investigatory fieldwork includes catching small mammals, watching badgers, dipping in ponds and doing a nocturnal census of wildlife noises. A small working farm encourages children to handle

and feed animals. Groups build raft from 45 gallon drums, planks, spars and ropes and then raft 3 miles downriver or on Lake Coniston learning canoeing en route. Prices from £115 per week. Binoculars should be brought if possible.
No experience needed.
Ages: 9-16 years and family groups.

## CONSTANCE ALLSTARS
**Grosvenor Hall, Bolmore Road, Haywards Heath, West Sussex RH!6 4BX. Tel: (0444) 458011.**
Multi-sport and specialist sports coaching holidays for young people in Bournemouth and Uppingham, July and August. Specialist courses in badminton, basketball, cricket, dance, golf, gymnastics, soccer, squash and tennis; multi-sports holidays involve choosing four from the above options or archery, badminton, canoeing, fencing, hockey, rugby and swimming. Expert coaching by sports personalities plus video analysis and individual assessment reports. Prices around £175 per week fully inclusive; reductions for second weeks and non-residency. Low cost escorted travel available. Holidays for adults also available: see *Multi Activity Holidays — England.*

## CRAG HOUSE FARM VENTURE CENTRE
**Crag House, Falstone, Hexham, Northumberland. Tel: (0660) 40259.**
In business since 1968.
Camping and pioneering holidays by the North Tyne River and on an adventure island. 6 days July-September. Price £65. Holiday includes opportunities for canoeing, archery, rifle shooting and orienteering.
Ages: 8-12 years and 13-16 years.

## THE DALES CENTRE
**Grassington, Skipton, N. Yorkshire. Tel: (0756) 752757.**
Multi activity holidays for teenagers in the Yorkshire Dales. A wide range of activities including climbing, caving, mountain walking, bivouacing, cycling and skiing. Based at Kettlewell hostel. Price: £100-£120 for 7 day or 9 day holidays.
No experience needed.
Ages: 11-14 years.

## DARTMOOR EXPEDITION CENTRE
**Rowden, Widecombe-in-the-Moor, Newton Abbot, Devon TO13 7TX. Tel: (036 42) 249.**
Warden: John Earle.
In business since 1971.
Holidays for 1,000 arranged annually.
Canoeing, caving, climbing, moorland hiking, orienteering, riding, sailing and Mountain Walking Leadership courses on Dartmoor and the South Devon Coast. Individuals and groups up to 30 for any length of time throughout the year. Prices from £120 for 6 days, including instruction, full board and bunkhouse dormitory accommodation in the converted barns of a thatched moorland farmhouse. Equipment provided. Riding £3 per hour extra. Sleeping bags needed. Participants contribute towards washing-up and general tidying. Highly experienced instructors. Sailing on historic 8 ton gaff cutter. Evening films of Warden's Himalayan and Patagonian expeditions. The Centre also offers 'Roving Moorland and Explorer Courses' based in tents for more experienced people.
Minimum age: 11 years.
Unaccompanied children: 11 years +.

## EASTERN SPORTS ACTIVITY HOLIDAYS
**3 Richard Avenue, Wivenhoe, Essex CO7 9JQ. Tel: (020 622) 4811.**
Proprietors: Mr & Mrs N F Smith.
In business since 1979.
Holidays for 500 arranged annually.
Canoeing, windsurfing, sailing, riding, soccer, tennis and other activities at Essex University in Colchester. One week in July or August £120, including instruction, all specialist equipment, accommodation and meals. Reduced rates for day campers.
No experience needed.
Ages: 7-18 years.

## EMSWORTH SAILING SCHOOL
**Northney Marina, Hayling Island, Hants. PO11 0NH. Tel: (0705) 468925.**
Junior adventure camp and sailing holidays including windsurfing, canoeing and evening barbecues. 7 days May-September. Price from £99 including accommodation.
Ages: 10-17 years.

*Canoe Acrobatics*                                                           *The Sports Council*

## ERA ADVENTURE HOLIDAYS LTD.
**18 Carr Field, Bamber Bridge, Preston, Lancs. PR5 8BS. Tel: (0772) 34998.**
Directors: R J Flynn, D J W Herdman, G Porritt.
In business since 1975.
Holidays for 600 arranged annually.
One week multi activity holidays in the summer for both children and adolescents. Based at a centre in the New Forest. Activities available include canoeing, archery, BMX, water skiing, sailing, riding, camp craft, windsurfing and other sports. Dormitory accommodation, full board and expert instruction included in price, from £125 per week. Multi activity day camp also available.
No experience needed.
Ages: 6-11 years and 11-16 years.
North American agent: B. Flynn, 1852 Fairfield Angling Road, North Fairfield, Ohio 44855, USA.

## EUROYOUTH
**301 Westborough Road, Westcliff on Sea, Essex SS0 9PT. Tel: (0702) 341434.**
Directors: E R, E and R Hancock.
In operation since 1961.
Recognised by FIYTO.
Holidays for 2,000 arranged annually.
Tennis, riding, sailing, windsurfing and canoeing holidays for individuals and groups of 15-45. Operating throughout the year. Accommodation arranged with families. Courses in individual sports available. Other activities include golf, football, landscape painting and drawing, educational and cultural visits.
No experience needed.
Minimum age: 14 years.
Unaccompanied teenagers: 16 years+.

## FOREST SCHOOL CAMPS
**Bourne Cottage, Park Lane, Heytesbury, Warminster, Wilts BA12 0HE. Tel: (0985) 40777.**
In operation since 1939.
Camping holidays including canoeing, cycling, hiking and potholing throughout the UK. 3 days to 2 weeks from February to October. Most parties travel with an escort from London but can be joined en route. Camping equipment must be

provided by the participant. Price around £98 for 2 weeks including fare from London.
Experience needed for some camps.
Ages: $6\frac{1}{2}$-18 years.

## KIDS INTERNATIONAL
**106 Seymour Place, London W1H 5DG. Tel: 01-723 2434.**
Directors: R D Tobias, J A Coronna, M S Wheeler.
In business since 1983.
Holidays for 4,500 young people arranged each year.
Multi activity holidays for children at both day camps and residential centres in London, Dorset, Hampshire, Kent, Surrey and Sussex. Abseiling, archery, badminton, canoeing, sailing, shooting, swimming, tennis, trampolining and windsurfing; plus computer, drama, music and video workshops. All equipment provided. Holidays operated during all school holiday and half-term periods, and in June primarily for overseas visitors. Prices (residential) from £149.50 plus VAT including all meals and accommodation; day camps from £59.50 plus VAT including lunch and snacks.
"Total 'no extras' vacations for children from all over the world."
Age limits: 4-14 years for day camps, 7-16 for residential centres. Information available from address above, BTA offices abroad or Kids International overseas booking offices.

## LAKELAND TRAINING
**Ashmeadow, The Promenade, Arnside, Cumbria LA5 0AD. Tel: (0524) 761710.**
Cumbria Services Ltd.
Directors: J E Foulerton, J Strachan.
In business since 1976.
Recognised by RYA.
Holidays for 5,000 arranged annually.
Multi activity holidays specialising in outdoor pursuits and 'Now get out of that' challenges.
The programmes are designed for either primary and secondary schools or individuals. Activities include board sailing, canoeing, caving, rock climbing,

expeditions, abseiling, archery, orienteering, gorge walking and mountaineering. Accommodation is in the Ashmeadow Centre, set in private grounds with a heated swimming pool. Course fee includes full board, in-course transport, instruction, equipment hire and use of all facilities.
Age limits: 8-18 years.

## MATHON LODGE ADVENTURE CAMP
**Harcourt Road, West Malvern, Worcs WR14 4DW. Tel: (06845) 67406.**
Partners: Mandy and Peter Scott.
In business since 1972.
Recognised by ETB.
Holidays for about 1,000 each year.
Multi activity holidays during Easter and summer vacations for individuals, and throughout the year for school groups. BMX riding, archery, pony rides, 75 ft water slide, grass sledging and local excursions. Prices for individuals from £140 per week inclusive; substantial reductions for groups.

**MAKE THE MOST OF YOUR SUMMER OR EASTER BREAK!**
Join us in the beautiful city of Oxford for fun and adventure

**Computing** – get acquainted with the latest technology
**Watersports** – expert supervision for punting, canoeing and windsurfing
**Field sports** – football, tennis, rounders, volleyball, swimming...
**Adventure** – orienteering, nature trails and horse riding

*English language tuition available for visitors from abroad*

Send for our free brochure now, or ring **(0865) 247115** anytime

**Oxford Activity Camps
99 Divinity Road, Oxford OX4 1LN**

"No timetable — the freedom to do what you want, when you want."
Age limits: 6-12 years.

## OXFORD ACTIVITY CAMPS
**99 Divinity Road, Oxford OX4 1LN. Tel: (0865) 247115.**
Operated by Camptour Computers Ltd.
Directors: M M Forkun, J H Forkun.
In operation since 1982.
400 holidays arranged annually.
Sport and educational holidays in the City of Oxford. A mixture of computing (in various applications, including a robot arm) and a wide variety of sports, including canoeing, horse riding, tennis and windsurfing. English language tuition is available to visitors from abroad.
Prices: residential — about £130 per week, with reductions for stays of two weeks or more. Non-residential — for half-day courses (9 am to 12.30 pm), about £39 per week; for full-day courses (9 am to 5 pm), about £54 per week; for 'multi-day' courses (9 am to 9.15 pm), about £69 per week. Accommodation for residential holidays is provided at the Centre or with local families.
"The sport is different every day and includes full monitoring and inexhaustible energy from the staff."
No experience necessary for any activity; all equipment provided.
Ages: 8-18 years.

## PEAK ADVENTURE HOLIDAYS
**28 Ampthill Road, Liverpool L17 9QW. Tel: (051) 727 0189.**
Partners: S J Lenord, R G Larkins.
In business since 1979.
Rock climbing, canoeing, caving, mountaineering and hill walking in the Peak District, Lake District and Snowdonia for individuals and school groups of 6-60, throughout the year. Accommodation in various youth hostels with full board. Price from £120 per week including accommodation, food, instruction and equipment.
No experience needed.
Ages: 10-20 years.

## QUEST ACTIVITY COURSES
**43 Belsize Lane, London NW3 5AU. Tel: 01-794 0427.**
Directors: Nigel Ragg, Norman Allum, Philip Davies, Tim Halford.
In business since 1982.
Holidays for 2,500 arranged annually.
Multi activity courses including water sports, problem solving exercises, environmental awareness and mountain activities in the Lake District and Dorset. Long weekend, midweek or full week March-November for individuals and groups of up to 50. Price from £36 for long weekend and from £72 for full week includes instruction, equipment, evening entertainment, accommodation and meals. Participants must be able to swim 50 metres.
Ages: 8-12 years and 12-16 years.

## ROCKLEY POINT SAILING SCHOOL
**Rockley Sands, Hamworthy, Poole, Dorset. Tel: (0202) 677272.**
Windsurfing, water-skiing and sailing holidays in Poole harbour March-October. Accommodation with families or in school caravans.
No experience needed.
Minimum age: 8 years.
Unaccompanied children: 10 years+.

Treasure Island holidays based in Poole Harbour. 6 days camping, price from £115 including food and equipment. Opportunities for sailing, windsurfing, canoeing and orienteering.
Ages: 10-17 years.

## VENTURE CREEK
**The Old Solent, Cross Street, Cowes, Isle of Wight. Tel: (0983) 297831/760915.**
Proprietors: Mark & Jane Board.
In business since 1977.
Holidays for children including sailing, canoeing, rowing, fishing, assault courses, swimming, outdoor games, camping and barbeques, in the Newtown Estuary on the Isle of Wight. Individuals and groups of up to 12. Camping accommodation and full board. Price £135 all inclusive. All equipment provided.

No experience needed.
Ages: 8-15 years.

## WOODSIDE ADVENTURE CENTRE
**First Raleigh, Bideford, Devon. Tel: (02372) 74496.**
Director: Christopher Reynard.
In business since 1968.
Holidays for 1,000 arranged annually.
Multi activity holidays including surfing, waterskiing, sandyachting, skatesailing, canoeing, climbing, abseiling, swimming and grass skiing. Dormitory accommodation, all meals, equipment and instruction included in prices: 2 days £39-£45, 4 days £59-£67, 5 days £67-£98 (all subject to VAT). Horse riding is an optional extra at about £3 per hour.
Minimum age: 8 years.
Unaccompanied children accepted.
Book through head office at 6 Kew Green, Richmond, Surrey TW9 3BH. Tel: 01-940 7782.

## YOUNG LEISURE ACTIVITY HOLIDAYS
**PO Box 99, Tunbridge Wells, Kent TN1 2EL. Tel: (0892) 31504.**
Partners: Elizabeth and Bill Higginson.
In business since 1982.
Recognised by the Sports Council.
Holidays for around 1,000 arranged annually.
Multi activity holidays at five centres in the Home Counties. Archery, computing, cricket, football, gymnastics, swimming and riding. One week holidays during Christmas, Easter and Summer vacations. Day camps: £59 (4-6 years) or £75 (7-16 years) for five days. Residential: £111 for five nights or £121 for six nights all inclusive. Watersports participants must have a certificate of ability to swim 50 metres.
Age limits: 4-16 years.

## YOUNGSTERS OUT OF DOORS
**72 Street Lane, Roundhay, Leeds, West Yorkshire LS8 2AL.**
Proprietor: David Higgins.
In business since 1959.
Multi activity adventure holidays including walking, caving, cycling, cleaning out canals

and other conservation projects, throughout the UK but mainly in England for individuals and groups of 10-20. Weekend day trips throughout the year and 4-7 day expeditions during the school holidays. Youth hostelling and camping accommodation. Prices around £8-£12 per day. Little specialised equipment is necessary and can be hired.
No experience needed.
Ages: 8-14 years.

# Scotland

## CRAIGOWER LODGE
**Golf Course Road, Newtonmore, Inverness-shire PH20 1AT. Tel: (05403) 219.**
Outdoor activities for young people in the Highlands. Pony trekking, rambling, canoeing, cycling and skiing. Holidays of 2, 5 or 7 days throughout the year. All activities paid for individually. Bed and breakfast £8 per night, half board £10.50.
Age limits: 9-17 years.

## GLENMORE LODGE NATIONAL OUTDOOR TRAINING CENTRE
**Glenmore Lodge, Aviemore, Inverness-shire PH22 1QU. Tel: (047 986) 256.**
Weekly courses in the Highlands include: hill walking, canoeing, kayaking and rock climbing. Sampling courses in summer, taking in several activities. Prices from around £180 including instruction, comprehensive evening programme, accommodation and meals.
No experience needed.
Minimum age: 14 years.

## HOBBY HOLIDAYS
**Glencommon Farm, Inchmarlo, Banchory. Tel: (03302) 2628.**
Proprietor: Penelope Wardle.
In business since 1975.
Holidays for 300 young people each year.

Multi activity holidays based on farmhouse accommodation, June-September. English language tuition available for foreign children. One week from £85 inclusive.
"We are a small organisation giving individual attention to those who don't like mass holiday camps."

## LOWER ARDENTALLEN HOUSE
**By Oban, Argyll PA34 4SF. Tel: (0631) 62070.**
Proprietor: Susan M Barnes.
In business since 1983.
Holidays for 20/30 arranged annually.
Recognised by Scottish Tourist Board.
Outdoor educational activities for about four young people at a time, in a comfortable house on the West Coast of Scotland. Wildlife study, boating, swimming, fishing, hiking, cycling and racquet sports. Pony trekking, climbing and canoeing at local centres for additional charge; English language tuition is also an option. Basic cost of £20 per day includes full board in twin-bedded rooms. Programmes of 7, 14 and 21 days, April-October.
"The small numbers are designed to allow for a high degree of care and attention to safety."
Age range: 8-17 years.

## SHS EXPEDITIONS
**Walcot Church House, 38 Paragon, Bath, Avon BA1 5LY.**
The Schools Hebridean Company Ltd.
Outdoor pursuit and field study expeditions in the Hebrides. Rock climbing, canoeing, survival, birdwatching and botany. 2-3 weeks in July and August for £155-£175. Backpack, sleeping bag and suitable clothing required. Rota system for cooking and washing up.
"Fantastic scenery and wildlife... the magical qualities of living on an island."
Age limits: 13-18 years.
Book through Mr G Smith, 54 Walker Avenue, Pedmore, Stourbridge, West Midlands.

# Wales

**CELMI**
**Llanegryn, Tywyn, Gwynedd. Tel: (0654) 710609.**
Director: D H Charlton.
In business since 1970.
Emphasis on outdoor adventure with imagination. Rock climbing, abseiling, mountain walking, canoeing, orienteering, windsurfing, mine exploration and night exercises. £150 for six nights full board with reductions for longer stays. Holidays operate mid-July to late August. Riding and deep sea fishing are optional extras. Weatherproof clothing and sleeping bags may be hired.
"It is not what we do, but the way we do it. Celmi is not the standard adventure holiday . . . abseiling down a candle-lit slate mine and then having a Chinese meal underground at midnight gives a small flavour."
Age limits: 14-19 years.
Book through: Melanie Granger, 5 Faenol Isaf, Tywyn, Gwynedd LL36 9DW. Tel: (0654) 711504.

**CHRISTIAN MOUNTAIN CENTRE**
**Tremadog, Porthmadog, Gwynedd. Tel: (0766) 2616.**
Chairman: G Stickley.
In business since 1965.
Holidays for 800 arranged annually.
Rock climbing, hiking, canoeing and environmental studies in Snowdonia and on the north coast of Wales. Open throughout the year. Dormitory accommodation and full board. All equipment provided; boots may be hired.
No experience needed.
Minimum age: 10 years.

**LONGTOWN OUTDOOR EDUCATION CENTRE**
**The Court House, Longtown, Hereford. Tel: (087 387) 225.**
Administered by Northamptonshire County Council.
In operation since 1967.

Courses for 1,500 arranged annually.
Canoeing, caving, rock climbing, mountain walking and pony trekking courses at all levels in the Black Mountains, Brecon Beacons and Wye Valley for individuals (during summer) and groups of up to 34 (during rest of year). Full board and dormitory accommodation in Centre. Participants expected to help with chores. Prices approximately £85 per week; discounts for Northamptonshire students. Experience needed for some courses.
Ages: 13-21 years.
Places are allocated between November and January.
Book through Education Department, Northamptonshire County Council, Northampton House, Northampton NN2 2HX.

# Isle of Man

**CAMPAMARENA HOLIDAYS LTD.**
**Falcon's Nest Hotel, Station Rd, Port Erin, Isle of Man. Tel: (0624) 834077.**
Directors: R Potts, M Hurley.
Holidays for 4,500 arranged annually.
Canoeing, sailing, windsurfing, archery and abseiling holidays on the Isle of Man for children. 1 week April-September. Prices from £110 including hotel or hostel accommodation and all meals.
Ages: 7-17 years.

**THE VENTURE CENTRE**
**Lewaigue Farm, Maughold, Isle of Man. Tel: (0624) 814240.**
Operated by: Compass Trading Co Ltd.
Directors: D Read, P Read, C J Foster, J Foster.
In operation since 1981.
750 residential course holidays arranged annually.
Sailing, canoeing, shooting, archery, camping, photography, pony trekking and orienteering holiday courses for individuals and groups of up to 60. 3-7 days March-November. Courses also include old mine exploration, survival instruction, deep sea fishing, raft building and "now get out of

that"-style day exercises. Price £13 per day including instruction, equipment, accommodation and meals. Bunk house accommodation for children, chalets for adults.
Ages: 9-15 years (16-19 years for Spring and Autumn Youth Training Courses).

# Europe

## ACCUEIL DES JEUNES EN FRANCE
12 rue des Barres, 75004 Paris. Tel: (+33) 1-278 04 82.
President: M Tessier.
Recognised by the Ministry for Youth, Sport and Leisure. Multi activity holidays for young people in the Auvergne, southern France. Canoeing, cycling, hang gliding, martial arts, riding, sailing and other activities. 20/21 day holidays in July and August. Prices depend upon activities selected, but range from 3400-4400 F inclusive (aout £290-380) plus travel to the centre.
"In the heart of the Auvergne, in the land of lakes and volcanoes."
Age limits: 11-17 years.
Watersports participants must be able to swim 50 metres.

## LENZERHEIDE — VALBELLA
Tourist Office, 7078 Lenzerheide, Switzerland. Tel: (+41) 81-34 15 89 or 34 19 59.
An innovative programme for young people during July, August and part of October. Mountain craft, camping and wildlife study, plus visits to a plant nursery, a cheese maker, a hotel kitchen and a trout farm. Breakfast is provided (7am-8am) and is followed by the day's activities. The programme is free; the only qualification for participants is that must by staying at hotels or apartments in the twin villages of Lenzerheide and Valbella.
"The children will get to know about various aspects of rural life; at the same time their team spirit and creative abilities are being developed." Age limits: 4-16 years; for windsurfing, 14-16 years.

## NSTS — STUDENT & YOUTH TRAVEL MALTA
220 St Paul Street, Valletta, Malta. Tel: 624 983.
Director: Francis Stivala.
In operation since 1968.
Holidays for 3,000 arranged annually.
Riding, tennis, sailing, windsurfing, scuba diving and waterskiing for individuals and groups of 10-30. One week from June to September. Choice of accommodation in guest houses, youth centres or with local families. Price about £90 Sterling.
Ages: 15-29 years.

## QUEST ACTIVITY COURSES
43 Belsize Lane, London NW3 5AU. Tel: 01-794 0427.
Windsurfing, cycling, waterskiing, sailing, canoeing and mountain hiking holidays in the Southern French Alps. Also water sports holidays including windsurfing, sailing, waterskiing and scuba diving on the Cote d'Azur in the South of France. Camping village accommodation May-September for groups of up to 50. All meals, instruction and travel by coach included in the price starting at £169.
Applicants must be able to swim 50 metres.
Ages: 11-15 years and 16-18 years.

# Americas

## SUPERCAMP USA
Ram Travel, PO Box 34, London SW14. Tel: 01-948 2488.
In business since 1979.
Member of ASTA.
Adventure summer camp holidays for unaccompanied children. Over 100 camps in 30 states of the USA. One to eight weeks June-August. Accommodation in cabins sleeping 6-8; all meals provided. Instruction in wide range of activities including rock climbing, waterskiing, horse trekking, scuba diving, computer camps, etc. depending on camp chosen. Prices £600-£2,500, including return flight.
"Experiencing adventure in its natural environment."
Ages: 7-17 years.

# Canoeing
# and Rafting

Canoeing is an ideal recreational activity, open to all ages and involving relatively little expense. It is also a highly competitive sport with world championships in all sections. The type of canoe used and the techniques involved are almost as diverse as the locations and types of water encountered.

Novices should first take a course to master the basic principles of embarking, disembarking, paddle control and righting the canoe after a capsize. More advanced courses include instruction in how to execute an Eskimo Roll, which is very important in whitewater canoeing. The majority of multi activity centres offer a basic introduction to canoeing and in some cases advanced tuition. Beginners can then practise the skills they have learned by touring on a wide variety of waters such as the gently flowing Wye and Dordogne Rivers or the placid lake networks in the Norwegian and Minnesota wilderness areas. The more advanced canoeist can experience the thrills of shooting rapids or racing in turbulent whitewater in the Cairngorms, Rockies or Andes. In the UK kayaks are used for this type of canoeing. Kayaks are derived from Eskimo canoes and are lightweight, very stable and easily portable. In North America touring canoes are used which have larger cockpits and can accommodate luggage.

Coastal or Sea Touring is to the canoeist what mountain expeditions are to the rock climber, combining planning, skill and stamina. The kayak is adapted for the sea by adding a rudder and sometimes inflatable buoyancy bags to provide stability when swamped. Surf canoeing is for those who have mastered the basic skills and is best done from coasts with a gently shelving beach and reasonably sized waves; an offshore breeze also helps. Slalom racing is another kind of canoeing which consists of manoeuvring the canoe through a series of suspended posts and requires special techniques.

Many holidays abroad feature a rafting expedition as well as hiking, riding, cycling, etc. River rafting outfitters allow the adventure-seeker to enjoy the thrill of turbulent waters without having to master the finer techniques of canoeing himself. Rafting expeditions, often known as Float Trips, are particularly popular in North America but can be practised on the rivers of Chile, Nepal and other exotic places. The rafts are generally made of inflatable rubber or neoprene and are powered by oars or a motor. Although there is an element of danger, the rafts are virtually unsinkable.

**Safety and Equipment.** The majority of canoeing courses will stipulate that you be able to swim at least 50 metres and that you wear a buoyancy aid. The best types of aid are those which are made to British Standards Specifications. It is inadvisable to go out alone; indeed canoeing in a group of three is ideal. In addition to the basic canoe and paddle, a waterproof cover which fits around the cockpit called a spray deck is required. A wet suit and plastic sandals are ideal for canoeing but a shirt, shorts, waterproof anorak and gym shoes are usually sufficient. In cold weather a jersey is necessary as this will keep you warm even when wet. A new canoe costs from £150, paddles £15, spray decks £10 and bouyancy aids £20.

The British Canoe Union (BCU) is the governing body of the sport of canoeing and supplies current lists of recognised clubs, courses, competitions and publications. It also publishes a number of handbooks and maps for canoeists, including the essential reference book for anyone planning a canoe journey in the UK: *Guide to the Waterways of the British Isles.* Star (the first level), Proficiency and Advanced Canoeing Tests have been established by the Union to set standards for the sport within Britain. The Senior Instructor Award is the basic qualification for group instructors and is recognised by the Department of Education as the minimum requirement for teachers and youth leaders. Further details can be obtained from the BCU at Flexel House, 45/47 High Street, Addlestone, Weybridge, Surrey KT15 1JV. Tel: (0932) 41341.

# England

## BOWLES OUTDOOR PURSUITS CENTRE (4)
**Eridge Green, Tunbridge Wells, TN3 9LW. Tel: (089 26) 4127.**
Canoeing courses. Basics taught in the Centre swimming pool, then progressing to the River Medway and the Sussex Coast. Advanced courses on British whitewater and in the Alps. Price per weekend from £34.

No experience needed. Participants must be able to swim 50 metres.
Ages: 10-65 years.
Unaccompanied children accepted.

## BRADWELL FIELD STUDIES & SAILING CENTRE
**Bradwell Waterside, near Southminster, Essex CM0 7QY. Tel: (0621) 76256.**
Owned by Essex County Council Education Department.
In operation since 1964.
Canoeing instruction for individuals and groups of up to 40. Courses daily/

weekend/midweek/weekly April-October. Board and accommodation provided. Instruction is given in a variety of single seater kayaks. Camping expeditions can be arranged. Price from £7 per day. Participants must be able to swim 50 metres.
Minimum age: 13 years.

## CALSHOT ACTIVITIES CENTRE
**Calshot Road, Calshot, Southampton SO4 1BR. Tel: (0703) 892077/891380.**
Recognised by BCU.
Sea canoeing at the largest sea canoeing centre in Britain offering all types of courses from novice to coach. Fleet of 150 canoes with special escort vessels for advanced canoeing. Weekends and weeks throughout the year. Prices from £38 for a weekend including accommodation, food, use of equipment and instruction. Reductions for those under 19 years.
No experience needed.
Minimum age: 11 years.
Unaccompanied children accepted.

## EUROYOUTH
**301 Westborough Road, Westcliff on Sea, Essex SS0 9PT. Tel: (0702) 341434.**
Canoeing courses at Thorpe Bay for individuals and groups. 3 weeks June-July. Accommodation arranged with families.
No experience needed.
Minimum age: 14 years.
Unaccompanied teenagers: 16+.

## HOLME PIERREPONT NATIONAL WATERSPORTS CENTRE
**Adbolton Lane, Holme Pierrepont, Nottingham NG12 2LU. Tel: (0602) 821212.**
In business since 1972.
Canoeing holidays at large purpose-built watersports centre for individuals and groups of up to 60. Available from April to September. Water-skiing, boardsailing, sailing and fishing also available.
Ages: 12-60 years.

## OUTDOOR ADVENTURE
**Atlantic Court, Widemouth Bay, nr. Bude, Cornwall EX23 0DF. Tel: (028 885) 312.**
Beginners, surf, sea and white water

canoeing courses for individuals and groups. One week October-April. Price £115 self catering and £157 full board, includes all equipment, instruction and local transport. Sea and inland canoeing expeditions also arranged. On all courses there is an opportunity to gain the BCU awards from One Star to Advanced Proficiency depending on the course taken.
No experience needed.
Minimum age: 16 years.

## PGL YOUNG ADVENTURE LTD.
**128 Station Street, Ross-on-Wye, Herefordshire HR9 7AH. Tel: (0989) 64211.**
Canoeing courses based on the River Wye near Ross-on-Wye. Elementary, intermediate, advanced and instructor's BCU-recognised courses are under personal direction of Senior Instructor.
No experience needed.
Ages: 8-16 years and families.

## WELLINGTON WATERSPORTS
**Reeds, Three Stiles Road, Farnham, Surrey GU9 7DE. Tel: (0252) 724433 or (0734) 884438.**
Canoeing courses on country park lake for individuals in groups of five per instructor. Half day and BCU two day courses April-October. Prices from £20 per day.
Minimum age: 8 years.

# Scotland

## ABERNETHY OUTDOOR CENTRE
**Nethy Bridge, Inverness-shire PH25 3ED. Tel: (047 982) 279.**
Canoeing courses on Loch Morlich and the River Spey for individuals and groups up to 24. 1 week June-September. Prices from £99 including accommodation, meals and equipment. Basic instruction using GRP slalom kayaks by BCU-trained staff. White water techniques, an overnight river expedition and (weather permitting) canoe surfing on the Moray coast. "The staff are committed Christians and enjoy sharing their faith with visitors to the Centre."

Ability to swim 50 metres required. All ages. Unaccompanied children: 12 years +.

## ARDFERN SEA SCHOOL
**The Galley of Lorne Inn, Ardfern, by Lochgilphead, Argyll PA31 8QN. Tel: (085 25) 664.**
Proprietor: Nigel Boase.
In business since 1970.
Canoe rental and instruction available on Argyll loch. Accommodation can be arranged locally.
No experience needed.
Minimum age: 16 years.

## CARNOCH OUTDOOR CENTRE
**Carnoch House, Glencoe, Argyll PA39 4HS. Tel: (08552) 350/374.**
Elementary and proficiency canoeing courses and canoe expeditions on the sea Loch Leven progressing through the Strait of Ballachulish to the open sea. For individuals and groups of up to 36. Holidays of 7 days from May to October. Accommodation and full board at the Centre. Price from around £82 per week. Opportunities to obtain BCU certificates. Handicapped people catered for.
No experience needed.
Minimum age: 10 years.

## CROFT NA CABER WATERSPORTS CENTRE
**Kenmore on Loch Tay, Perthshire PH15 2HW. Tel: (08873) 236.**
Canoeing courses from May to September. All equipment and instruction included in price of around £60 for five days; shorter courses can be arranged. Upon completion of the five day course, participants have the opportunity to negotiate white water. Sailing and windsurfing also available. Accommodation not included in price, but various alternatives available locally.
"The majority of canoeists will be capable of taking national awards at the end of the five day course."
Minimum age: 8 years.
Unaccompanied children accepted.

## LOCH INSH WATERSPORTS AND SKIING CENTRE
**Insh Hall, Kincraig, by Kingussie, Inverness-shire, PH21 1NU. Tel: (054 04) 472.**
Whitewater canoeing and canoe touring holidays for individuals and groups of up to 50. 1-3 weeks May-September. Beginners and advanced courses available. Good waterproof anorak and trousers and several changes of clothing required. Wet weather gear available for hire. Students are expected to keep their own rooms tidy, prepare packed lunches and help in turn to serve and clear meals in the dining room. Self-catering terms on request. Price £132-£141 per week. Dinghy sailing and windsurfing holidays also available.
No experience needed.
Minimum age: 12 years.
Unaccompanied children: 12 years +.

Canoe expeditions from Fort William to Inverness. 1 week July-September. Travelling in double kayaks carrying all camping equipment and food aboard. Accommodation in 3-man tents. Sleeping bag, waterproofs, swimming trunks and insect repellent needed. Price £141.
No canoeing experience required. Participants must be good swimmers.
Minimum age: 16 years.

## OUTWARD BOUND TRUST
**Chestnut Field, Regent Place, Rugby CV21 2PJ. Tel: (0788) 60423.**
Sea canoeing around the west coast of Scotland, and white water canoeing in the Scottish rivers around Fort William. One week courses.
Some experience needed.

## SCOTTISH YOUTH HOSTELS ASSOCIATION
**7 Glebe Crescent, Stirling FK8 2JA. Tel: (0786) 72821.**
Canoe touring among Scottish lochs. One week June-August. Self-catering hostel accommodation. Chance to try canoe surfing if weather permits. Price from £69.
Minimum age: 12 years.

# Wales

## MAESLLWCH RIVER AND MOUNTAIN CENTRE

**Glasbury on Wye, Herefordshire. Tel: (04974) 226.**
Proprietors: Graham and Sheila Williams.
In business since 1969.
Holidays for 3,000 arranged annually.
Canadian canoe expeditions along the Wye for $\frac{1}{2}$, 1, 2, 3, 4 or 7 days. All instruction and equipment provided. Prices from £6-£105 (plus VAT) including meals and accommodation. Canoeing may be combined with trail riding and/or caving.
Age limits: 7-10 years.
Minimum age for unaccompanied young people: 16 years.

# Ireland

## ASSOCIATION FOR ADVENTURE SPORTS

**Tiglin Adventure Centre, Ashford, Co. Wicklow, Ireland. Tel: (+ 353) 404-4169.**
Whitewater and introductory canoeing courses at the Tiglin Adventure Centre near Dublin. The Centre is situated near a lake and only 8 miles from the sea. Weekends February-May and October-November. Instruction by experienced and qualified staff. Youth hostel type and guest house accommodation with all meals provided. Prices from £36, all equipment provided.

Canoe touring on the River Barrow in Southern Ireland. 1 week July-August. Prices from £117. "The tours are conducted by friendly and very experienced guides who are also excellent outdoor cooks. The informality of our small groups generates friendliness and enthusiasm."
Minimum age: 16 years.

# Europe

## AQUA VIVA ADVENTURE CLUB

**Carsac, 24200 Sarlat, France. Tel: (+33) 53-592109.**
Canoeing and camping expeditions with guide/instructor through the Dordogne Valley. Departures every week between June and September. Camping accommodation with meals. All local transport and equipment supplied. English speaking staff. Price Fr. 1700.
Minimum age: 17 years.

## ACCUEIL DES JEUNES EN FRANCE

**12 rue des Barres, 75004 Paris. Tel: (+33) 1-278 04 82.**
Canoeing in the Haute Savoie, the Gorges du Tarn and the Ardeches from June to September. Full board in youth hostels. Six, seven and 12 day holidays costing 1400-2400 F (about £120-200), plus travel to site.
Age limits: 16-30 years.

Rafting in four areas of France. Two, three and six day holidays from March to September with all equipment provided and accommodation in youth hostels. Prices from 600 F (£50) for two days.
Minimum age: 16 years.

## NUH REISEBYRA

**Norwegian Youth Hostels Association, Dronningensgate 26, 0154 Oslo 1, Norway. Tel: (+47) 2-42 14 10.**
Established 1930.
Holidays for 10,000 arranged annually.
Canoeing on the Telemark waterways of Southern Norway from May to September. All equipment (except sleeping bag provided). Overnight stay at Dalen youth hostel, then camping *en route*. Prices Nkr 500-700 according to season.
Minimum age: 12 years.
Book direct or through national YHA offices abroad.

## SPORTING TRAVEL SERVICES

**9 Teasdale Close, Royston, Herts, SG8 5TD. Tel: (0763) 42867.**

Proprietor: Alan Miller.
In business since 1978.
Recognised by BCU.
A variety of canoeing and rafting holidays in Sweden, mostly for one week from June to September. Prices include ferry travel, equipment, most meals and camping, hostels or hotels. Canoe safari: £240-£280; family canoeing trip £230-£260 with reductions of up to 40% for children; canoeing and wilderness trip, about £280; whitewater canoeing and rafting, £190-£400.

Arctic canoe race, beginning late July, for competitors and non-racers: 320 miles (200 of which are above the Arctic Circle); prices around £230.

Timber rafting — an unusual trip in which you build your own raft from three layers of logs (timber and ropes supplied) and drift downstream at 1mph. Camping either on board or at river bank. At the end of the trip the raft is dismantled and the logs float further downriver to be used for papermaking. Price £205-£270 with reductions of up to 60% for accompanying children. Food provision pack (£40) and fishing gear (£8) available.
"For people who need to get away from town and stress ... the most tranquil holiday anywhere."

**SSR-REISEN**
**Bäckerstrasse 52, 8026 Zurich, Switzerland. Tel: (+41) 1-2423000.**
Beginners and advanced canoe courses on the quiet stretches and the wild waters of the River Inn (on the Austrian-Swiss border). One week June-August. Half-board and hotel accommodation provided. Price from S.Fr. 640 including 5 days of lessons and all equipment.

River rafting tours in Europe. 9 or 14 days, on the Tarn, Dordogne, Vézère, Var and Verdon Rivers (France); Drina and Tara Rivers (Yugoslavia) and Reuss, Thur and Vorderrhein Rivers (Switzerland). Transport to and from river by bus. Campsite accommodation. No experience needed. Ages: 16-35 years.

**WEXAS**
**45 Brompton Road, London SW3 1DE. Tel: 01-589 0500.**
Rafting in inflatables on Swiss rivers. One week, July and August. Around £265 including flights plus £12 per day kitty. Membership required.

# Americas

**EXPEDITIONS INC.**
**Rt. 4, Box 755, Flagstaff, Arizona 86001, USA. Tel: (+1) 602-774-8176.**
Proprietors: Dick & Susan McCallum.
In business since 1970.
Grand Canyon river trips in groups of up to 25. 5-18 days April-October. Camping equipment provided and meals cooked. Price $525-$1350.
All ages.

**GOWAY TRAVEL LTD.**
**40 Wellington Street East, Toronto, Ontario, Canada M5E 1C7. Tel: (+1) 416-863-0799.**
President: Bruce Hodge.
In business since 1970.
Holidays for 1,200 arranged annually.
Wilderness canoe trips for individuals and groups in Ontario's Algonquin Park. 8 days departing from Toronto June-September. All camping and canoeing equipment (except sleeping bag) provided. Participants share cooking and camping chores. Leisure time available for hiking, fishing and swimming. Price from Toronto is £179.
No experience needed.
Minimum age: 18 years.

**LIBERTY BELL ALPINE TOURS**
**Star Route, Mazama, WA 98833, USA. Tel: (+1) 509-996 2250.**
Rafting through the Black Canyon of the Methow River, May-August. Price $21, including picnic lunch. "You will get real wet, so bring a change of clothes for the end, and prepare to have a blast."

Kayaking courses for beginners in Washington State. Weekend ($125) and one week courses ($345) in July and August, all equipment provided. May be combined with windsurfing instruction.

## SOBEK EXPEDITIONS, INC
**One Sobek Tower, Angels Camp, CA 95222, USA. Tel: (+1) 209-736 4524.**
Directors: Richard Bangs, John Yost, George Wendt.
In business since 1973.
Recognised by ASTA, IATA and others.
Expeditions for 32,000 arranged annually. Whitewater rafting from Alaska to Chile, including the Tatshenskini, Alaska (12 days July-August, about $1,600 plus air travel); Tuolumne, California (2/3 days, March-October, $250-$350); Bio-Bio, Chile (14 days, December-March, $2,000).

Sobek Expeditions is associated with Sobek's International Explorers Society (SIES), who publish the *Adventure Book* of expeditions arranged by Sobek and other operators. Members of SIES receive a free copy and get a discount on the trips listed.

For further details, write to SIES at Sobek Expeditions.

## WHITEWATER ADVENTURES
**1616 Duranleau St, Vancouver, British Columbia V6H 3R5. Tel: (+1) 604-669-1100.**
President: Dan Culver.
In business since 1973.
Holidays for 6,000 arranged annually.
Inflatable raft trips on the Thompson, Fraser and Chilcotin rivers in British Columbia and the North West Territories for individuals and groups of up to 150. 1-12 days April to October. Camping accommodation and meals provided. Price around $70 per day all inclusive.
No experience needed.
Ages: 10-85 years.
Unaccompanied children: 12 years+.

## WHITE WATER RIVER EXPEDITIONS
**PO Box 1269, Mariposa, CA 95338, USA. Tel: (+1) 209-742 6633.**

*Rafting on the Penobscot River, Maine*                    *Northern Whitewater Outdoors*

Directors: Henry & Grace Falany.
In business since 1963.
River trips by inflatable motor rafts in the Grand Canyon in Arizona starting and terminating in Las Vegas for individuals and groups of up to 36. Seven days May-September. Camping accommodation with meals cooked outside. Price from $935 per week, includes all meals, wine, equipment and transport. Geology professor accompanies most trips.
No experience needed.

**WILDERNESS RIVER OUTFITTERS & TRAIL EXPEDITIONS INC.**
PO Box 871, Salmon, Idaho 83467, USA. Tel: (+1) 208-756-3959.
Director: Joseph Tonsmeire.
In business since 1969.
Holidays for 300 arranged annually.
Whitewater raft trips on the rivers of Idaho, Montana, Oregon, Alaska and Peru. 5-9 days throughout the year. Camping accommodation and outdoor meals. Price approximately $120 per day.
No experience needed.
Minimum age: 12 years.

**WILDERNESS SOUTHEAST**
711 Sandtown Road, Savannah, GA 31410, USA. Tel: (+1) 912-897-5108.
Director: Richard Murlless.
In business since 1971.
Naturalist-led holidays for 900 conducted annually.
Canoeing in the Okefenokee Swamp of Georgia. Weekends or 6 day trips October-April. Camping accommodation and meals. Opportunities to observe alligators and wading birds. Price $315 for 6 days.
No experience needed.
Minimum age: 12 years.

**WOLF RIVER LODGE, INC.**
White Lake, Wisconsin 54491, USA. Tel: (+1) 715-882 2182.
President: George Steed.
In business since 1925.
Recognised by BCU, American Canoe Association.
Holidays for 2,500 arranged annually.
Whitewater canoeing and kayaking instruction in Wisconsin for individuals or groups of 10-12. 5 days May-September.

Accommodation and food provided at the lodge. Price from around $400 per week all inclusive. Good physical fitness required.
No experience needed.
Ages: 12-65 years.

# Africa

**ABERCROMBIE & KENT TRAVEL**
Sloane Square House, Holbein Place, London SW1W 8NS. Tel: 01-730 9600.
Whitewater rafting holidays and canoe safaris in Zimbabwe and 'Mokoro' (dugout canoe) safaris in the Okavanga Delta in Botswana.
Minimum age: 12 years.
North American headquarters: 1000 Oak Brook, Illinois 60521, USA.

# Asia

**SOBEK EXPEDITIONS, INC.**
One Sobek Tower, Angels Camp, CA 95222, USA. Tel: (+1) 209-736 4524.
Rafting on the Alas River in Sumatra, 15 days in October. Price around $2,000 plus air travel.

Rafting the Curoh River in Asiatic Turkey, 16 days May-June. Price around $1,550 plus air travel.

# Australasia

**SOBEK EXPEDITIONS, INC.**
One Sobek Tower, Angels Camp, CA 95222, USA. Tel: (+1) 209-736 4524.
River safari on the Sepik River in Papua New Guinea, 9 days in early summer. Included stays in native villages and travel in dugout canoes. Price around $1,200 plus air fare.

Rafting on the Watut River in central New Guinea, 6 days April-May. Price around $900 plus air fare.
"The wildest river run in the pacific."

# Climbing
# and Mountaineering

There was a fashion in the late eighteenth century to find mountains grotesque and distasteful. But today mountains are a very popular destination for adventurous travellers, and the post war period has seen the establishment of many new climbing centres in the Scottish Highlands, the Canadian Rockies, the Himalayas and elsewhere. The most popular areas have schools and guiding facilities for all grades of climber.

It is not necessary to be a technical rock climber to enjoy moving among mountains. Conversely it is possible to become an expert rock climber without going above 100 ft. The British have distinguished themselves as rock climbers principally because there is no range of towering mountains but plenty of challenging crags from Cornwall to Skye. Whereas some relish the challenge of climbing steep and difficult cliffs, others are intimidated not only by the feeling of exposure but by the cumbersome hardware necessary for rock climbing. There are opportunities for people of either persuasion to learn new skills and explore new areas of the world.

**Safety and Equipment.** When practised with the appropriate equipment and precautions, climbing is not as dangerous as it may seem to the uninitiated. Most accidents are the result of inexperience, inadequate equipment or an error of judgment. Even easy hills can be dangerous when the weather changes unexpectedly and the climbers are caught unprepared. Warm and waterproof clothing with a high wool content should be carried even in summer (see wind chill chart below) and boots with tough rubber soles which minimise slipping should be worn.

At least one member of a mountaineering party should have a working knowledge of maps and compass navigation, survival and rescue procedures and first aid. A sample equipment checklist for an ascent of Mont Blanc (at 15,871 ft, the highest peak in the Alps) would include crampons, ice axe, a rope for every three climbers, glacier cream, sunglasses and three layers of woollen clothing. Bivouac gear, which consists of a light waterproof body-length bag, is necessary when there is a high chance of not being able to complete a climb during daylight.

Most holiday organisers will provide or hire the specialised equipment needed for the purpose. Climbing and the related activity of abseiling (or rappelling) are included as part of almost all multi activity holidays. Abseiling is the "walking" down a rock face with your weight borne by a rope attached to a secure anchor at the top. Organisations such as the Sports Council, the Youth Hostels Association and the Outward Bound Trust offer introductory and specialist courses in all aspects of mountaineering.

The British Mountaineering Council (BMC) is the national body for climbing and can provide details of clubs and holidays throughout Britain and some abroad. They carry a large stock of mountaineering books and publish their own set of climbing guides to the Peak District. The authoritative book on the sport is called *Mountaineering* by Alan Blackshaw; a revised edition was published by Penguin in 1984. Advice on all aspects of climbing can be obtained from the BMC by sending a stamped addressed envelope to them at Crawford House, Precinct Centre, Booth Street East, Manchester M13 9RZ. Tel: 061-273 5835.

# England

## BOWLES OUTDOOR PURSUITS CENTRE (4)
**Eridge Green, Tunbridge Wells, TN3 9LW. Tel: (089 26) 4127.**
Climbing courses throughout the year. Weekend "taster" course in the basics and longer courses giving a fuller introduction to mountaineering. Courses in North Wales and the Alps also available. Price from £92 per week.
No experience needed.
Ages: 10-65 years.
Unaccompanied children accepted.

## CALSHOT ACTIVITIES CENTRE
**Calshot Road, Calshot, Southampton SO4 1BR. Tel: (0703) 892077/891380.**
Climbing courses run throughout the year using six indoor climbing walls and the sea cliffs at Swanage on the Dorset coast. Evening courses. Prices in range £20-£40

including use of equipment and instruction. Minimum age: 13 years.

## HF HOLIDAYS
**Dept 43, 142 Great North Way, London NW4 1EG. Tel: 01-203 3381.**
Mountain leadership courses at Derwentbank in the Lake District. Designed to increase enjoyment of mountain areas by instruction and practice in the use of map and compass, fell walking, scrambling techniques and party leadership. Equipment, first aid, safety and emergency procedures dealt with.

# Scotland

## ASSOCIATION FOR ADVENTURE SPORTS
**Tiglin Adventure Centre, Ashford, Co. Wicklow, Ireland. Tel: (+353) 404-4169.**
Winter mountaineering in the Ben Nevis and

Glencoe regions. One week in January to learn the skills of general winter mountaineering, survival, movement with axe and crampons and classic ridge traverses. Also one week in March for those with previous rock experience and a knowledge of ropework.
Minimum age: 16 years.

## CARNOCH OUTDOOR CENTRE
**Carnoch House, Glencoe, Argyll PA39 4HS. Tel: (08552) 350/374.**
Winter and summer climbing, backpacking and mountaineering courses in Glencoe, Ben Nevis and the surrounding area for individuals and groups of up to 36, throughout the year. Full board and accommodation at the Centre. Price from around £79 per week.
No experience needed.
Minimum age: 10 years.

## CUILLIN GUIDES
**Stac Lee, Glenbrittle, Isle of Skye IV47 8TA. Tel: (047 842) 289.**
Proprietor: Gerry Akroyd.
In operation since 1970.
Recognised by Skye Tourist Board.
Mountaineering and rock climbing courses in the Cuillin Mountains of Skye and backpacking holidays on the West Coast of Scotland for individuals and groups. 5 days throughout the year. Price from £75 per week, winter and summer, not including accommodation. Alpine courses also available.
Hill walking experience and physical fitness essential.
Ages: 16-65 years.

## HF HOLIDAYS
**Dept 43, 142 Great North Way, London NW4 1EG. Tel: 01-203 3381.**
Mountain leadership courses based at Loch Awe. See entry under *England* above for details of coverage.

## SCOTTISH YOUTH HOSTELS ASSOCIATION
**7 Glebe Crescent, Stirling FK8 2JA. Tel: (0786) 72821.**
Climbing instruction for novice and advanced climbers and ridge walkers.

Seven-day holidays from April to September at a choice of hostels. Price from £114 for basic rock climbing course.
Minimum age: 12 years.

# Wales

## ASSOCIATION FOR ADVENTURE SPORTS
**Tiglin Adventure Centre, Ashford, Co. Wicklow, Ireland. Tel: (+353) 404-4169.**
Rock climbing courses in Wales. One week at Easter and in the summer. Courses run to suit individual abilities with an emphasis on technique, safety and belaying.
Minimum age: 16 years.

## PLAS Y BRENIN
**The National Centre for Mountain Activities, Capel Curig, Betws-y-Coed, Gwynedd. Tel: (069 04) 214 or 280.**
Rock climbing courses in Snowdonia for individuals and groups. Weekly April-October. Board and accommodation provided at Centre. Instruction given in the latest belay techniques and use of equipment. Emphasis is placed on developing a higher personal skill level and sound judgement in the student. Multi activity holidays also arranged.
No experience needed. Some intermediate-level and instructor training courses are available in summer.
Minimum age: 16 years (14 years for courses in July and August).

# Ireland

## ASSOCIATION FOR ADVENTURE SPORTS
**Tiglin Adventure Centre, Ashford, Co. Wicklow, Ireland. Tel: (+353) 404-4169.**
Rock climbing courses. Weekends and weeks based at Tiglin Adventure Centre. Instruction by experienced and qualified staff. All specialist equipment provided. Prices from IR£36.
No experience needed.

## NORTHERN IRELAND MOUNTAIN CENTRE, TOLLYMORE

**Bryansford, near Newcastle, County Down.**
Mountaineering courses throughout the year but especially in July and August. Self-catering accommodation at the Centre. Most equipment and supplies such as food, sleeping bag, first aid kit, compass and 1:50,000 Ordnance Survey map of the Mournes needed; specialist equipment provided. On request transport can be provided from Newcastle bus station. Mountaineering instruction can be combined with a canoeing course. Comprehensive range of specialist courses on techniques of navigation, winter mountaineering, rock climbing, mountain rescue and equipment making. Mountain Leader courses also available.
Bookings through the Sports Council for Northern Ireland, The House of Sport, Upper Malone Road, Belfast BT9 5LA. Tel: (0232) 661222.

# Europe

## ASSOCIATION FOR ADVENTURE SPORTS

**Tiglin Adventure Centre, Ashford, Co. Wicklow, Ireland. Tel: (+353) 404-4169.**
Mountaineering courses in the Alps. 2 weeks in August. Instruction and ascent of four or five routes including Mont Blanc. Some experience necessary.
Minimum age: 16 years.

## AUSTRIAN ALPINE CLUB

**13 Longcroft House, Fretherne Road, Welwyn Garden City, Herts AL8 6PQ. Tel: (0707) 324835.**
Secretary: Mrs D M Dorward.
Established 1948.
Operated by Ramblers Holidays Ltd.
The aim of the club is to "promote all forms of mountain activity and to increase knowledge and appreciation of mountains." Activities include creating and improving waymarked footpaths, preserving alpine wildlife, testing and improving equipment for mountaineers, rescue work and providing an independent mountaineering rescue service. The UK branch has a regular newsletter and offers a lift-sharing service to the Alps.

Mountaineering courses in the Austrian Alps lasting 2 weeks July-September. Accommodation in mountain huts. Basic Rock and Ice course, led by professional Austrian guides. Suitable protective clothing, boots and a comfortable rucksack are essential. Chest sling, karabiners, ice axe, and crampons are provided. Rock climbing and scrambling experience needed.
Club membership required.
Minimum age: 18 years.

## BERGSTEIGERSCHULE PONTRESINA

**7504 Pontresina, Switzerland. Tel: (+41) 82-66444.**
Director: Paul Nigg.
In business since 1961.
A full programme of mountaineering expeditions in the Alps with experienced guides. February-October. Prices from SFr450 (about £103); equipment may be hired.
"Be friends with nature and the mountains."

Expeditions to East Africa, Alaska, the Andes and the Soviet Union also arranged: prices from SFr3000 to SFr6000 inclusive from Zurich.
Minimum age: 16.

## BERGSTEIGERSCHULE ROSENLAUI

**3860 Meiringen, Bernese Oberland, Switzerland. Tel: (+41) 36-711653.**
Partners: B Scheller, R Frutiger.
In business since 1945.
Holidays for about 200 arranged annually. Rock and ice climbing courses for beginners and advanced climbers in the Swiss, French and Italian Alps. One week holidays June-September. Boots, ice-axe, crampons, etc. can be hired; sling, karabiner and pitons needed. Prices from SFr635 to SFr1250 (about £200-£400) plus travel, depending on location and degree of difficulty.
No experience needed.
Age limits: 14-70 years.

**BERGSTEIGERZENTRUM GRINDELWALD**
**2818 Grindelwald, Switzerland. Tel: (+41) 36-532021.**
Director: Edi Bohren.
In business since 1970.
Instruction on rock and ice climbing, and guided climbing and glacier hikes in the Jungfrau region. Winter season January-May, summer season July-October.
Minimum age: 12.
No experience needed for climbing courses and glacier hikes. Information and bookings through Swiss Tourist Offices abroad.

**PSOM/MGS INC.**
**Palisade School of Mountaineering/ Mountaineering Guide Service.**
PO Box 694, Bishop, CA 93514, USA. Tel: (+1) 619-873 5037.
Director: John Fischer.
In business since 1958.
Rock climbing in Bavaria, Switzerland and Italy, September 13-27 1986. Trip concludes with visit to Munich Oktoberfest.

Price $1,600-$2,000 depending on numbers taking part, plus travel to Alps.
Some experience necessary.
Minimum age: 16 years.

# Americas

**AMERICAN ALPINE INSTITUTE**
**121 24th St, Bellingham, WA 98225, USA. Tel: (+1) 206-671-1505.**
Treks and ascents in the Andes of Argentina, Bolivia and Peru, including optional ascents above 20,000 feet. All programmes should be preceded by a set period of altitude acclimatisation, which can be provided by a special AAI programme. Fees range from $900-$1400 plus air fares.

**EXUM GUIDE SERVICE & SCHOOL OF MOUNTAINEERING**
**PO Box 56, Moose, Wyoming 83012, USA. Tel: (+1) 307-733-2297.**

# Wind Chill Chart

As wind has an important effect on the temperature it is most advisable to use a tent or bivouac shelter when sleeping in cold weather or at high altitude in windy weather.

| ESTIMATED WIND SPEED IN MPH | ACTUAL THERMOMETER READING (°F) | | | | | | | | | | |
|---|---|---|---|---|---|---|---|---|---|---|---|
| | 50 | 40 | 30 | 20 | 10 | 0 | −10 | −20 | −30 | −40 | −50 |
| | EQUIVALENT TEMPERATURE (°F) | | | | | | | | | | |
| calm | 50 | 40 | 30 | 20 | 10 | 0 | −10 | −20 | −30 | −40 | −50 |
| 5 | 48 | 37 | 27 | 16 | 6 | −5 | −15 | −26 | −36 | −47 | −57 |
| 10 | 40 | 28 | 16 | 4 | −9 | −21 | −33 | −46 | −58 | −70 | −83 |
| 15 | 36 | 22 | 9 | −5 | −18 | −36 | −45 | −58 | −72 | −85 | −99 |
| 20 | 32 | 18 | 4 | −10 | −25 | −39 | −53 | −67 | −82 | −96 | −110 |
| 25 | 30 | 16 | 0 | −15 | −29 | −44 | −59 | −74 | −88 | −104 | −118 |
| 30 | 28 | 13 | −2 | −18 | −33 | −48 | −63 | −79 | −94 | −109 | −125 |
| 35 | 27 | 11 | −4 | −20 | −35 | −49 | −67 | −82 | −98 | −113 | −129 |
| 40 | 26 | 10 | −6 | −21 | −37 | −53 | −69 | −85 | −100 | −116 | −132 |

(wind speeds greater than 40 mph. have little additional effect)

LITTLE DANGER (for properly clothed persons)

Increasing DANGER

GREAT DANGER

Danger from freezing of exposed flesh.

Directors: Rod Newcomb, Peter Lev, H Dean Moore, W Al Read.
In business since 1929.
Member of American Alpine Club.
Holidays for 4,000-5,000 arranged annually.
Climbing instruction and guided mountain travel in the Grand Teton National Park. 1 or 2 day trips for small parties. Camping facilities in the park plus overnight in hut on the Grand Teton mountain. Also 1 day courses in basic and advanced climbing including snow work. Price from $45 a day. Minimum age: 14 years.

## INTERNATIONAL MOUNTAIN CLIMBING SCHOOL
PO Box 239, Conway, NH 03818, USA.
Tel: (+1) 603-447 6700.
President: Paul Ross.
In business since 1974.
Recognised by the American Professional Mountain Guide Association.
Courses for 400 arranged annually. Rock and ice climbing instruction on faces of up to 1,000ft in the White Mountains of New Hampshire. All equipment included in price of around $50 per day; accommodation extra (about $25 night).
Minimum age: 12 years.
Handicapped people catered for.

## LIBERTY BELL ALPINE TOURS
Star Route, Mazama, WA 98833, USA.
Tel: (+1) 509-996 2250.
Proprietor: Eric Sanford.
In business since 1975.
Member of the American Professional Mountain Guides Association.
Programmes for 1,500 arranged annually; most based in the North Cascades National Park, Washington State. Basic 5 day mountaineering course, June-August. Includes all basics for safe and efficient mountain travel, and culminates in an ascent of a major peak. Price $325 inclusive, plus travel to Mazama.

Guided 2 day climbs up the Easton Glacier to the 10,700ft summit of Mt Baker: $150.

Intensive 5 day rock climbing course, culminating in ascent of 7,800ft Liberty Bell Mountain. June-August, $325.

Snow and ice climbing course on the glaciers of Mt Baker. 5 days June-August, $345.

"While none of our programmes are survival ordeals, you should be in good physical shape to enjoy them. Applicants should be able to run two miles easily, and we discourage smokers."

## MOUNTAINEERING SCHOOL AT VAIL, INC.
PO Box 3034, Vail, Colorado 81658, USA.
Tel: (+1) 303-476 4123.
Director: Ted Billings.
In business since 1970.
Holidays for 100 arranged annually.
Mountaineering, rock climbing, snow climbing and backpacking courses in the Gore Range Vail Valley in Colorado. 6 and 10 days basic and advanced courses for groups of 4 to 8, June-September. Tented accommodation. Prices from $300 for 6 days all inclusive. Specially arranged trips to Alaska, British Columbia and Mexico also available. Ski touring and winter climbing available in the winter.
No experience needed.
Minimum age: 12 years.

## MOUNTAIN PEOPLE SCHOOL
157 Oak Spring Drive, San Anselmo, CA 94960, USA. Tel: (+1) 415-450 3664.
Director: Terry C Halbert, CCD.
In business since 1974.
Rock climbing in the Sierra Nevada mountains of California throughout the year. Prices start at $65 for a two day course.
No experience necessary.
Minimum age: 11 years.
Unaccompanied children accepted.

## MOUNTAIN TRAVEL, INC.
1398 Solano Avenue, Albany, CA 94706, USA.
Britain: 22 Church Street, Twickenham TW1 3NW.
Directors: L Lebon, B Lyons.
In business since 1967.
Holidays for 1,000 arranged annually.
Volcano climbing in Mexico and the Andes of Ecuador. Some of the climbing may

involve the use of crampons and ice axes. Instruction given in snow climbing techniques. Prices from $975 for 14 days, air fare not included. Basic mountaineering experience preferred.

**NORTHERN LIGHTS ALPINE RECREATION**
**Box 399, Invermere, British Columbia V0A 1K0, Canada. Tel: (+1) 604-342-6042.**
Director: A Larson.
In business since 1970.
Holidays for 60 arranged annually.
Mountaineering courses for beginners and experts in the Southern Canadian Rockies and Purcell Range. For groups of 2-4 led by expert mountaineers. Accommodation in tents can be arranged separately. Alpine hiking, basic mountaineering, exploratory climbing expeditions and snow-shoeing treks are all arranged. Instruction in route finding, rescue techniques and rock climbing. Basic equipment needed, although ice axes, crampons, stoves and some tents may be hired. Prices from C$400 for 8 days.

Expeditionary mountaineering seminar, $500 for 10 days April-June. Intended for experienced mountaineers.
"It is amazing that in an age when trips by the score head for Nepal and Patagonia, it is still possible, with expert guidance, for the mountaineer to experience first ascents or new routes in Western Canada".
Minimum age: 14 years.

**PSOM/MGS INC. PO Box 694, Bishop, CA 93514, USA. Tel: (+1) 619-873 5037.**
Director: John Fischer.
In business since 1958.
Mountaineering and rock climbing courses in the Sierra Nevada, California from April to October. Basic mountaineering course (six days, around $500) includes equipment, instruction and meals. Basic two-day rock climbing course around $150 including equipment and instruction. Ice climbing course operates January-February ($190). Advanced mountaineering and mountain medicine courses also available. No experience necessary.

Cordillara Blanca Expedition to Peru, July 6-29 1986. Includes Huascarau (22,204ft) and visits to Lima and Huaraz. Price $1,785 plus air travel.

Climbing the volcanoes of Mexico: February 16-March 1 and October 26-November 8 1986. Includes three volcanoes over 17,000ft. Price $885 plus travel to Mexico.
"An excellent introduction to high altitude climbing."
Some experience and equipment required.

# Israel

**JABALIYA TREKKING LTD.**
**36 Keren Hayesod Street, Jerusalem 92426, Israel. Tel: 699385.**
Directors: G Sternbach, M Savir.
In business since 1977.
Recognised by: Israel Ministry of Tourism.
Holidays for 500-1,000 arranged annually.

Discover the Himalayas
with the Experts

**INTERNATIONAL TREKKERS**

*Trekking and Mountaineering in Nepal, Sikkim, Ladakh and Bhutan*

●Fully inclusive tours from $200●

Our tours are accompanied by teams of guides, cooks and sherpa-porters. Clients do not have to do anything but walk!

For reliability, value and experience, contact:

**International Trekkers (Pvt) Ltd**

**Durbar Marg, Post Box 1273 Kathmandu, Nepal**

Tel: 215594     Telex: 2353 INTREK NP

Rock climbing holidays in the mountains of the Sinai. For individuals and groups of 6-20 all year round. Camping accommodation and meals provided plus rental of camels and Bedouin guides if necessary and coordination of rescue facilities. Price on application.
Experience needed.
Ages: 18-75 years.

# Asia

## INTERNATIONAL TREKKERS (PVT) LTD.
**PO Box 1273, Durbar Marg, Kathmandu, Nepal. Tel: (+977) 215594.**
Directors: P T Ongdi, B Whyte.
In business since 1967.
Member of Trekking Agents' Association of Nepal, Nepal Mountaineering Association.
Expeditions for 1,000 people arranged annually.
Mountaineering and trekking in Nepal, Sikkim, Bhutan and Ladakh. Throughout the year in Bhutan, in summer in Ladakh and year-round except for the summer monsoon season in Nepal and Sikkim.
Prices from US$200 include food, tents, sleeping mats and bags etc.
Experience required for treks involving mountaineering; equipment available on request.
Minimum age: 5 years (16 years unaccompanied).
Book direct or through DAV Furstenfeldstr 7, D-8000 München 2 or Adventure Travel Centre, 117 York St, Sydney Australia.
"The grandeur of the mightiest mountains in the world, and the experience of meeting a culture far different from elsewhere in the world."

## MOUNTAIN TRAVEL INDIA PVT. LTD.
**1/1 Rani Jhansi Road, New Delhi 110055, India. Tel: (+91) 11-523057.**
Climbing trips arranged in all accessible areas of India and Nepal for any level of competence, for any length of time.
British agent: ExplorAsia, 13 Chapter Street, London SW1P 4NY. Tel: 01-630 7102.
North American agent: Tiger Tops International (U.S.A.) Inc., 2627 Lombard Street, San Francisco, CA 94123. Tel: (+1) 415-346 3402.

## PSOM/MGS INC.
**PO Box 694, Bishop, CA 93514, USA. Tel: (+1) 619-873 5037.**
High altitude expedition to Langtang in central Nepal, including Ganja La Chuli (19,181 feet). April 14-May 15 1986; price $2,000-$2,500 (depending on numbers taking part) plus air fare.
Some experience and equipment required.

## TRAVELLERS
**Waterside, Kendal, Cumbria LA9 4HE. Tel: (0539) 28334.**
Director: John Noble, FRGS.
In business since 1980.
Climbing and mountaineering in Nepal, India and Sikkim led by well-known mountaineers.

# Cycling

Cycling is an activity which is far more accessible than many other adventure holidays. Since almost everybody learned to ride a bicycle when young, the prospect of a cycling holiday is less daunting than one which involves hang gliding or camel caravanning. It may sound less adventurous than taking to the air or the desert, but freewheeling down a mountain road can be as exhilarating (and dangerous) as gliding or sailing.

Ten years ago, the vogue was for racing machines sporting ten or fifteen gears. Now "mountain bikes" are all the rage: tough enough for a mountainside or a pot-holed city street. In North America it is rare to see an adult riding an "ordinary" bicycle, and bells and baskets-on-the-front are unknown. But it is not necessary to own the sportiest or toughest machine to enjoy country cycling. The Dutch are avid cyclists and yet because of their terrain don't need fancily-geared bicycles. Or you might be inspired to imitate Dervla Murphy, the traveller and author who cycled from her home in Ireland to India on a "boneshaker" in the mid-sixties.

Most organisers of cycling holidays offer sturdy 3-speed bicycles equipped with rack, panniers and repair kit for touring, though some do hire out sports cycles. Some holidays described in this chapter are designed for the independent cyclist; maps and route suggestions are provided, but it is up to the individual to decide whether he stays in a tent or a hotel. Others organise the accommodation along a set route, and still others arrange group cycling with a leader who is knowledgeable both about bicycles and about the area. So whether it is East Anglia or East Africa you wish to explore, consider taking to the back roads on a bicycle.

The Cyclists' Touring Club (see entries below) is the organisation to contact for all cycling information both in Britain and the Continent. Membership costs around £12 per year for adults, half for young people under 21. This includes a cycling magazine, a free technical, legal and touring information service, and the opportunity to join one of 200 local cycling groups in Britain.

# England

## BIKE EVENTS
**PO Box 75, Bath, Avon. Tel: (0225) 310859**
Proprietor: John Potter
In business since 1975.
Holidays for 3,000 arranged annually.
Cycling holidays and events organised throughout Britain. Weekends June-September cycling holiday based at Bath. Price from £40 including mechanic, courier, accommodation and meals. Bike events include riding from Lands End to John o'Groats, Bath to London and London to York. Also days out from £10.
Minimum age: 12 years.

## CALSHOT ACTIVITIES CENTRE
**Calshot Road, Calshot, Southampton SO4 1BR. Tel: (0703) 892077/891380.**
Cycling on the only indoor cycling track in Britain, moved from Earls Court.
Instruction for beginners and cycle teams. Weekend and evening courses. Prices from £46 for a weekend including accommodation, food, use of equipment and instruction.
Minimum age: 13 years.

## CYCLISTS' TOURING CLUB
**69 Meadrow, Godalming, Surrey GU7 3HS. Tel: Godalming (048 68) 7217.**
Established 1880.
Cycle touring in the British Isles April-September. Organised tours for groups of about 16 led by enthusiastic members of the Club. 3-9 day tours around the most scenic areas of Britain such as the New Forest, West Country and Galloway. Itineraries are rated according to strenuousness. Accommodation in youth hostels, guest houses and occasionally tents. Food and accommodation are the only costs.
Cycling experience required.
Minimum age: 11 years. Age limits vary with itineraries.
Bookings through individual tour organisers. Addresses available from Cyclists' Touring Club (enclose SAE).

## CYCLORAMA HOLIDAYS (V)
**The Grange Hotel, Grange over Sands, Cumbria LA11 6EJ. Tel: (04484) 3666.**
Proprietor: G C Thompson MA.
Member of Cumbria Tourist Board.
Cycle touring holidays in the Lake District and along the Cumbrian Coast based at 5 hotel centres for individuals and groups. 5, 7 or 8 days (although longer trips can be arranged) from late March to end of October. Luggage is transported for cyclists between hotels. Hotel, guest house and inn accommodation. Prices from £116 for 6 nights including accommodation, breakfast, evening meal, transfer of luggage, use of bicycle and accessories, maps, route guides etc. Reduced prices for those bringing their own bicycles. Also Cumbria Cycleway Tours for groups.
Cycling and map reading experience needed.
Minimum age: 9 years.

## EACH CYCLING HOLIDAYS LTD.
**Tempo House, 15-27 Falcon Road, London SW11 2PH. Tel: 01-223 7662.**
Directors: D Smith, G P Robinson.
Cycling holidays in East Anglia, West Country, Yorkshire Dales, Scottish Borders and Highlands for individuals but not groups. Accommodation at pubs, inns, youth hostels, farms, etc. on half board or bed and breakfast basis. Fully equipped touring and sports cycles provided. Prices from £78 per week + VAT.
Minimum age: 11 years.
Unaccompanied children: 14 years+.

## FLATFORD MILL FIELD CENTRE
**East Bergholt, Colchester CO7 6UL. Tel: Colchester (0206) 298283.**
Administered by the Field Studies Council.
Warden and Director of Studies: Dr A Hodges.
Courses on "Cycling in Constable Country" through Suffolk with the opportunity to learn about the natural and local history while cycling. Bicycles may be hired. Four day courses about £78.50 including tuition, accommodation and meals.

## HF HOLIDAYS
Dept 43, 142 Great North Way, London NW4 1EG.
One week tours based on HF holiday centre at Alnmouth in Northumberland led by a specialist. Cycling is at a leisurely pace with time to visit places of interest. Price around £170, less £15 if you take your own bicycle. Reduced rate rail travel available.

## JUST PEDALLING
The Glass House, Wensum Street, Norwich, Norfolk. Tel: (0603) 615200.
Partners: Adelin & Tony Johnson.
In business since 1979.
Holidays for up to 1,000 arranged annually. Cycling holidays in East Anglia for individuals throughout the year. Bed and breakfast accommodation provided in farms and guest houses. Suggested itineraries to suit specialist interests such as historic buildings, wildlife or real ale pubs. 3- or 5-speed bicycles with lights, panniers, tools, waterproofs and maps. Price £120 per week.
Minimum age: 12 years.

## PEAK NATIONAL PARK STUDY CENTRE
Losehill Hall, Castleton, Derbyshire S30 2WB. Tel: (0433) 20373.
Cycling holidays for beginners and more experienced cyclists in the Peak National Park. Price from £123 per week including accommodation and full board. Cycle hire can be arranged.
Minimum age: 8 years.
Unaccompanied children: 16 years+.

## YHA TRAVEL
14 Southampton Street, London WC2E 7HY. Tel: 01-240 5236.
Cycling holidays in North Norfolk and Wales. 7 days July-August. Average of 35 miles cycling per day. Bicycles must be in good condition and cyclists are advised that small wheel bicycles are not suitable. Price £95.
Also cross-country cycling using mountain bikes in the Peak District.
Unaccompanied children: 11-15 years.

# Scotland

## BIKE EVENTS
PO Box 75, Bath, Avon. Tel: (0225) 310859.
Cycle tours of the Highlands and Islands. 13 days August-September. Price around £300 including ferry charges, mechanic, courier, accommodation and meals. Travelling through Arran and Kintyre and on the islands of Mull and Skye.
Minimum age: 12 years.

## EACH CYCLING HOLIDAYS LTD.
Tempo House, 15-27 Falcon Road, London SW11 2PH. Tel: 01-223 7662.
Cycling holidays in various parts of Scotland for individuals for one week. Bed and breakfast or half board accommodation in hotels, inns, farmhouses and youth hostels. Fully equipped touring and sports cycles provided. Price from £82 per week.
Minimum age: 11 years.
Unaccompanied children: 14 years+.

## HIGHLAND CYCLE TOURS
Highland Guides, Aviemore, Inverness-shire. Tel: (0479) 810729.
Proprietor: Chris Hawson.
In business since 1980.
Holidays for 200 arranged each year. One week cycle tours in the Highlands, June-September. Accommodation in youth hostels (about £100 per week), or in bed and breakfast (about £215, including support vehicles). Most meals not included. Bicycles provided; reductions for those who bring their own cycles. Rail is used to reduce cycling distances and must be paid for separately. Self-led tours and cycle hire also available.
"On these tours, the cycling 'is the time not spent eating or drinking', to quote one satisfied customer."

## SCOTTISH CYCLING HOLIDAYS
Ballintuim Post Office, Blairgowrie, Perthshire PH10 7NJ. Tel: (025 086) 201.
Proprietor: Kenneth Todd.
Cycling tours of the Borders and Highlands of Scotland for individuals and groups. 1-2

weeks throughout the year but length of tours flexible. Short break and "stay-put" holidays available. Accommodation in guest houses, hotels or youth hostels. Price from £90 to £170. Fully equipped adult and children's touring cycles and tandems available for hire. Advice is given to those who wish to plan their own tours.
No experience needed.
All ages.

### SCOTTISH YOUTH HOSTELS ASSOCIATION
**7 Glebe Crescent, Stirling FK8 2JA. Tel: (0786) 72821.**
Cycling trips based at youth hostels from the Isle of Skye to Glencoe. One week May-September. Prices from £84.50 include 10-speed bike, experienced leader and hostel accommodation.
Minimum age: 12 years.

# Wales

### JOYRIDES
**The Old Station, Machynlleth, Powys. Tel: (0654) 3109.**
Proprietor: Alun Williams.
In operation since 1981.
Cycling holidays throughout rural Wales. 1-2 weeks Easter-September. Self-catering youth hostel accommodation or bed and breakfast arranged. 10-speed bicycles and all equipment are provided.
All ages.

### NEUADD ARMS HOTEL
**The Square, Llanwrtyd Wells, Powys. Tel: (05913) 236.**
Mountain bicycle holidays in the Cambrian Mountains at Britain's first centre for the sport. Weekends and weeks throughout the year. Price from £35 for weekend, £110 for one week including accommodation and all meals. Mountain bicycles may be hired.
Unaccompanied children: 14 years+.

# Ireland

### BIKE EVENTS
**PO Box 75, Bath, Avon. Tel: (0225) 310859.**
Cycle tours of County Kerry. One week in September. Price around £170 including ferry from Liverpool, courier, route maps, accommodation and breakfast. Based at Kenmare in the Kerry Hills with the Killarney Mountains to the north.
Minimum age: 12 years.

### MOUNTAIN LODGE
**Bridia Valley, Glencar, Co. Kerry, Ireland.**
Proprietors: Bernard & Gina Edwards.
In business since 1981 (under present name since 1985).
Recognised by Cyclists Touring Club.
Cycling tours of Kerry arranged for individuals and groups of up to 12 throughout the year. Accommodation — and meals made from home grown produce — in traditional Irish farmhouse. Cycles can be hired locally. Price £85 per week inclusive.
Minimum age: 16 years.

# Europe

### ACCUEIL DES JEUNES EN FRANCE
**12 rue des Barres, 75004 Paris. Tel: (+33) 1-278 04 82.**
Cycling holidays in the Gorges du Tarn, the lakes of Auvergne and the Lot valley, from late June to late August. Between 30-50km covered each day. Bicycles provided except in Auvergne. Camping or youth hostel accommodation and all meals included in price of 1,350-1,500F (about £110-120) plus travel to site.
Minimum age: 18 years.

### BIKE EVENTS
**PO Box 75, Bath, Avon. Tel: (0225) 310859.**
Cycle tour of the vineyards of the Dordogne

in France. 2 weeks June-July. Price £360 including ferry and accommodation. Grand tour from London to Venice around £300. Minimum age: 12 years.

## CYCLISTS' TOURING CLUB
**69 Meadrow, Godalming, Surrey GU7 3HS. Tel: (048 68) 7217.**
Cycle touring in Western Europe for groups of about 16. 9-16 days May-September. Itineraries include Northern France, Southern Ireland, Black Forest of Germany, Holland and Northern Spain. Accommodation in hostels or hotels. Pace varies from leisurely to about 70 miles per day, according to preference of individual tour leader.
Cycling experience required.
Minimum age varies with itinerary.
Bookings through individual tour leaders whose addresses are available from the Cyclists' Touring Club (enclose S.A.E.).

## EACH CYCLING HOLIDAYS LTD.
**Tempo House, 15-27 Falcon Road, London SW11 2PH. Tel: 01-223 7662.**
Cycling holidays in various parts of Holland and Denmark for individuals for one week. Bed and breakfast or half board accommodation in hotels, inns, farmhouses and youth hostels. Fully equipped cycles with panniers, maps, etc. Price from £175 including return travel.
Minimum age: 11 years.
Unaccompanied children: 14 years+.

## INTERNATIONAL BICYCLE TOURING SOCIETY
**2115 Pasoe Dorado, La Jolla, CA 92037, USA. Tel: (+1) 619-459 8775.**
President: Clifford Graves.
A non-profit organisation in operation since 1864.
Tours for 450 people arranged annually. Cycling tours throughout Europe planned for 1986: Italy (May), southern France (May/June and September/October), Brittany (June), Austria (July), Holland to Denmark (July), Sweden (August), Yugoslavia (September), Greece (October) and northern Spain (October). Itineraries are graded according to difficulty. Average price of $40 per day for food, hotel accommodation and support vehicle. Participants must provide their own bicycles.
Volunteer leaders are invited to submit proposals for tours and to lead them in return for a reduction in price.
Minimum age: 21 years.

## NEUCHATEL TOURIST OFFICE
**rue du Trésor 9 (Place des Halles), Neuchâtel 2001, Switzerland. Tel: (+41) 38-251789.**
Director: René Leuba.
Nine cycling itineraries and five tours prepared and maintained around the canton of Neuchâtel, totalling 360 kilometres. Participants arrange their own accommodation.

## SUSI MADRON'S HOLIDAYS
**11 Norman Road, Manchester M14 5LF. Tel: 061-225 0739.**
Directors: Susan Madron, Roy Madron.
In business since 1979.
Holidays for around 1,000 arranged annually.
Cycling holidays in various parts of France. 1-2 weeks May-September. Hotel accommodation prearranged on cycling circuits. Bicycles and equipment provided. Participants proceed at their own pace without group leaders. Price from £200 per week including all travel and accommodation.
All ages.

## YHA TRAVEL
**14 Southampton Street, London WC2E 7HY. Tel: 01-240 5236.**
Cycling in Luxembourg planning own route and making own reservations in youth hostels. 10 days April-October. Full board and hire of cycles provided.
Cycling holidays in the Loire Valley in France for individuals and small groups. 9 or 15 days from July to September. Accommodation in youth hostels or camping with full board. Cycles provided. Average distance 30-35 km per day.
Cycling across Holland. 13 days March-November. Youth hostel accommodation with breakfast. Cycles not provided. 20-40 km covered per day.

All holidays include travel from England.
Prices from £165.
Minimum age: 16 years.

# Americas

## BIKECENTENNIAL INC.
PO Box 8308P, Missoula, Montana 59807, USA. Tel: (+1) 406-721 1776.
Director: Gary MacFadden.
In business since 1975.
Cycling camping and country tours in the USA and Canada for groups of 9-11. 6 to 90 days from late May to November. Price from around $330 for 12 days includes maps, services of leader, food, camp sites, some equipment and insurance. Participants must supply own bicycles.
No experience needed, but may be useful on more arduous trips.
"A member-supported non profit organisation for touring bicyclists."
Minimum age: 18 years.

## BIKE EVENTS
PO Box 75, Bath, Avon. Tel: (0225) 310859.
Cycle Tour of New England, USA. 15 days September-October. Price around £700 including air, train and bus fares, courier, maps, accommodation and meals. Travelling through upstate New York, Vermont, New Hampshire to Cape Cod in the 'fall'.
Minimum age: 12 years.

## BIKE VERMONT
PO Box 207 AH, Woodstock, VT 05091, USA. Tel: (+1) 802-457-3553.
Director: R R McElwain.
In business since 1975.
Holidays for 1,000 arranged annually.
Bicycle tours in Vermont for individuals and groups of 10-15. Weekends or 5 days from mid-May to October. Support van for luggage and assistance. Rentals available. Accommodation in small country inns with breakfast and evening meal. Price from around $400 for 5 days all inclusive.
No experience needed.

## CYCLISTS' TOURING CLUB
69 Meadrow, Godalming, Surrey GU7 3HS. Tel: (048 68) 7217.
Cycle touring in Atlantic Canada. 22 days July-August. Average mileage of 50 per day with 3 rest days. Travelling through Nova Scotia and Prince Edward Island.
Cycling experience required.
Bookings through individual tour leaders whose addresses are available from the Cyclists' Touring Club (enclose S.A.E.).

## INTERNATIONAL BICYCLE TOURING SOCIETY
2115 Paseo Dorado, La Jolla, CA 92037, USA. Tel: (+1) 619-459 8775.
Cycling tours in scenic areas of the USA and Canada. Price around $50 per day, for food, accommodation and support vehicle. Participants must provide their own bicycles.
Minimum age: 21 years.

## LIBERTY BELL ALPINE TOURS
Star Route, Mazama, WA 98833, USA. Tel: (+1) 509-996 2250.
Cycling tours in Washington State featuring 18 speed Bianchi mountain bikes. All equipment, meals and accommodation (six nights) included in prices. Travel to tour location extra. Methow Valley, $325; San Juan Islands, $345; Cascade Mountains, $275; wineries tour (including private tours and wine tastings), $475.

## OPEN ROAD BICYCLE TOURS
1601-AH Summit Drive, Haymarket, VA 22069, USA. Tel: (+1) 703-754 4152.
Director: Bryon E Reed.
In business since 1982.
Bicycling holidays in the mid-Atlantic USA and Nova Scotia, Canada, March-November. Ten historic and scenic itineraries in the States range in length from two to five days in areas such as the Pennsylvania Dutch Country, the Shenandoah Valley, and Colonial Williamsburg, Virginia. The Nova Scotia tour is ten days in length and includes the "Lighthouse Route" along the seacoast. Lodging is in country inns, bed and breakfasts and small hotels; tours feature regional meals. Experienced leaders and

support vans accompany all trips; bicycles are available for hire. The selection of cycling routes on each day will accommodate any ability, and participants always ride at their own pace. Prices from $179 for a weekend.
Minimum age (unaccompanied): 18 years.

**ROCKY MOUNTAIN CYCLE TOURS**
**PO Box 895, Banff, Alberta, Canada T0L 0C0. Tel: (+1) 403-762 3477.**
Proprietors: Larry & Mary Jane Barnes.
In business since 1976.
Cycle touring holidays in Banff National Park, Jasper National Park, Alberta and Eastern British Columbia for individuals and groups of up to 20. Holidays of 5-18 days from June to September. Camping or mountain lodge accommodation with all meals and support vehicle provided. Price from C$470. Bicycles can be hired. Self-guided tour map available by air mail for C$8.95.

EXPO 86 ride across British Columbia to the World Fair in Vancouver, September 8-21 1986. C$1290 plus C$125 bicycle rental.
Participants should be fit.
Minimum age: 15 years.

**VERMONT BICYCLE TOURING**
**Box 711-GA, Bristol, VT 05443, USA. Tel: (+1) 802-453 4811.**
Director: John S Freidin.
In business since 1972.
Holidays for 5,000 arranged annually.
Bicycle touring holidays in the State of Vermont for individuals and groups of 12-35. Weekends, weeks or longer from May to October. Accommodation and meals in country inns. Prices from $150-$450 include accommodation, breakfast, evening meal and guides. Bicycles can be hired for an additional charge.
All ages.

# Israel

**JABALIYA TREKKING LTD.**
**36 Keren Hayesod Street, Jerusalem, Israel. Tel: (+972) 2-699385.**
Cycling tour of Central and Northern Israel for individuals and small groups all year round. Accommodation in tents, on a kibbutz, in a village or hotel. All equipment provided. Prices on application.
Ages: 18-75 years.

# Africa

**CYCLISTS' TOURING CLUB**
**69 Meadrow, Godalming, Surrey GU7 3HS. Tel: (048 68) 7217.**
Cycle touring in Kenya. 18-25 days December-January. Travelling from Mombasa on the coast to Mounts Kenya and Kilimanjaro. Optional 1 week camping safari available.
Cycling experience required.
Bookings through individual tour leaders whose addresses are available from the Cyclists' Touring Club (enclose SAE).

# Asia

**EXODUS EXPEDITIONS LTD.**
**All Saints Passage, 100 Wandsworth High Street, London SW18 4LE. Tel: 01-870 0151.**
In operation since 1973.
Holidays for 2,000 arranged annually.
Cycling tours in China. 2-4 weeks throughout the year. Hotel accommodation and meals provided. Prices from £1,620-£2,190 inclusive.
Reasonable fitness required.

**OPEN ROAD BICYCLE TOURS**
**1601 Summit Drive, Haymarket, VA 22069, USA. Tel: (+1) 703-754 4152.**
Six itineraries in China of 18-26 days including the Great Wall, the Yangzi Valley, Beijing and Shanghai. Prices up to $3,400 excluding air travel.

**SACU TOURS**
Society for Anglo-Chinese Understanding.
152 Camden High Street, London NW1
0NE. Tel: 01-482 4292.
Chairman: Jim Pennington.
In business since 1967.
Holidays for 400 arranged annually.
Cycling tours of the Yangzi Delta. 24 days
May, August and September. Price of
around £1,800 includes air travel,
insurance, meals in China, accommodation
and the services of a tour leader and guide.
Meals in Hong Kong are extra. Cycling
through a countryside of mulberry bushes,
cotton and green rice paddy, visiting the
Summer Palace at Beijing, the Ming Tombs
and Great Wall, the Buddhist carvings of
Sinian and to Suzhon, the 'Venice of the
East'. SACU holds preparatory study
weekends six weeks prior to departure.

No experience needed.
All ages.

# Australasia

**INTERNATIONAL BICYCLE
TOURING SOCIETY
2115 Paseo Dorado, La Jolla, CA 92037,
USA. Tel: (+1) 619-459 8775.**
Cycling tour of New Zealand scheduled for
February 1986. Three weeks on South
Island, optional extra week on North Island.
Price around US$45 per day plus air fare.
Participants must provide their own
bicycles.
Minimum age: 21 years.

# Flying

Most people's experience of flying is confined to the inside of a jet airliner. Several more intimate forms of flying, however, have developed into increasingly popular leisure pastimes. Airborne activities are extremely varied in terms of length of time in the air, duration of necessary training, expense, amount of technical equipment and knowledge required, participation involved, risks entailed and excitement experienced. Among all those who fly there is a great sense of comradeship and a strong addiction to altitude.

BALLOONING was man's first experience of flight over 200 years ago. However, it was not until the late 1960s that hot-air ballooning really developed in Britain. It is a very tranquil experience and virtually passive as you are expected only to stand and look at the receding countryside, the mechanics of the flight being handled by experts. If you wish to learn to fly a balloon yourself and can afford it (they cost several thousand pounds), it is possible to buy your own, usually as part of a syndicate. Some manufacturers provide instruction or you can learn on an hourly basis at a club. The minimum age is 17 and you must provide a medical certificate. Further information can be obtained from the British Balloon and Airship Club, Kimberley House, 47 Vaughan Way, Leicester LE1 4SG. Tel: (0533) 531051.

GLIDING is a very graceful sport. Gliders are usually made of wood and covered with fabric. They fly as a bird does when soaring, that is when the speed of the air flowing over the wings is enough to cause it to lift. While training you will fly in a two seater with a qualified pilot and the first flight will last about 15-20 minutes. During a week's course with average weather conditions you can expect to do about 20 launches and it will take an average of 50 to be at the standard to enable you to fly solo. Occasionally novices can learn to fly solo by the end of a one-week holiday course. The minimum age for solo flying is 16. Introductory courses include subjects such as aerodynamics, navigation and meteorology. All equipment is usually provided by the club or can be hired. Suitable warm and waterproof clothing is very important as airfields are very exposed places and the air at 2000 feet can be quite cool even in summer. Sunglasses are essential on a sunny day. Further information can be obtained from the British Gliding Association, Kimberley House, 47 Vaughan Way, Leicester LE1 4SG. Tel: (0533) 531051.

**HANG GLIDING** is the fulfilment of man's dream of stepping off a hill or mountain and flying like a bird. It has made flying a possibility for almost everyone since it is relatively inexpensive and involves very little equipment. Training includes ground instruction in aerodynamics, wind conditions and possible hazards as well as learning how to manoeuvre with the glider. This is done from a hill facing into the wind and by the end of the course you should be able to make flights from the hilltop, turn left and right, land accurately at the bottom of the hill. By doing so, you should qualify for a Pilot 1 certificate which will enable you to hire or buy a hang glider and use it without supervision. A five-day course is normally needed to reach this standard. The minimum age for flying solo is 16. You should wear warm and waterproof clothing and a helmet.

**PARACHUTING**, although terrifying at first, is probably one of the most thrilling and exhilarating of the airsports. It is not as dangerous as it may seem as very thorough training is given and high standards of safety are met. The training which usually takes place over 2 days includes study of the equipment used, exit drill from the aircraft, theory and practice in a suspended harness, canopy handling, landing falls and emergency procedure. The first jump is made from about 2,500 feet with an automatically opening parachute attached to the aircraft by a static line, and a reserve in case of malfunction. After 6 static line jumps you may progress to free fall descents.
You should wear a one-piece boiler suit, helmet without a peak and boots with ankle support but no lace hooks. Use of all equipment is included in the price. The minimum age is 16 and you must provide a medical certificate. The course fee usually includes membership of the British Parachute Association, which is the governing body of all clubs and can provide insurance cover. The address is Kimberley House, 47 Vaughan Way, Leicester LE1 4SG. Tel: (0533) 59778.

**PARASCENDING** is similar to parachuting with the major difference being that no aircraft is needed. The parascender is launched into the air, underneath an already open parachute, by being towed behind a landrover or speed boat. After only a few steps he or she becomes airborne; the expert can gently ascend to about 1,000 feet where he releases the tow line to make a normal parachute descent.
Beginners start with thorough ground training before making low ascents (about 100 feet), while remaining on the tow line. Higher and longer flights come later in the training programme. Parascending is probably the most economical way of becoming airborne. Most British Association of Parachute

Clubs (BAPC) member clubs run one-day courses for around £25. This includes training, use of equipment and four or five flights. Subsequent flights usually cost around £3. The only equipment a beginner needs is strong ankle-supporting boots and old outer clothing for land and a swimming costume or wet suit and plimsolls for water. The minimum age is 14 years.

It is very important that you should take a course only at a member club of the BAPC which will have qualified instructors. The BAPC, Room 6, Exchange Buildings, 34-50 Rutland Street, Leicester LE1 1RD; tel: (0533) 530318, will provide a list of clubs and any further information you may require.

POWER FLYING is the most expensive way to take to the air and it takes 3-4 weeks of intensive training to complete the course for a Private Pilot's Licence (although an experienced glider can qualify in less). Many clubs offer instruction on an hourly basis but holiday courses are sometimes arranged. The PPL training consists of both flying practice including take offs, landings and cross-country navigation, and ground instruction in related subjects. The minimum age is 17 and before embarking on a course you must have a medical examination by a Civil Aviation Authority doctor. Further information — and details of clubs and schools offering instruction — can be obtained from the Aircraft Owners and Pilots Association, British Light Aviation Centre, 50a Cambridge Street, London SW1V 4QQ.

# Ballooning

## England

**ELCOT PARK HOTEL**
**near Newbury, Berkshire RG16 8NJ. Tel: (0488) 58100.**
Director: H. P. Sterne.
Balloon flights arranged at weekends throughout the year. Price £50 per person per flight. Accommodation and meals not included.

**SKYSALES BALLOONING HOLIDAYS LTD.**
**249 Passage Road, Bristol BS10 7JB. Tel: (0272) 501196.**
Directors: M J Moore, E M Moore.
In business since 1977.

Member of: British Balloon & Airship Club.
Flights for 150 arranged annually.
Introduction to hot air ballooning based at Bristol, London, Nottingham and Leicester on various days from April to October. £60 per flight.
Minimum age: 12 years.

## Europe

**THOMAS COOK HOLIDAYS — MARLBORO ADVENTURE TRAVEL**
**Thorpe Wood, PO Box 36, Peterborough, Cambs PE3 8LB. Tel: (0733) 64200.**
Hot air ballooning in the foothills of the Jura mountains in eastern France, from June to October. Hotel and auberge accommodation. Prices from £450 include four flights and six nights half-board; travel to and from destination extra.

# Americas

**BALLOON CORPORATION OF AMERICA**
**2084 Thompson Road, Fenton, MI 48430, USA. Tel: (+1) 313-629 0040.**
Director: Dennis Floden ("Captain Phogg").
In business since 1970.
Member of Flint Convention and Visitors Bureau.
Flights for 700-1,000 arranged annually.
Hot-air balloon champagne flights throughout the year. The three hour ballooning adventure includes a one hour flight followed by a champagne celebration.
Prices: $200 for 1 to $400 for 4; reductions for groups of ten or more.
"We set down gently in a lake and pretend to be a sail boat — this we call a Splash and Dash".
Handicapped people catered for during ideal weather.
Minimum age: 5 years. Unaccompanied children accepted.

**SCORPION BALLOONS INC.**
**246 Lomita Drive, PO Box 147, Perris, CA 92370, USA. Tel: (+1) 714-657 6930.**
Directors: A, F and H Kregg.
In business since 1969.
Flights for 300 arranged annually.
One hour demonstration flights at sunrise in southern California. One or two passengers — $180; three — $240; four — $280.
Champagne is served after landing. Private Pilot Course from around $1,500.

# Gliding

## England

**CAMBRIDGE UNIVERSITY GLIDING CLUB**
**55 Moorfield Road, Duxford, Cambridge.**
Established 1935.
Recognised by BGA.
Gliding courses near Cambridge for individuals and groups of up to 6. 5 days from June to September. All types of accommodation available locally. Course includes 10 aerotow launches to 2,000' and 5 hours flying, weather permitting.
No experience needed.
Ages: 15-65 years.

**CORNISH GLIDING CLUB**
**Travellas Airfield, Perranporth, Cornwall.**
**Tel: (087 257) 2124.**
Chairman: J Trenchard.
In business since 1957.
Member of BGA.
Holiday courses for 150 arranged annually.
Gliding holidays for individuals and groups of up to 6. 5 days May-October. Price £150 for all flying fees, accommodation not included.
No experience needed.
All ages.
Unaccompanied teenagers: 16 years+
Bookings through: Ruth B Phillips (Course Secretary), Cornish Gliding Club, 14a Kenwyn Street, Truro TR1 1DF. Tel: (0872) 73892.

**DERBYSHIRE AND LANCASHIRE GLIDING CLUB LTD.**
**Camphill, Great Hucklow, Buxton, Derbyshire SK17 8RQ. Tel: (0298) 871270.**
Directors: P Gray, J Humpherson.
Secretary: P Hubbard.
In business since 1935.
Holidays for 200 arranged annually.
Member of BGA.
Training holiday courses in gliding for individuals and groups of up to 16. 5 full days May-September. Price of approximately £175. Course members help with all aspects of the flying operation, especially with the driving of tractors used to tow cables and gliders. Course members automatically become temporary members of the Club.
Minimum age: 16 years.

**ESSEX GLIDING CLUB**
**North Weald Airfield, near Epping, Essex.**
Directors: C Nicholas, J Critch.

In business since 1963.
Recognised by BGA.
Holiday gliding courses from April to the end of September. Courses operate Monday-Friday inclusive. Accommodation not included in price of £95-£130 but is available locally.
Minimum age: 16.

**KENT GLIDING CLUB LTD.**
**Squids Gate, Challock, Ashford, Kent TN25 4DR. Tel: (023 374) 274.**
Directors: R Cousins, H Gardiner, R Neame, R Hubble.
In business since 1965.
4 and 5 day holiday flying courses for beginners, April-October. Up to 20 winch launches and instruction of basic manoeuvres. All equipment, tuition, meals and dormitory accommodation included in prices from £160 to £200.
Minimum age: 16 years.

**LAKES GLIDING CLUB**
**Walney Airfield, Barrow in Furness, Cumbria LA14 3RN.**

In business over 20 years.
Gliding courses June-August; six days from Sunday night to Saturday. Price around £180 including all instruction, equipment, meals and dormitory accommodation.
"A bird's eye view of the beautiful Lake District."
Minimum age: 16 years.
Book through Peter Lewis (Course Secretary), Greenock Sweet Store, 166 Dalton Road, Barrow in Furness, Cumbria LA14 1PU. Tel: (0229) 39494.

**LASHAM GLIDING SOCIETY**
**Lasham Airfield, near Alton, Hampshire GU34 5SS. Tel: (025 683) 270/322.**
General Secretary/Manager: Phil Phillips.
Over 20 years in operation.
Member of BGA.
Gliding instruction all year round. Accommodation in double or single bunkrooms, and all meals provided. Price per week from £215 inclusive. Weekend courses also available.
Minimum age: 10 years.

## DERBYSHIRE & LANCASHIRE GLIDING CLUB LIMITED

MEMBER OF THE BRITISH GLIDING ASSOCIATION

Situated high in the Peak National Park, close to Edale.

5 day Training Holiday Courses from June to September. Approx £180.

Full board and accommodation included.

**Camphill,
Great Hucklow,
Buxton,
Derbyshire SK17 8RQ
Tel: 0298 871270**

Come Gliding with the

# LAKES GLIDING CLUB

**Summer Gliding Holidays in the beautiful Lake District**

Six-day Holidays for only £180 including instruction, accommodation and all meals

**For our brochure, contact the Course Secretary:**
Mr Peter Lewis, Greenock Sweet Store, 166 Dalton Road, Barrow in Furness, Cumbria LA14 1PU
**Tel: Barrow (0229) 37494 or 23457**

**MIDLAND GLIDING CLUB LTD.**
**The Long Mynd, Church Stretton,**
**Shropshire SY6 6TA. Tel: (058 861) 206.**
Course Secretary: Mr P V Strickland.
Gliding holidays for individuals or groups.
5 days April-October. Accommodation, all
meals, expert instruction and temporary
club membership provided. Prices on
application. Beginners are given instruction
in modern two-seater gliders.
No experience needed.
Minimum age: 16 years.

**YHA TRAVEL**
**14 Southampton Street, London WC2E**
**7HY. Tel: 01-240 5236.**
Gliding in the Lake District for 7 days. Price
from £175 inclusive. Flying in T49 two
seaters.
No experience needed.
Minimum age: 16 years.

**YORKSHIRE GLIDING CLUB LTD.**
**Sutton Bank, Thirsk, Yorkshire. Tel: (0845)**
**597 237.**

In business since 1935.
Member of BGA.
Holidays for 250 arranged annually.
Gliding instruction for individuals and
groups of up to 12. Open throughout the
year. 5-day courses for beginners and
experts available April-October. Accommodation in modern clubhouse with meals,
from £90 per week. Gliding charges from
£12 per hour including instruction. The
sheer escarpments of Sutton Bank facing the
prevailing winds provide hill, wave and
thermal soaring over an unspoiled part of
Yorkshire. "Gliding is a sport of
participation: launch cables have to be
retrieved, gliders returned to launch points,
logs to be kept, etc. Yet there is the joy of
launching into motorless flight, and
climbing to heights of several thousand feet
powered only by currents of air, while
enjoying views extending from the coast to
beyond the Pennines."
Minimum age: 15 years.
No experience needed.

**Reach for the Skies!**

# MIDLAND
# GLIDING CLUB

Spend a holiday with us, gliding over
the outstanding scenery of the
Welsh Borders.

*Expert instruction in*
*modern two-seaters*

For full details and bookings,
contact the Course Secretary

**Midland Gliding Club**
**The Long Mynd, Church Stretton,**
**Shropshire SY6 6TA**

**Telephone: (058 861) 206**

# YORKSHIRE
# GLIDING CLUB

*Take a holiday gliding*
*course at Sutton Bank.*

The Y.G.C. offers 5 day courses
with full-time professional
instruction at its superb site in the
North Yorkshire National Park.
Residential licensed clubhouse,
modern aircraft and unrivalled
freedom from airways are all yours
at surprisingly low rates.
**For details contact:**
**Miss V. W. Woodhead,**
**Yorkshire Gliding Club,**
**Sutton Bank, Thirsk, North Yorkshire.**
**Telephone: (0845) 597237**

# Americas

## SIERRA NEVADA SOARING
**PO Box 60036, 4895 Texas Avenue, Reno-Stead Airport, Reno, NV 89506, USA. Tel: (+1) 702-972 7757.**
President: James D Richardson
In business since 1976.
Gliding instruction around Reno near the Sierra Nevada range of mountains for individuals throughout the year. Price for course to reach level to fly solo from $695. Advanced instruction, glider rentals and sightseeing trips also available for one or two people.
No experience needed.
Minimum age: 14 years.
Unaccompanied children accepted.

# Hang Gliding

## England

## ISLE OF WIGHT HANG GLIDING CENTRE
**Rose Cottage, Clay Lane, Newbridge, Isle of Wight PO41 0UA. Tel: (0983) 78488.**
Proprietor: M D McMillan.
In business since 1981.
Recognised by: ETB, BHGA.
Holidays for 300 arranged annually.
Hang gliding training, weekly courses all year round. Price from £135 for instruction and all equipment hire and island transportation. Tuition by winch now makes learning quicker and easier. Camping or bed and breakfast accommodation available. Other sports also arranged.
Minimum age: 16 years.

## NORTHERN HANG GLIDING CENTRE
**155 Filey Road, Scarborough, North Yorkshire YO11 3AE. Tel: (0723) 353077.**
Proprietor: Richard Ware.

In business since 1978.
Registered with BHGA.
Holidays for 200-250 arranged annually.
Hang gliding courses over the Yorkshire coast. 5 days throughout the year. Accommodation can be arranged locally. Price of £120 for certificate course includes all instruction and equipment.

Multi activity holidays arranged including surfing, boardsailing, parascending and waterskiing. Based at Killerby Park, Cayton Bay near Scarborough. Weekly from April; details from Northern Hang Gliding Centre.
No experience needed.
Ages: 16-60 years.

## SKYRIDERS BRITISH HANG GLIDING SCHOOLS
**15 St Mary's Green, Biggin Hill, Kent. Tel: (095 94) 73996.**
Proprietor: Derek Bond.
In business since 1976. First UK school.
Approved by BHGA.
Holidays for 1,000 arranged annually.
Hang gliding instruction for individuals and groups of up to 18. Introductory courses of 1-2 days. BHGA Pilot 1 course takes 4-6 days. Open throughout the year for weekly holidays. Accommodation available locally. All equipment provided. Price from £26 per day. 15% discount for groups.
No experience needed.
Minimum age: 16 years.

## SUSSEX COLLEGE OF HANG GLIDING
**49 Church Street, Brighton, Sussex. Tel: (0273) 24151/609925/733914.**
Proprietor: Captain V Hallam.
In business since 1979.
Registered by: BHGA, Federation of British Hang Gliding Schools.
Hang gliding courses on the Sussex Downs with occasional group visits to Wales and Ireland. Individuals or groups of up to 6. 3 day basic course £80, 5 days or more to reach Pilot 1 standard £180. Tuition and equipment provided. Accommodation must be arranged independently. Equipment may be hired or further instruction received for £25 per day.

No experience needed.
Ages: 16-73 years.

## Scotland

### CAIRNWELL HANG GLIDING SCHOOL
**Cairnwell Mountain, Braemar, Aberdeenshire AB3 5XS. Tel: (033 83) 331.**
Proprietor: Gustav Fischnaller (Scottish champion in 1977).
In business since 1973.
Approved by BHGA.
Hang gliding holidays in the Grampian Mountains for individuals and groups of 6-8. 2, 4 and 7 day courses from May to the end of September. The 7 day course leads toward a Pilot One licence. Accommodation can be arranged locally.
Price from £46.50 for 2 days.
No experience needed.
Ages: 16-55 years.

**CAIRNWELL**
**HANG GLIDING**
B.H.G.A. REGISTERED
Gustav Fischnaller

Cairnwell Mountain Braemar
Aberdeenshire AB3 5XS
Telephone Braemar 331

***BASED IN THE SCENIC GRAMPIAN RANGE OF THE EASTERN SCOTTISH HIGHLANDS***

In operation for over ten years under the guidance of Gustav Fischnaller, the Chief Flying Instructor who pioneered the sport in Scotland in the early 1970s and was Scottish Champion in 1977

Specifically designed training gliders which fly low & slow

***2 and 4 DAY COURSES***

**PILOT ONE SCHEME**

BUDGET AND HOTEL ACCOMMODATION ARRANGED LOCALLY

## Wales

### WELSH HANG GLIDING CENTRE
**'The Ranch', Llangattock, Powys. Tel: (0873) 810019.**
Proprietor: L P Farley.
In business since 1974.
Member of BHGA.
Holidays for 500 arranged annually.
Hang gliding holidays and instruction for the BHGA Pilot One Certificate. Two or more days throughout the year. Price from £58 for instruction. Accommodation available in converted stable at £3.50 per night. BHGA membership required (£6.50 for three months). The Centre also has a registered riding school on the premises.
Minimum age: 14 years.

## Europe

### ACCUEIL DES JEUNES EN FRANCE
**12 rue des Barres, 75004 Paris. Tel: (+33) 1-278 04 82.**
Hang gliding courses in the Haute Savoie and Massif Central from June to October. Instruction, all equipment, meals and youth hostel accommodation included in price of 1,620-2,000F (about £140-£180), plus travel to site.
Minimum age (Massif Central): 18 years.
Age limits (Haute Savoie): 17-30 years.
IYHF membership card required.

### DISTRICT OF NEUCHATEL TOURIST OFFICE
**9 rue du Trésor (Place des Halles), Neuchâtel 2001, Switzerland. Tel: (+41) 38-251789.**
Hang gliding courses in Neuchâtel, Switzerland for beginners. 4 days June-September. Region offers good hang gliding conditions with winds blowing down from the mountains surrounding Lake Neuchatel and Lake Biel. Instructors are fully qualified members of the Fédération Suisse de Vol Libre. Prices from £130.

# Parachuting and Parascending

## England

### BRITISH PARACHUTE SCHOOLS
The Control Tower, Langar Air Field, Langar, Nottinghamshire. Tel: (0949) 60878.
Directors: D T Hickling, J Fletcher.
In business since 1976.
Recognised by BPA and BAPC.
Parachuting courses in Nottinghamshire for individuals and groups of up to 50, throughout the year. Camping or local bed and breakfast accommodation available. Price £65 for the course all inclusive. £10 for each subsequent jump. All equipment provided except boots.
Minimum age: 16 years.

Parascending courses throughout the year. Price £20 for course, £3 for each subsequent flight.
Minimum age: 14 years.
No experience needed.

### DUNKESWELL INTERNATIONAL SKYDIVING CENTRE
Dunkeswell Airport, near Honiton, Devon. Tel: (040 489) 350.
Chief Instructor: Ian Louttit.
Parachute training in East Devon. 2 day courses throughout the year. Rudimentary accommodation available in clubhouse. Camping permitted on airfield and bed and breakfast can be arranged locally. Courses include documentation, orientation and equipment, aircraft and exit drills, canopy control and how to steer the parachute, parachute landing falls, use of the reserve parachute and collapsing the canopy after landing. Introductory and more advanced instruction up to competition standard. Equipment needed: rubber-soled boots with ankle support, one-piece overalls, crash-

# We Promise You The Experience of A Lifetime PARACHUTING

First Jump Courses, using automatically opened Parachutes
**£65.00!!**

**PARASCENDING**
First Flight Courses
**£20.00!!**

£20.00

£65.00

## British Parachute Schools

LANGER AIRFIELD, Langer, Nottingham
Tel: HARBY 60878

**EXCITEMENT!
EXHILARATION!
IN EAST DEVON!**

Try our two-day beginner's

**PARACHUTING COURSE**

*Send SAE for details:*

DUNKESWELL INTERNATIONAL SKYDIVING CENTRE
DUNKESWELL AIRFIELD
HONITON, DEVON

Telephone: Luppitt (040 489) 350

helmet and (for contact lens wearers) goggles. The first jump will take place when the surface wind is less than 10 mph, usually in early morning or late evening. Price about £50 plus £7 for subsequent descents. Minimum age: 16 years.

## HEADCORN PARACHUTE CLUB
**Headcorn Airfield, Headcorn, Kent TN27 9HX. Tel: (0622) 890862.**
Director: P D N Parker.
In business since 1979.
Approved by BPA.
Parachuting courses throughout the year. First jump course takes one or two days and costs £70 (midweek, summer only) or £75 (weekend). All reserve chutes used by first-timers have automatic opening device. Accommodation in bunk house (50p per night) or adjacent campsite.
Maximum weight: 15 stones.
Age limits: 16-50 years. Those under 18 require parental consent. Those over 40 require a medical certificate.

## IPSWICH PARACHUTE CENTRE
**Ipswich Airport, Nacton Road, Ipswich, Suffolk IP3 9QF. Tel: (0473) 76547.**
Proprietor: A G Knight.
In business since 1981.
Recognised by BPA.
Parachute courses throughout the year. Two days, midweek or weekend. Courses cost between £52 and £70 and include all training and equipment to the first jump. Subsequent jumps £10 each. Accommodation on adjacent campsite or at nearby guest houses.
Age limits: 16-55 years.

## MANCHESTER FREE FALL CLUB
**9 St. Andrews Road, Stretford, Manchester M32 9JE. Tel: 061-865 3912.**
Proprietor: N Law.
In business since 1963.
Member of BPA.
Weekend sport parachuting courses for individuals and groups of up to 20 in Whitchurch, Shropshire. Bed and breakfast accommodation available at local hotel. Price of £60 includes basic training, first jump and use of equipment. Subsequent

jumps £8. Overalls or track suit, and boots with ankle support essential.
No experience needed.
Minimum age: 16 years.

## NORTH WEST PARACHUTE CENTRE
**Cark Airfield, Flookburgh, near Grange-over-Sands, Cumbria. Tel: (044 853) 672.**
Partners: J D Prince, A W Morris.
In business since 1971.
Member of BPA.
Weekend sport parachuting courses for individuals and groups of up to 50 throughout the year.
Weight limit: 15 stones/210 lb/95 kg.
Age limits: 16-50 years.
No experience needed.

## THRUXTON PARACHUTE CLUB
**Thruxton Airfield, Andover, Hants SP11 8PW. Tel: (0264 77) 2124/2154.**
Directors: J E Ball, Miss J J Wright.
In business since 1973.
Recognised by BPA.
Two-day parachuting courses for individuals or groups of up to 35 throughout the year. Price of £75 includes hire of equipment, third party insurance, club membership and one descent. Bed and breakfast accommodation available locally for extra charge.
Age limits: 16-55 years.

## YHA TRAVEL
**14 Southampton Street, London WC2E 7HY. Tel: 01-240 5236.**
Parachuting courses at the British Sky Sports Parachute Centre in the Yorkshire Wolds. 6 days June-September. Progressive training course with 6 descents by static line from 2,000 ft. Stout boots, one-piece boiler suit and helmet required.
No experience needed.
Minimum age: 16 years.

# Ireland

## WILD GEESE PARACHUTE CLUB
**27 Drumeil Road, Aghadowey, Coleraine,**

Co Londonderry, Northern Ireland. Tel: (026585) 669.
Proprietor: David Penny.
In business since 1978.
Recognised by BPA.
Parachute, parascending and survival courses throughout the year for 1, 2, 7, or 14 days. All equipment, instruction to certificate standard and accommodation provided. Prices start at £38 per day for parascending, £66 for parachuting.

## Americas

**PARACHUTE CENTRE**
**23597 N Highway 99, PO Box 423, Acampo, CA 95220 USA. Tel: (+1) 209-369 1128.**
Year-round parachuting courses using larger aircraft — DC3, Twin Beech etc. $125 covers all instruction, equipment and first jump. Subsequent jumps $30. Accelerated freefall programme for $250 including jump from 10,000 feet (allowing 45 seconds of freefall time).

# LEARN TO FLY
### We have a school near you...

London School of Flying
Elstree 01-953 4343/4

Biggin Hill School of Flying
0959 73583

Denham School of Flying
0895 833327

Blackbushe School of Flying
0252 879449

*PHONE TODAY FOR A TRIAL FLIGHT*

# Power Flying

## England

**IPSWICH SCHOOL OF FLYING**
**Ipswich Airport, Nacton Road, Ipswich, Suffolk IP3 9QF. Tel: (0473) 79510.**
Directors: J F Thurlow, J H Pickering.
In business since 1971.
Recognised by AOPA.
Flying training for PPL throughout the year. Full time residential courses arranged for rapid qualification if required. Trial lessons (15 or 25 minutes) also available.

**LONDON SCHOOL OF FLYING**
**Elstree Aerodrome, Borehamwood, Herts. Tel: 01-953 4343/44.**
In business since 1967.
Member of Aircraft Operators and Pilots Association.
Flying training and aircraft hire for individuals and groups of up to 10. 3-4 week Private Pilot's Licence course in the summer. Price from £2,095 plus VAT including 38 hours flying, club membership, ground lectures and exams, radio telephone licence, flight case and equipment. Introductory lesson available, price £30. Two full lessons — 'the double' — for £65. Also at Biggin Hill, Blackbushe and Denham Aerodromes.
No experience needed.
Minimum age: 17 years.

**WYCOMBE AIR CENTRE LTD.**
**Wycombe Air Park, Booker, Marlow, Bucks SL7 3DR. Tel: (0494) 25378.**
General Manager: R K Gyselynck.
In business since 1968.
Power flying holidays for individuals and groups of up to 6. 1-4 weeks throughout the year. Prices upon application for 10 hours flying plus accommodation. Meals are available at the airfield restaurant. Instruction in Cessna 152 training aircraft. Equipment is provided or can be bought from the Cessna Pilot Centre.
Minimum age: 17 years.

# Hiking
# and Orienteering

The rediscovery of the skill of walking appears to spring from two main modern causes: the public's growing awareness of the importance of the countryside as an antidote to city life, and secondly of the advantages of keeping fit. Most doctors agree that the cheapest, easiest and safest way to improve health is to walk. Hiking is also a very cheap activity requiring little equipment and can be enjoyed throughout the year. As so many more people are walking — there are an estimated 800,000 hill walkers in the UK — it is important that walkers help to maintain the countryside. The Country Code provides a good common sense guide: guard against fire hazard, fasten all gates, keep to paths across farm land, avoid damaging fences, hedges, etc., leave no litter, and respect the plant and animal life of the countryside. The Ramblers Association, 1-5 Wandsworth Road, London SW8 2LJ, plays a prominent part in the campaign to protect places of natural beauty, preserve public rights of way and establish national parks (see map).

**Clothing and Equipment.** Even for guided hikes when the route is known and planned, it is important to be suitably and comfortably equipped. Walkers should have a windproof jacket or anorak, loose fitting trousers and a good pair of well broken-in boots, a size larger than normal shoe size to be worn over two pairs of woollen socks. A good pair of walking boots will cost at least £30 and should have one-piece leather uppers, a waterproof outside tongue and thick moulded rubber soles with a deep tread of the "Vibram" type which will give up to 1,000 miles of service before resoling becomes necessary. Detailed maps are essential when hiking. A compass, torch, whistle, spare woollens, waterproof cape, bivouac bag and high calorie provisions are advisable for mountain hiking. It is a good idea to carry a first aid kit containing elastoplast, gauze, a selection of bandages, antiseptic, antihistamine cream and aspirins. If you are hiking in the midge or mosquito season, don't forget your insect repellent.

**Rucksacks and Pack Frames.** Whether you are carrying a small day pack or 70 lbs. on a frame, the weight needs to be carried high on the back with the heaviest objects at the top close to the body. Such problems as straps that get twisted or are too widely spaced make all the difference to your hiking comfort. A hip belt is highly recommended for carrying heavy loads.

Britain has over 100,000 miles of public footpaths and bridleways, in some of the most varied and beautiful landscape to be found in such a small area of the world. The variety is matched by the different types of walking holiday available, from leisurely afternoon rambles to extended backpacking expeditions over moor and mountain.

Travelling on foot is arguably the most rewarding way to see a foreign country. A reasonable level of fitness is often the one requirement for joining a group of travellers in the Alps, the Himalayas or the Andes. It is said that there are tracks in the Annapurna and the Mont Blanc massifs which are as crowded as Oxford Street on the last Saturday before Christmas. But there are also magnificently remote areas throughout the world for the adventurous hiker. The most recent and exciting possibility for hikers is to explore the Tibetan side of Mount Everest. Because of the relaxation of tourist restrictions in China, a few tour organisers have obtained permission to escort parties of walkers into this hitherto inaccessible region.

Orienteering is a specialised form of hiking which combines a high degree of navigational skill with (at a competitive level) the fitness of a cross-country runner. Details of local clubs and a list of publications may be obtained from the British Orienteering Federation, 41 Dale Road, Matlock, Derbyshire DE4 3LT.

# England

**BRATHAY EXPLORATION GROUP**
**Brathay Hall, Ambleside, Cumbria LA22 0HN. Tel: (0966) 33042.**
Administered by the Brathay Hall Trust. In operation since 1947.
Holidays for 270 arranged annually.
Adventure/scientific expeditions in the Lake District in March-April and August. Price £69-£75. Opportunities to learn campcraft, map reading and navigation, mountain safety and field project skills.
No experience needed; expert tuition provided.
Ages: 16-23 years.

**COTSWOLD RAMBLING**
**A29 "Petty Croft", Hillesley, Wotton-under-Edge, Gloucestershire GL12 7RB. Tel: (0453) 842920.**
Partners: Ian and Julie Dickens.
One year in operation.
Leisurely walking holidays in the South Cotswolds. Dinner, bed and breakfast is provided in inns and guesthouses in the area, never more than 12 miles apart. Luggage is transported from one nightstop to the next. Free car parking or transport from Bristol Parkway Station included in the price of £65 (3 days) or £130 (6 days). Reductions for children and groups of up to 15 people.
"Designed for those who neither wish to carry a backpack nor want to go in a guided party."

# The National Parks
# and Long Distance Paths
# of England and Wales

Kelso

Northumberland

*The Pennine Way*

North York Moors

*The Cleveland Way*

Lake District

Helmsley

Yorkshire Dales

*The Ebor Way*

Prestatyn

Edale

Peak District

*The Viking Way*

*The Staffordshire Way*

*Offa's Dyke Path*

Snowdonia

Peddars Way

*The Wye Valley Way*

*The Pembrokeshire Coast Path*

*The Cotswold Way*

Chepstow

*The Oxfordshire Way*

*The Essex Way*

Ivinghoe

Brecon Beacons

*The South-West Peninsular Coast Path*

Marlborough

*The Ridgeway Path*

Minehead

Farnham

*The North Downs Way*

Dover

Exmoor

Petersfield

*The South Downs Way*

Dartmoor

Eastbourne

Swanage

*The South-West Peninsular Coast Path*

National Parks

Long Distance Paths

Other Paths

## THE COUNTRYWIDE HOLIDAYS ASSOCIATION
**Birch Heys, Cromwell Range, Manchester M14 6HU. Tel: 061-225 1000.**
President: Lord Sandford.
Founded in 1893.
Member of ABTA.
Holidays for 30,000 arranged annually.
Walking holidays in Cornwall, Devon, Exmoor, the New Forest, the Forest of Dean, the Cotswolds, the Lakes, the Yorkshire Moors and the Isle of Wight. Also hill walking in the Lakes, the Peaks and the Pennines. 7 days April-October. Well broken-in strong shoes or boots needed. All ages.
Unaccompanied children: 15 years +.

## CYCLORAMA HOLIDAYS (V)
**The Grange Hotel, Grange over Sands, Cumbria LA11 6EJ. Tel: (04484) 3666.**
Walking holidays in the Lake District based at five hotel centres for individuals and groups. 5, 7 or 8 days (although longer trips can be arranged) from late March to end of October. Luggage is transported for walkers between hotels. Hotel and guest house accommodation. Price from £110 per 6 nights including accommodation, breakfast and evening meals, maps, etc.
Map reading ability needed.
Minimum age: 8 years.

## THE DALES CENTRE
**Grassington, near Skipton, N. Yorkshire. Tel: (0756) 752757.**
Hiking in the Yorkshire Dales and Moors, the Lake District and Arran. 1-3 weeks April-November. Hotel and guest house accommodation with full meals. Parties consist of 12 walkers with guide who carries safety equipment. Choice of 8 or 12 miles per day depending on holiday. All equipment provided. Price £220 per week. "The main aim will be to explore the countryside, not to race over it!"
No experience needed.
All ages.
North American agent: Paul Gessford, PO Box 1203, Twain Harts, CA 95383, USA.

## EDEN TOURS
**Old School, Long Marton, Appleby, Cumbria CA16 7JP. Tel: (0930) 61685.**
Partners: V C and H C Bendelow.
In business since 1973.
Guided walking holidays in Cumbria from Easter to October. Accommodation about £13 per night for bed, breakfast and evening meal. Walking £10 per day including guide, transport and packed lunch.
"Peaceful, relaxed holiday in varied and little known area."

## ENGLISH WANDERER
**13 Wellington Court, Spencers Wood, Reading RG7 1BN. Tel: (0734) 882515.**
Directors: Tom Harrison, Ian Robertson.
In business since 1978.
Holidays for 800 arranged annually.
Walking holidays and weekends in scenic areas of England and Scotland. Prices from £42 (weekend) and £133 (one week) including meals and farmhouse accommodation.
Minimum age (unaccompanied): 16 years.
Blind people catered for.

## FIELD STUDIES COUNCIL
**Information Office (AHF), Preston Montford, Montford Bridge, Shrewsbury SY4 1HW. Tel: (0743) 850674.**
Director: A D Thomas, BA, CertEd, Acad DipEd.
Registered charity, established 1945.
Various opportunities include "Walking in the Yorkshire Dales" while learning about the landscape and its wildlife; "Exploring with Map and Compass" and "Backpacking in the Borderland" from the centre in Shropshire. Price around £50 for a weekend, £125 for a week including tuition, accommodation and meals.

## HEAD FOR THE HILLS
**The Recreation Hall, Garth, Builth, Powys. Tel: (05912) 388.**
Organiser: L Golding.
In business since 1976.
Holidays for around 100 arranged annually.
Gentle but challenging walking expeditions throughout selected areas of England and Wales. 5-14 nights Easter to October for individuals and groups of up to 12. Price £11 per day including wholefood meals. Camping at farms on the route. A Land-Rover carries all the luggage.

"The emphasis is on a prehistoric perspective of the landscape."
Ages: Mainly adults but older children welcome.

## HF HOLIDAYS
**Dept 43, 142 Great North Way, London NW4 1EG. Tel: 01-203 3381.**
Walking along long distance footpaths and in areas of scenic beauty throughout England. One or more weeks March-October. Food and lodging are provided in HF's own country houses, youth hostels or guest houses. Many grades of walks are arranged, from the leisurely to the strenuous (for example walking 12-17 miles and ascending 1,000-2,000 ft per day). Walking is done under competent and informal leadership, stopping at places of interest. Prices from £99; reduced rate rail travel available.
No experience needed.
All ages (except on strenuous itineraries).

## HIDEAWAY HOTEL
**Phoenix Way, Windermere, Cumbria LA23 1DB. Tel: (09662) 3070.**
Proprietor: Tim Harper.
In business since 1975.
Holidays for 3,000 arranged each year. Informal "Hideaway Hikers Club" (membership: a pint for the proprietor) which arranges fell walking around the Lake District. Prices from £150 per week include dinner, bed and breakfast and guidance on walks.
Minimum age: 10 years.

## MOUNTAIN GOAT HOLIDAYS
**Victoria Street, Windermere, Cumbria LA23 1AD. Tel: (09662) 5161.**
In business since 1972.
Member of Cumbria Tourist Board.
Fell walking in the Lake District for individuals and groups preferably in multiples of 12. Weekly from May to October. Accommodation in hotels or guest houses in Windermere or Keswick. Four graduated walks culminating in ascents of Helvellyn or Scafell Pike, both over 3,000ft led by experienced guides. Required equipment includes hiking boots, anorak, waterproof trousers and a small rucksack all

of which can be hired. Price from around £160 per week all inclusive.
No experience needed, but fitness essential.
All ages.

## RAMBLERS HOLIDAYS
**Longcroft House, Fretherne Road, Welwyn Garden City, Herts. AL8 6PQ. Tel: (0707) 331133.**
Holidays of one week duration range from gentle rambling to more strenuous hill and mountain walking in the Lake District, Peak National Park and other parts of Great Britain. Prices from around £65 include accommodation and the services of a Rambler leader.

## STAFFORDSHIRE MOORLANDS DISTRICT COUNCIL
**New Stockwell House, Stockwell St, Leek, Staffs ST13 6HQ. Tel: (0538) 385181.**
Walking weekends in the southern Peak District and Churnet valley. April-June and from September to December. Accommodation in local hotel; additional fee for guide.
Minimum age: 10 years.

## YHA TRAVEL
**14 Southampton Street, London WC2E 7HY. Tel: 01-240 5236.**
Splendid range of walking holidays in the most scenic and interesting areas of England; from the Exmoor National Park to the Lake District, covering parts of the major long distance footpaths including the complete length of the Pennine Way. Weekly throughout the summer. Accommodation and board arranged in youth hostels along route. Walking 10-12 miles per day, though distance varies with holiday. Good waterproofs and broken-in walking boots are essential. Price from £90. Recent walking experience recommended.
Minimum age: 16 years.

# Scotland

## ABERNETHY OUTDOOR CENTRE
**Nethy Bridge, Inverness-shire PH25 3ED. Tel: (047 982) 279.**

Mountain craft courses in the Cairngorm Mountains for individuals and groups of up to 24. 1 week June to September. Prices from £99 including accommodation, meals and equipment. Emphasis is placed on navigational and safety skills. Subjects covered include map and compass work, river crossing, abseiling and simple rock climbing. High level bivouac camping can be arranged. "The staff are committed Christians and enjoy sharing their faith with visitors to the Centre."
All ages.
Unaccompanied children: 12 years +.
Bookings through: Abernethy Outdoor Centre.

**BRATHAY EXPLORATION GROUP**
**Brathay Hall, Ambleside, Cumbria LA22 0HN. Tel: (0966) 33042.**
Adventure/scientific expeditions in the Highlands and Islands. 11-15 days camping

April, July and August. Activities include camp and mountain craft, recording fauna and flora and in April, learning ice axe and crampon techniques.
No experience needed.
Ages: 16-23 years.

**THE COUNTRYWIDE HOLIDAYS ASSOCIATION**
**Birch Heys, Cromwell Range, Manchester M14 6HU. Tel: 061-225 1000.**
Mountain walking holidays in Scotland. 7 days May-September. Opportunities to visit the numerous glens and lochs of the region. Strong well broken-in boots needed.
All ages.
Unaccompanied children: 15 years +.

**HF HOLIDAYS LTD.**
**Dept 43, 142 Great North Way, London NW4 1EG. Tel: 01-203 3381.**
Walking excursions on the Isle of Arran, along the Firth of Clyde and the Highlands.

*Sharing the load*                    *Barnaby's Picture Library*

1 or more weeks March-October. Meals and accommodation provided in HF country houses. Itineraries include Ben Nevis, Ben Lawers and other Scottish peaks, as well as gentler routes for the less experienced. Hiking under competent and informal leadership. Prices from £99; reduced rate rail travel available.
All ages, except on strenuous excursions.

**OUTWARD BOUND TRUST**
**Chestnut Field, Regent Place, Rugby CV21 2PJ. Tel: (0788) 60423.**
Walking expeditions through some of Britain's wildest country. 12 days from the Loch Eil Centre to the Isle of Skye.
No experience needed.
Ages: 16-25 years.

# Wales

**THE COUNTRYWIDE HOLIDAYS ASSOCIATION**
**Birch Heys, Cromwell Range, Manchester M14 6HU. Tel: 061-225 1000.**
Mountain walking holidays in Snowdonia. 7 days June-September. Mountain boots needed.
All ages.
Unaccompanied children: 15 years +.

**THE DRAPERS' FIELD CENTRE**
**Rhyd-y-creuau, Betws-y-coed, Gwynedd LL24 0HB. Tel: (069 02) 494.**
Administered by the Field Studies Council. Various opportunities include "Walking in Snowdonia" where, for the fit and active, there will be a thorough exploration of the Cardennau, Glyderau and Snowdonia or, for those who want a less strenuous time, walks in the woods, valleys and lower mountains of the National Park. Price around £44 for a weekend, £116 for a week including tuition, accommodation and meals.

**HF HOLIDAYS**
**Dept 43, 142 Great North Way, London NW4 1EG. Tel: 01-203 3381.**
Guided walks in the scenic areas of Wales, especially the coasts and mountains throughout the year. Accommodation and meals are arranged in HF's own country houses and local guest houses. All grades of walking excursion. Prices vary according to season from £99. Reduced rate rail travel available.
No experience needed.
All ages, except on more demanding routes.

**NEUADD ARMS HOTEL**
**The Square, Llanwrtyd Wells, Powys. Tel: (05913) 236.**
Proprietors: Gordon and Diana Green.
In business since 1975.
Holidays for 1,000 arranged annually.
Walking and training for runners in the Cambrian Mountains. Weekends and weeks throughout the year. Price from £35 for weekend, £110 for one week including accommodation and all meals. Mountain cycling and pony trekking also available.
No experience needed.
Unaccompanied children: 14 years+

**OUTWARD BOUND TRUST**
**Chestnut Field, Regent Place, Rugby CV21 2PJ. Tel: (0788) 60423.**
Walking 'Rover' expeditions from Wales and the Lake District.
No experience needed.
Ages: 16-25 years.

**PLAS Y BRENIN**
**The National Centre for Mountain Activities, Capel Curig, Betws-y-Coed, Gwynedd. Tel: (069 04) 214 or 280.**
Hill walking and mountain craft courses in Snowdonia. 6 days throughout the year. Board and accommodation provided in Centre. Instruction in navigation with maps and compass, basic mountain safety techniques, introduction to basic rock climbing, ridge scrambling and mountain walking and overnight camping. In winter, courses are offered in basic snow and ice craft. Mountain leadership courses are available throughout the year. Minimum age for registration is 18 years.
Minimum age: 16 years (14 years for young people's courses).

Orienteering: Plas y Brenin is the BOF's National Orienteering Centre in Wales. Weekend courses for beginners. Board and accommodation provided. Instruction given in navigation techniques, course planning, simple map-making and event organisation. No experience needed. Minimum age: 16 years.

# Ireland

## ASSOCIATION FOR ADVENTURE SPORTS
**Tiglin Adventure Centre, Ashford, Co. Wicklow, Ireland. Tel: (+353) 404-4169.**
Orienteering courses for novice and advanced students. The Tiglin Centre has permanently marked orienteering routes. Map-making instruction available. Orienteering at night is also taught. Minimum age: 16 years.

# Europe

## ACCUEIL DES JEUNES EN FRANCE
**12 rue des Barres, 75004 Paris. Tel: (+33) 1-278 04 82**
Hiking tours of the Lakes and volcanoes of the Auvergne June-September. About 6-8 hours walking per day, with gite accommodation and all meals provided. Prices depend on whether you carry your backpack (1,410F, about £125) or it is transported for you (1,550F, about £140). Minimum age: 18 years. Good physical condition required, but "ce n'est pas une performance sportive!"

## AQUA VIVA ADVENTURE CLUB
**Carsac, 24200 Sarlat, France. Tel: (+33) 53-592109.**
Trail hiking in the Dordogne Valley. One week mid-June to mid-September. Camping accommodation and meals with hikers helping with chores. Price from Fr.1,400 (about £120). All equipment supplied.

English speaking staff. A visit to prehistoric cave paintings and a day canoeing included with optional horse riding. Minimum age: 17 years.

## AUSTRIAN ALPINE CLUB
**13 Longcroft House, Fretherne Road, Welwyn Garden City, Herts AL8 6PQ. Tel: (0707) 324835.**
Mountain walking in the Austrian Alps, Italian Dolomites and French Pyrenees. 2 weeks July-September. Energetic hut to hut tours led by experienced leaders. Accommodation in mountain huts. Maximum of 8 hours walking per day in the Venediger, Pyrenees, Dolomite, Glockner, Schober and Dachstein Mountains. These tours involve some scrambling and easy glacier crossings; ice axe recommended. Club membership needed. Minimum age: 18 years.

## EXPLORE WORLDWIDE LTD.
**7 High Street, Aldershot, Hampshire GU11 1BH. Tel: (0252) 319448/9.**
16 day Cretan expeditions May-October, exploring villages, beaches and gorges and staying in small hotels and tavernas. Trekking through the Samaria Gorge and in the Ida Mountains. Price from around £300 includes flights, local transport by bus and ferryboat and guide. Minimum age: 18 years.

## LENZERHEIDE — VALBELLA
**Tourist Office, 7078 Lenzerheide, Switzerland. Tel: (+41) 81-34 15 89 or 34 19 59.**
Guided and self-guided hikes and mountain excursions in the Graübunden Alps. No charge except for travel by cable car, rail or road.

## MOUNTAIN TRAVEL, INC.
**1398 Solano Avenue, Albany, CA 94706, USA.**
Trekking in Greece. 16 days in September. 3 day trek across Spartan warrior paths in the Taiyetos Mountains and 3 day trek through the Gorge of Samaria to the coast of Crete, plus visits to Sparta and Khania. Accommodation in villagers' homes. Price $1,790 plus air fare.

## NORWEGIAN MOUNTAIN TOURING ASSOCIATION
**(Den Norske Turistforening)**
**Boks 1963, Vika N-0125, Oslo 1, Norway.**
Founded in 1868.
Mountain hiking and rambling in Norway. Any number of days from end of June to mid-September. Guided tours and courses available in varying degrees of difficulty. Most tours are based on walking from hut to hut, some of which are staffed. The Association operates a network of lodges and chalets, marks summer routes and winter ski trails, arranges guided tours and offers practical courses.
No experience needed.
All ages.
Unaccompanied children accepted.

## NSTS — STUDENT AND YOUTH TRAVEL MALTA
**220 St Paul Street, Valletta, Malta. Tel: (+356) 624983.**
Rambling holidays for groups of minimum 10. One week October to April. Accommodation in youth centre on bed and breakfast basis. 30 hours of accompanied rambling through Malta's countryside plus visit to Valletta. Sterling price about £50 in shared apartments and £66 in single bedroomed apartments; air travel extra.
Ages: 15-29 years.

## NUH REISEBYRA
**Dronningesgate 26, 0154 Oslo 1, Norway. Tel: (+47) 2-42 14 10.**
Hiking through the mountains of South Western Norway. Tours start at Oslo and Bergen and travel by train to start at Mjolfell youth hostel. Full board and accommodation in hostels and mountain cabins. Prices around Nkr 2500; reductions for holders of Inter Rail cards.
Minimum age: 12 years.
Book direct or through national YHA offices abroad.

## RAMBLERS HOLIDAYS
**Longcroft House, Fretherne Road, Welwyn Garden City, Herts. AL8 6PQ. Tel: (0707) 331133.**
Hiking in most of the scenic areas of Western and Eastern Europe. Usually 2 weeks. Accommodation in small hotels and mountain huts. Choice of hiking from one or two centres or on continuous tours. Most itineraries include some sightseeing. All holidays are graded according to strenuousness and specialisation of equipment needed, and vary between 5 and 9 hours of walking per day. On more serious mountain expeditions, ice axes may be required. For all but the easiest holidays, worn-in hiking boots with moulded rubber soles are essential and previous mountain walking experience is recommended.

## RIEDERALP VERKEHRSBURO
**CH-3981 Riederalp, Switzerland. Tel: (+41) 28-271365.**
Director: E Kummer.
In business since 1972.
Hiking in the Berner Alps of the Valais Canton in Switzerland. 6 days June-October. Hotel accommodation at Riederalp which is at an elevation of 6,342 ft. Guided hikes in the Aletsch Glacier area and surrounding countryside. Prices from SFr390 (around £130) including guide, accommodation and half board; travel to and from Switzerland not included.
All ages.

## SHERPA EXPEDITIONS
**Link Travel Ltd.**
**131A Heston Road, Hounslow, Middlesex TW5 0RD. Tel: 01-577 2717.**
Hiking expeditions in the Pindos Mountains of Greece. 2 weeks May-September. Combination of camping accommodation, local inns and mountain refuge huts. The expedition begins in Ioannina by Lake Pamvotis and continues through the mountains (some reaching an elevation of 8,000 ft) and finishing on the beaches of Parga. An experienced expedition leader accompanies each group of 10-15 people. The trails are usually grass-covered, so walking is not too demanding. A support vehicle carries the luggage. Prices from £385-£405 all inclusive.
Minimum age: 18 years.

**WAYMARK HOLIDAYS**
**295 Lillie Road, London SW6 7LL. Tel: 01-385 5015.**
Directors: G Chamberlain, P Chapman, M Hounslow, N Vincent.
In business since 1973.
Holidays for 2,500 arranged annually.
Walking tours throughout Europe in parties of up to 16. 8-15 days in spring, summer and autumn. Accommodation varies with terrain and type of walk, from good hotels to mountain huts.
Experience required for more difficult walks.
Minimum age (unaccompanied): 16 years.

**WEXAS**
**45 Brompton Road, London SW3 1DE. Tel: 01-589 0500/3315.**
Tour Director: Judy Sykes.
In operation since 1970.
Holidays for 2,000 arranged annually.
Trekking in unusual areas of Europe and North Africa, including Algeria, Greece and Corsica. 10 or16 days in summer. Price from £285 including return travel by air.
Membership required.

**YHA TRAVEL**
**14 Southampton Street, London WC2E 7HY. Tel: 01-240 5236.**
Walking holidays in Luxembourg with youth hostel accommodation. 10 days from April to October. Full board provided. Walking about 10-15 miles per day.

Walking in the Mosel, Eifel, Rhine and Black Forest areas of Germany. 15 days April-October. Bed and breakfast accommodation in youth hostels. Some tours include German Railways 10 day Regional Touring Card.

Walking in the Bernese Oberland in Switzerland. 15 days June-October. Half or full board in youth hostels and mountain huts. Some ascents are 5,000' and participants should be used to strenuous walking.
Minimum age: 16 years.

# Arctic

**DICK PHILLIPS**
**Whitehall House, Nenthead, Alston, Cumbria CA9 3PS. Tel: (0498) 81440.**
In business since 1970.
Holidays for 300 arranged annually.
Hiking tours in Iceland. 2-3 weeks May-August. Maximum of 13 miles walking per day in the mountains of the South or North-West. Rucksack and sleeping bag needed. Prices from £360 including return air fare from Glasgow. "We are genuinely concerned to avoid the tourist routes. We still have parties who walk for 10 days without seeing another person."
Membership of the YHA required.
Minimum age: 17 years.

**ERSKINE EXPEDITIONS**
**14 Inverleith Place, Edinburgh, EH3 5PZ. Tel: 031-552 2673.**
Director: Commander Angus Erskine.
In operation since 1976.
Recognised by: Scottish Tourist Board.
Holidays for 200 arranged annually.
Trekking trip of about 80 miles led by experienced guides on Baffin Island in the Canadian Arctic for individuals or groups of up to 14. 2 or 3 weeks July-August. Camping accommodation. Spectacular mountain scenery; interesting for botanists and birdwatchers with opportunities to see snowy owls and lapland buntings. Trip begins flying to an eskimo village and taking a boat up the Pangnirtung Fjord. Price £1,600 all inclusive. Sleeping bags should be taken.
Similar treks to remoter Greenland for £950.
No experience needed.
Ages: 16-60 years.

**TWICKENHAM TRAVEL**
**33 Notting Hill Gate, London W11 3JQ. Tel: 01-221 7278.**
Camping and walking tours in Iceland. Eight, 13, 15 and 21 day holidays June-August. Meals and tents provided; sleeping bags may be hired. Prices of £420-£800

include flights from London or Glasgow and services of English-speaking guide. Additional extensions and tours available. "Organised camp sites are avoided wherever possible . . . there is plenty of time available for long walks in solitary landscapes."

**YHA TRAVEL**
**14 Southampton Street, London WC2E 7HY. Tel: 01-240 5236.**
Hiking and camping tour in the mountain area of South Greenland. 8 days in July. Visits to glaciers, fjords and Eric the Red's Farm. Sleeping bag required.
Minimum age: 16 years.

# Americas

**THE DALES CENTRE**
**Grassington, nr Skipton, N. Yorkshire. Tel: (0756) 752757.**
Hiking holidays in California lasting three weeks.
Accommodation in motels and cabins. Itinerary begins in San Francisco and includes part of the Sierra Ridge trail, Yosemite National Park, Death Valley and the Grand Canyon. Cost of £1,500 includes air fare from London, transport, porters, guides and accommodation.
No experience needed.
All ages.

**EXODUS EXPEDITIONS LTD.**
**All Saints Passage, 100 Wandsworth High Street, London SW18 4LE. Tel: 01-870 0151.**
Trekking in the mountains of Peru and Bolivia for 22-28 days from June to October. Camping accommodation. Price from £1,390.

**EXPLORE WORLDWIDE LTD.**
**7 High Street, Aldershot, Hampshire GU11 1BH. Tel: (0252) 319448/9.**
22 days from Lima in April and July-September including trekking the old Inca Trail from Cuzco to Machu Pichu in small groups. All equipment provided. Price from

Lima around £700 including a trip into the Amazon jungle.
Minimum age: 18 years.

**MOUNTAIN PEOPLE SCHOOL**
**157 Oak Spring Drive, San Anselmo, CA 94960, USA. Tel: (+1) 415-450 3664.**
Backpacking in the Sierra Nevada mountains of California throughout the year. Prices: 7 days, $305; 14 days $600.
Minimum age: 11 years.

**MOUNTAIN TRAVEL, INC.**
**1398 Solano Avenue, Albany, CA 94706, USA.**
**Britain: 22 Church Street, Twickenham TW1 3NW.**
Hiking in the Hawaiian Islands. 15 days in April, October and December. Exploring the islands of Maui and Hawaii, visiting 2 active volcanoes and Haleakala National Park. Price $975 not including air fare.

Hiking in the Peruvian Highlands, in Patagonia and Ecuador. 14-29 days April-June or November. Accommodation in small pensions and camps. Prices from $1,000.

**NORTHERN LIGHTS ALPINE RECREATION**
**Box 399, Invermere, British Columbia V0A 1K0, Canada. Tel: (+1) 604-342-6042.**
Alpine hiking in the rugged areas of Alberta and British Columbia for groups of 2-6. 8 days June-October. Routes range from well-groomed park trails to severe cross-country tours designed to suit various abilities. Opportunities for photography of alpine flowers and for exploration of ruined mines.
Prices from $350 for 8 days.
Minimum age: 14 years.

**PERUVIAN ANDEAN TREKS**
**Ave Pardo 575, Casilla 454, Cuzco, Peru. Tel: 225701.**
Director: Thomas Hendrickson.
In business since 1979.
Expertly-led treks into some of the most curious and rewarding destinations in the Andes. Horsebacking, whitewater rafting, orchid hunting, gold panning, glacier scrambling and 'just plain knocking about in

the mountains.' Prices from $200 excluding travel. Mountaineering basecamp support and guiding in southern Peru and Aconcagua.
"We deliver comprehensive, high-quality trek guiding and logistics by professionals."
UK bookings through Sherpa Expeditions, 131a Heston Road, Hounslow, Middlesex TW5 0RD. Tel: 01-577 2717.

**PSOM/MGS INC. PO Box 694, Bishop, CA 93514 USA. Tel: (+1) 619-873 5037.**
'In the footsteps of the Inca' — a trek across the Andes and in the Amazon rain forests. Two weeks, departing May 25 and November 16, 1986. Price $985 plus travel to Ecuador.
Previous backpacking and climbing experience necessary.

**SOBEK EXPEDITIONS, INC.**
**One Sobek Tower, Angels Camp, CA 95222, USA. Tel: (+1) 209-736 4524.**
Wilderness trek at the base of Mt McKinley in the Denali National Park of Alaska; 12 days in August, around $1,300 plus travel to Anchorage.
Trek along the spine of the Andes in Cordillera Blanca, Peru. Pack animals carry luggage and equipment. 8 days from April to October. Price around $700 plus air travel to Lima.
Walking options from gentle strolls to challenging treks in the Torres del Paine national park in southernmost Chile. 9 days in January. Price around $1,000 plus air travel to Santiago.

**WEXAS**
**45 Brompton Road, London SW3 1DE. Tel: 01-589-0500/3315.**
Trekking in Peru. 20, 22 or 27 days in June, July and August. Mainly camping. Length of trek varies from 8 to 15 days, shorter treks are combined with visits to Inca sites. Price from $1,227; membership required.

# Israel

**JABALIYA TREKKING LTD.**

**36 Keren Hayesod Street, Jerusalem, Israel. Tel: (+972) 2-699385.**
Trekking in the Judean desert or the Galilee for groups. 4-10 days throughout the year. Varied accommodation from camping to kibbutz or hotel. Equipment and food carried by support truck in the Galilee, and by camel in the Judean desert. Tours accompanied by guides with knowledge of history, geology, botany and archaeology of the regions. Prices on application.
Ages: 18-75 years.

**SOCIETY FOR THE PROTECTION OF NATURE IN ISRAEL**
**13 Helene Hamalka Street, PO Box 930, Jerusalem 91008, Israel. Tel: (+972) 2-249567.**
In operation since 1955.
Hiking and nature trips throughout Israel for individuals and groups. 1-14 days throughout the year. Accommodation ranges from sleeping in the open to rooms in Field Study Centres or hotels. Prices and itineraries on application.

**WEXAS**
**45 Brompton Road, London SW3 1DE. Tel: 01-589 0500/3315.**
Walking and driving in Israel with watersports and time in Jerusalem. 15 days throughout the year. Price from £425 plus US$110 kitty.
Membership required.

# Africa

**THE DALES CENTRE**
**Grassington, near Skipton, N. Yorkshire. Tel: (0756) 752757.**
Hiking holidays in Kenya and Tanzania. 3 weeks October-February. Accommodation in hotels, huts or tents. Itinerary begins on the traverse of Mt. Kenya or the climb of Mt. Kilimanjaro, with a safari expedition and visits to Nairobi and Mombasa. Price of around £1,500 includes air fare from London, transport, porters, guides and accommodation.
No experience needed.
All ages.

**EXODUS EXPEDITIONS LTD.**
**All Saints Passage, 100 Wandsworth High Street, London SW18 4LE. Tel: 01-870 0151.**
Trekking in the mountains of Tanzania or Ethiopia. 15-18 days in March, April, August, October and December. Accommodation mainly in lodges and mountain huts. Fully portered. Price from £1,220.

**EXPLORE WORLDWIDE LTD.**
**7 High Street, Aldershot, Hampshire GU11 1BH. Tel: (0252) 319448/9.**
15 days hiking in Morocco's High Atlas Mountains July-September. Average altitude of walk is 10,000 feet. Accommodation in alpine huts and Berber houses. Price from £295 including flights, transportation, mule hire and all equipment.

15 day Morocco Winter Breaks in the Anti-Atlas, October-March. Escorted walks to Berber villages from Tafraout. Price from £320 including flight to Marrakesh. Minimum age: 18 years.

**WEXAS**
**45 Brompton Road, London SW3 1DE. Tel: 01-589 0500/3315.**
Atlas Mountain treks and camping. 16 days April-September. Starting at Marrakesh. Trekking through the mountains, with a mule to help, camping or staying in mountain huts and Berber villages. Sharing in the routine chores, such as cooking. Price from £400 including return air fare.

Walking in Uganda, visiting forest pygmies and wildlife reserves. 15 days August-September. £565 including air travel plus £60 kitty.

22 days in Zambia on walking safari with visits to the Victoria Falls, a working African farm and a non-tourist traditional village. May, August and September, price from £365 plus £45 food kitty, air fare not included. Membership required.

# Asia

**CLUB MEDITERRANEE**
**UK Office: 106-108 Brompton Road, London SW3 1JJ. Tel: 01-581 1161.**
Trekking in Nepal for individuals or groups of 12-15. 15 days of walking with 6 days of travelling and sightseeing at beginning and end of holiday. Departing from Paris in April/May and October/November. Accommodation in 2-man tents with foam mattresses; simple but plentiful meals prepared by Sherpa cooks. Porters carry main luggage. Average of 5 hours of trekking daily, some quite strenuous. Walking through dense tropical forests and high barren plateaus at over 10,000 ft. above sea level.
Hiking experience needed.

**EXODUS EXPEDITIONS LTD.**
**All Saints Passage, 100 Wandsworth High Street, London SW18 4LE. Tel: 01-870 0151.**
Trekking in the Himalayas, Karakorum or Thailand. 16-39 days departing throughout the year. Choice of treks in Nepal, Pakistan, Kashmir, Garhwal, Bhutan, Sikkim and Ladakh. Price £1,090-£1,790 including flights, food, accommodation, equipment, trek leaders and porters.

**EXPLORE WORLDWIDE LTD.**
**7 High Street, Aldershot, Hampshire GU11 1BH. Tel: (0252) 319448/9.**
Treks and expeditions in Asia for small groups. 15 or 22 days in Kashmir & Ladakh, Gilgit and Hunza and the Nepalese Himalayas. Also an 18 day river journey and hilltribe walk in Thailand in October from about £700. Special 18 day expedition to the jungle villages of the "long-neck" Pad'aung tribe in May, October and December. Price about £800. Prices include flights from London, accommodation and all guides and equipment.
Minimum age: 18 years.

**MOUNTAIN TRAVEL, INC.**
**1398 Solano Avenue, Albany, CA 94706, USA. Tel: (+1) 415-527 8100.**
**Britain: 22 Church Street, Twickenham TW1 3NW.**
Hiking in the Karakoram Mountain wilderness of Northern Pakistan, in Nepal, Kashmir, Ladakh, China, Tibet, Mongolia, Bhutan and the Japanese Alps. 21-45 days throughout the year. Sleeping in huts or tents; full camp staff and cook provided. Highlights may include rocky glacier travel and difficult river crossings. Prices range from $1,665-$5,600 excluding air fare. Experience needed varies with expedition.

14 day trek below Mt. Muztagata in western Tibetan grasslands of Xinijang Province. Bactrian camels carry camping gear. Price $4,975 not including air fare.

**MOUNTAIN TRAVEL INDIA PVT. LTD.**
**1/1 Rani Jhansi Road, New Delhi 110055, India. Tel: (+91) 11-523057.**
Trekking in the Himalayas, especially Ladakh. Accommodation in tents which are adapted from the Mongolian "yurt". All food and equipment provided. Opportunities to see wild ass and Tibetan gazelle.
Bookings through: Mountain Travel India, c/o ExplorAsia, 13 Chapter Street, London S.W.1. Tel: 01-630 7102.
North American agent: Tiger Tops International (U.S.A.) Inc., 2627 Lombard Street, San Francisco, California 94123. Tel: (415) 346-3402.

**RAMBLERS HOLIDAYS**
**Longcroft House, Fretherne Road, Welwyn Garden City, Herts AL8 6PQ. Tel: (0707) 331133.**
Walking holidays in Turkey. 2 weeks in June and September. 2 centre holiday with hotel/motel accommodation. Walking over wooded hillsides to ancient sites and hidden villages. A maximum of 5 hours walking per day. Shoes with thick soles are adequate.

**SACU TOURS**
**Society for Anglo-Chinese Understanding, 125 Camden High Street, London NW1 ONE. Tel: 01-482 4292.**
Rambling tour of Northern China. 24 days in April. Starting in Beijing to Qufu (Confucius' birthplace), the sacred mountains of Daoism and along the coast to Shanghai.
Rambling tour of the lakes and mountains of north east China. 18 days July-August. Visiting Beijing, Harbin, the Long White Mountains, Changbaishan Nature Reserve and Tian Chi, the 'Lake of Heaven'.

**SHERPA CO-OPERATIVE (P) LTD.**
**Kamal Pokhari, P.O. Box 1338, Kathmandu, Nepal. Tel: (+977) 215887.**
Trekking in Nepal in groups of 10-20. 5 days September-May. 5-6 hours hill walking per day, accommodation in tents.
Minimum age: 10 years.
Book through Sherpa Co-operative or Roama Travels, Larks Rise, Shroton, Blandford, Dorset DT11 8QW.
Group bookings through Exodus Expeditions, All Saints Passage, 100 Wandsworth High Street, London SW18 4LE.

**SHERPA EXPEDITIONS**
**Link Travel Ltd.**
**131A Heston Road, Hounslow, Middlesex TW5 0RD. Tel: 01-577 2717.**
Trekking in Western or Central Nepal, as well as to Everest Base Camp. 24 days October-April. Choice of treks may include the Annapurna Sanctuary, Langtang Valley, the Pangboche and Thangboche monasteries and Sherpa villages of Solo Khumbu. Prices from £1,295, including return air fare and sightseeing excursion to the Taj Mahal.
High standard of fitness required for most treks.
Minimum age: 18 years.

**SITA WORLD TRAVEL (INDIA) PVT LTD.**
**F-12 Connaught Place, New Delhi-110 001, India. Tel: (+91) 11-3311133.**
Trekking holidays in the Himalayas for 5-27 days between April and mid-November. Tented and hotel accommodation with Indian and continental meals cooked by

trained staff.
Prices on application.

## SOBEK EXPEDITIONS, INC.
**One Sobek Tower, Angels Camp, CA 95222, USA. Tel: (+1) 209-736 4524.**
Treks in Nepal from September to May in conjuction with other activities including Everest flight and Chitwan National Park. Prices from around $2,000 including air fare from USA. Optional 10 day Everest trek $450.

## TRAVELLERS
**Waterside, Kendal, Cumbria LA9 4HE. Tel: (0539) 28334.**
Himalayan journeys and expeditions into Nepal, India and Sikkim. Many programmes led by well-known mountaineers or naturalists.

## WEXAS
**45 Brompton Road, London SW3 1DE. Tel: 01-589 0500/3315.**
Membership required for all holidays.
Jungle trek in Northern Thailand. 18 days throughout the year. Accommodation in hotels, native villages and under the stars. Exploring Bangkok and Chiang Mai, 5 days trekking in the mountainous jungles and the 'Golden Triangle' (with porters carrying the baggage). Sleeping bag needed. Price from £695 including return air fare.

Trekking in the Himalayas. 22, 24, 26 or 29 days October-April. A choice of eleven different holidays. The basic areas for trekking are Everest, Annapurna, Langtang, Kashmir, Makalu or Zanskar. The actual treks vary from 8 days to 22 days. The shorter treks are combined with two days at the Chitwan Wildlife Reserve and three days whitewater rafting. All treks are accompanied by Sherpas. Price from £1,290 including return air fare.

## WORLDWIDE STUDENT TRAVEL LTD.
**38/39 Store Street, London WC1E 7BZ. Tel: 01-580 7733.**
Trekking in the Chiang Mai district of Northern Thailand. 8 days departing every Saturday during the summer. Price £130 including hotel accommodation, experienced guides and all transportation, flight not included. Adventure trips to China, India and Russia also available. No experience needed.

# Overland

For an increasing number of young people, the modern alternative to the "Grand Tour" is the Overland Expedition. Travel may be by specially-modified coach or double-decker bus, 3-ton truck, 4-wheel drive vehicle or by public transport; under the leadership of a seasoned guide and organiser, overlanding can be an appealing and reasonably priced way of seeing new places and peoples.

There are three great overland trips: the trans-Asia to Kathmandu, the trans-Africa to Kenya or Johannesburg and across and around South America. On most overland trips, a food kitty is organised from which fresh food is bought en route and then prepared communally. Return travel from the destination is not always included in the prices quoted.

In the past few years, there has been much concern over the old trans-Asian route which crossed the Khyber Pass from Afghanistan to Pakistan and India. At present Afghanistan is completely off-limits. However, there is a more southerly route which crosses the wild and desolate tracts of Baluchistan between Isfahan in Iran and Quetta in Pakistan. Unless you're American, it is not difficult to get an Iranian visa. Women travellers should be prepared to go into temporary purdah to avoid difficulties with the Islamic authorities. A more recent impediment has been the intermittent closing of the Pakistan/Indian border near Lahore due to Sikh troubles in the Punjab.

Although the trip by public transport is possible and very cheap (about £50 Istanbul to Delhi), it is a tough trip and many people prefer to go with an overland company. The well-established companies will have a contingency plan in the event of political upheavals, such as to overfly from Damascus to Karachi. If all this sounds too risky and daunting a prospect, stick to the more politically stable countries of Africa and South America.

Further details about Overlanding can be obtained from WEXAS, 45 Brompton Road, London SW3 1DE. (Tel: 01-589 0500/3315). WEXAS publish a splendid book for people planning travels and expeditions of all kinds, called *The Traveller's Handbook* which contains several good articles on Overlanding.

## ADVENTURE AGENCY
**9 The Square, Ramsbury, Marlborough, Wiltshire SN8 2PE. Tel: (0672) 20569.**
Proprietors: Ben and Carole Satterthwaite.
5 years in business.
Adventure travel from one to forty weeks throughout South America, Africa and Asia. Free newsletter detailing the many tours available from Adventure Agency. Special escorted 21 day journey through Rajasthan, India during November to visit the annual Pushtar camel fair. Accommodation in Maharajah's palaces. Inclusive price £1,450.

Special Halley's Comet safari departs Johannesburg in March 1986, 18 days across Kalahari and northern Botswana; price £675.

## CONTIKI
**7 Rathbone Place, London W1P 1DE. Tel: 01-637 2121.**
Directors: Kit Nixon, Geoff Phillips, Alison Lloyd.
In business since 1960.
Member of: ABTA.
Holidays for 40,000 arranged annually.
Overland by coach through Europe, Russia and Scandinavia, U.S.A. and Canada, New Zealand and Australia. Tours last between 1 and 8½ weeks available throughout the year. Accommodation ranges from hotel/motel, chateau and dude ranch to Contiki tent villages. Activities available include: schooner sailing in Greece, white water rafting in New Zealand, reef exploring, horse riding and water sports in Australia, cycling in Amsterdam.
Ages: 18-35 years.
Bookings through: Contiki or ABTA agents.
USA agent: Contiki Travel America Inc., 1432 East Katella Avenue, Anaheim, California 92805. Tel: (714) 937 0611.

## EXODUS EXPEDITIONS
**All Saints' Passage, 100 Wandsworth High Street, London SW18 4LE. Tel: 01-870 0151.**
Long range overland expeditions across Asia (14 weeks), Africa (20-33 weeks) and South America (22 weeks). Travel is by specially built expedition truck carrying 20-25 people with an emphasis on exploration of the more remote regions as well as sightseeing. Trans Asia routes through Turkey, the Middle East, Iran, Pakistan, India and Nepal; trans Africa through Morocco, the Sahara, Chad, Upper Volta, Mali, Benin, Malawi, Central Africa, Zaire, east Africa, Zambia to Johannesburg; South American tours include the whole continent except the Guyanas. Shorter sections from 4-35 weeks may be taken on all expeditions. Cost approximately £100 (plus £10 food kitty) per week.

## EXPLORE WORLDWIDE LTD.
**7 High Street, Aldershot, Hants. GU11 1BH. Tel: (0252) 319448/9.**
Directors: T Cox, D Cook, P Newsom, D Moore.
A wide range of shorter overland journeys utilising different modes of transportation from small buses to 4-wheel drive desert

# EXPLORE
## small group holidays
Adventure holidays, treks and special expeditions. 2 & 3 weeks from £295, including travel by bus, unusual train rides and river explorations, camel safaris and hilltribe treks. Over 20 countries in Europe, Africa, Asia and Latin America. Contact us for brochure now.

Explore Worldwide, Dept AH, 7 High Street, Aldershot, Hants. GU11 1BH. Tel: 0252 319448

trucks, riverboats, camels and trains. Areas of exploration include Scandinavia, Morocco and Algeria, Anatolian Turkey, Egypt, Jordan, India, Yemen, Mexico, Russia, Peru and Bolivia. Most accommodation at small hotels; some camping (all equipment provided except sleeping bags). Length of trips varies from 15 days to 22 days. Prices from £300 to £900.
Minimum age: 18 years.

### GOWAY TRAVEL LTD.
**40 Wellington Street East, Toronto, Ontario, Canada M5E 1C7. Tel: (+1) 416-863-0799.**
Camping tours of North and South America for groups of up to 14 people. Itineraries in various parts of North America last from 1 to 10 weeks in the warmer months, and in South America from 3 to 10 weeks year round. Campers participate in cooking and camping duties. Food kitty of about $4 per day. Many choices of itinerary vary in cost from £179 for 1 week to £1,249 for 10

weeks in North America; from £1,035 for 23 days in South America to £1,315 for 70 days.
Ages: 18-35 years.

### GUERBA EXPEDITIONS LTD.
**Westfield House, Westbury, Wiltshire BA13 3EP. Tel: (0380) 830476.**
Directors: M Crabb, H D Gough, A Morgan, J Dunn.
In business since 1977.
Holidays for 2,000 arranged annually.
Overland expeditions and adventure holidays in Africa. Departures all year round from 1 to 40 weeks duration. Most trips use 4 wheel drive expedition trucks with a crew of 3; a leader, a second driver and a cook. All camping equipment supplied.
"The widest variety of routes and destinations in Africa."
Minimum age: 17 years.
Bookings through: Guerba, or Trailfinders (46 Earls Court Road, London W8.)
North American agents: Adventure Centre, 5540 College Ave, Oakland, CA 94618; Westcan Treks, 3415 W. Broadway, Vancouver, BC V6R 2B4.

### HANN OVERLAND
**185 Streatham High Road, London SW16 6EG. Tel: 01-769 6659.**
Director: Geoffrey Hann.
Highcrest Travel Ltd.
In business since 1973.
Holidays for 800 arranged annually.
Overland bus tours of the Middle East. 3 weeks departing April-November. Choice of visiting Syria, Jordan and Iraq, or concentrating on Iraq (Mesopotamia). Basically camping accommodation with some modest hotels. Group cooking with occasional meals out. Itineraries have cultural and historical emphasis, but also include relaxing and skin diving by the Red Sea. Prices from £560 including return flight to Amman; food kitty extra.

Adventure tours in India: 10 days Bombay to Delhi, 16 days Delhi to Kathmandu, 30 day tour of South India all overland. Flights can be arranged. Also 15 day tours of Sri Lanka, Madagascar, Burma etc.

# AFRICA

**EXPEDITIONS ACROSS AFRICA**

GUERBA have the widest choice of routes in Africa from 1 – 21 weeks.

GUERBA offer optional trekking, river exploration or mountain climbing on all major expeditions

GUERBA use vehicles fully equipped for safety, reliability and comfort

GUERBA expedition leaders are experienced and trained in Africa.

GUERBA - the specialists in AFRICAN ADVENTURE
For details of this and many other short and long expeditions send for our full colour brochure.

GUERBA EXPEDITIONS LTD. WESTFIELD HOUSE, WESTBURY, WILTSHIRE BA13 3EP, UK. TEL: BRATTON (0380) 830476

IN CANADA call WESTCAN TREKS
(Toll Free) 1-800-227-8747
IN U.S.A. call ADVENTURE CENTRE
(Toll Free) 800/227-8747
(Toll Free in C.A.) 800/661-7265

London-Kathmandu in 60 or 87 days. Travelling in small groups of 23. Mostly camping in 2-man tents with group cooking. Thorough exploration of the Middle East and one week stay in Kashmir with the option of going to Ladakh. Prices from £760 not including food kitty.
Minimum age: 16 years.
North American agent: Adventure Center, 5540 College Avenue, Oakland, CA 94618.

**HOBO TRANS-AFRICA**
**Wissett Place, Halesworth, Suffolk IP19 8HY. Tel: (09867) 3124.**
Hobo Trans-Africa Expeditions Ltd.
Directors: J M Jordan, N P Fisher.
In operation since 1974.
Departures from Britain each February taking an unusual route across the Sahara, £995 for five months' travel to Johannesburg, visiting more than a dozen African countries. Price including all ferries, transport and equipment. Food kitty (around £150) and visa fees are extra.
"Whether you are interested in the flora and fauna, landscape, geology, architecture, anthropology or simply the challenge, Africa is still able to offer something exciting and unique."

**HOBO TRAVEL LTD**
**Town Street, Swanton Morley, Norfolk NR20 4PF. Tel: (036283) 629.**
Directors: M McHugo, C Barry, T Rowell, K Reeve.
In business since 1976.
Tours to Morocco and the Pyrenees of Northern Spain for small groups of up to 18 people. Considerable experience in school tours — adventure and field studies. Prices include equipment, food, insurance, etc: Morocco from £284 per person; Pyrenees from £156 per person.

**JABALIYA TREKKING LTD.**
**36 Keren Hayesod Street, Jerusalem, Israel. Tel: (+972) 2-699385.**
Overland safari in the Sinai including swimming in the Red Sea, visiting the area where the Exodus took place, Mt. Sinai, and

# ADVENTURE

*Small group camping and hotel tours.*

**SYRIA, JORDAN, IRAQ/TURKEY**
3 week camping tours.
**INDIA-16 DAYS**
Delhi-Kathmandu
**INDIA-KASHMIR:**
21 day, hotel/houseboats.
**INDIA-RAJASTHAN/GOA;**
3/4/6 weeks.
**OVERLAND LONDON TO NEPAL:** 60 and 87 day tours.
**LONDON-DELHI**
By train-upto 50 days
**TREKKING IN NEPAL.**

*Consult us, the specialist operator.*

# HANN OVERLAND

**185 STREATHAM HIGH RD., LONDON SW16 6EG**
Telephone: 01-769 6659.
Telex: 8956502 CRESNT G.

### AFRICA

Five months of adventure with

# HOBO TRANS-AFRICA

— Annual February Departures —

Visiting: **Morocco** ... **Algeria** ... **Mali** ... **Upper Volta** ... **Niger** ... **Nigeria** ... **Chad** ... **Cameroon** ... **C.A.R.** ... **Zaire** ... **Rwanda** ... **Burundi** ... **Tanzania** ... **Kenya** ... **Zambia** ... **Botswana** ... **South Africa**

A small but well established organisation offering a **personal approach** as well as **value for money, flexibility** and **reliability**.

**Hobo Trans-Africa Expeditions**

Wissett Place, Halesworth
Suffolk IP19 8HY, Great Britain
Telephone: (09867) 3124

St. Catherine's Monastery and seeing Bedouin tribesmen and oases. 1-5 days all year round. Camping accommodation. Price from $115 includes transport, meals, equipment and English speaking guides.

## JOURNEY LATIN AMERICA LTD.
**16 Devonshire Road, Chiswick, London W4 2HD. Tel: 01-747 3108.**
Directors: J B Williams, C A Parrott, W Parrott.
In business since 1979.
Travel planned for 10,000 in 1986.
Overland adventure holidays in Latin America travelling by local transport. Departures throughout the year for groups of up to 15. Choice of ten itineraries lasting 14, 21, 28, 35, 42, 72 or 79 days starting in Lima, Santiago, or Rio de Janeiro, Caracas or Guatemala City. Highlights include hiking in the Andes, the glaciers of Patagonia, the Amazon and visiting pre-Columbian ruins of the Inca cultures. Budget hotels and restaurants are used, but individuals are free to stay anywhere. Price from £345 to £495 including all group

transportation on local trains, buses, taxis, boats or planes, plus a tour leader who will speak Spanish. Food and accommodation allow £8-£10 daily. Flights not included but Journey Latin America specialises in low cost flights, and is happy to advise clients who are buying air fares on the best way to travel independently in South America. Minimum age: 18 years.

## LONG HAUL EXPEDITIONS
**Tamar Travel Agents Ltd.**
**56 Bohun Grove, East Barnet, Herts EN4 8UB. Tel: 01-440 1582.**
Director & Tour Leader: T L Wilkinson.
In business since 1979.
Holidays for 250 arranged annually.
Trans-African overland expeditions for groups of 25 departing October, November and January. 5 months travelling by Bedford 4-wheel-drive safari truck from London to Nairobi. Camping in desert oases, mud-baked villages, dense tropical rain forest, open savannah or on the rim of a volcanic crater. The route will cross Tunisia, Algeria, Niger, Upper Volta, Togo,

*Exodus Expeditions Ltd*

90

Benin, Nigeria, The Cameroons, Central African Republic, Zaire, Rwanda, Tanzania and Kenya, and will cover approximately 14,000 miles. Opportunities for 2 or 3 day dugout canoe trips, climbing Mt. Kilimanjaro (19,349 ft.) with guides and porters, and snorkelling in coral reefs off the coast of Kenya. Itinerary arranged to coincide with special regional market days and with the migration of game animals. Price is £950 plus food kitty of £150. Travel insurance, visa costs and return air fare from Nairobi (about £200) not included. All equipment provided except sleeping bags, mosquito nets and individual's eating utensils. Participants take turns cooking and everyone helps with daily chores.

After Nairobi it is possible to continue on to South Africa (2/3 weeks for £75 plus £15 for group kitty). Also 4 week camping trips to Morocco and Turkey during summer. Price £245 and £275 fully inclusive. Ages: 18-40 years.

**MOUNTAIN TRAVEL, INC.**
**1398 Solano Avenue, Albany, CA 94706, USA. Tel: (+1) 415-527-8100; toll-free (USA only) 1-800-227-2384.**
**Britain: 22 Church Street, Twickenham TW1 3NW.**

Overland through Patagonia. 25 days in January and February. Starting and ending in Miami, U.S.A. Accommodation in simple inns and camps. Travelling by bus in Southern Argentina and Chile, a land of granite mountains, deep fjords, glaciers, rain forests and the pampas. The holiday includes a boat ride in the Beagle Channel and a visit to Ushuaia, "the southernmost town in the world". Price $1,890, not including air fare.

Overland tour and trek in the Peruvian Andes. 16 days in July-August. Starting and ending in Miami, USA. Visiting Lima and the mountain town of Huaraz and walking in the Cordillera Blanca. Price $1,290 not including air fare.
Recent hiking experience needed.

**SACU TOURS**
**Society for Anglo-Chinese Understanding**
**152 Camden High Street, London NW1 0NE. Tel: 01-482 4292.**
Overland to China on the Trans-Siberian railway from Moscow to Beijing in North West China and tours through China for individuals and groups. 25-30 days July-September. Accommodation is in 4-berth compartments on the train and in guest

GRANDSTAND TOURS FROM THE COMFORT OF YOUR TRAVELLING HOME
# GREECE ★ TURKEY ★ ITALY ★ PORTUGAL ★ MOROCCO
# EUROPEAN HIGHLIGHTS ★ AFRICAN SAFARIS
Fly to Italy or Portugal and then join a small party for the trek of a lifetime. Live and sleep aboard our specially converted double-decker motor caravans stopping when and where you please.
Sightseeing and meals included. **2 or 3 weeks from £249**

**TENTREK DECKERTREKS**
BROCHURE FROM: TENTREK  152 MAIDSTONE ROAD, SIDCUP, KENT. 01-302 6426
ABTA ATOL 806

houses in China. Price from around £1,400 includes all travel, accommodation, meals in China, the services of a tour leader and Luxingshe guide. Meals on the train are extra. Preparatory study weekends are held six weeks prior to departure to meet the tour leaders and other participants. All ages.

**SOBEK EXPEDITIONS, INC.**
**One Sobek Tower, Angels Camp, CA 95222, USA. Tel: (+1) 209-736 4524.**
'Patagonian Express' overland tour from Santiago de Chile to Buenos Aires, using sleeper trains and steamboats through the Andean Lake District. 8 days from October to May. Price around $900 plus air travel.

'Patagonia Overland' tour using heavy duty van: south from Santiago into Patagonia taking in mountains, fjords and pampas. 16 days in December. Price around $1,800 plus air travel to Santiago.

**SSR-REISEN**
**Bäckerstrasse 52, Zurich, Switzerland. Tel: (+41) 1-242 3000.**
Overland holidays in open-topped double-decker buses carrying up to 24 people. 9 different itineraries from 9-50 days with 80 departure dates April-October. To Greece, Scandinavia, Sardinia/Corsica, Spain, Portugal, Southern France, Morocco, round the Mediterranean and the North African Sahara. Camping accommodation. Prices from S.Fr.720.
Ages: 16-35 years.

**TENTREK EXPEDITIONS LTD.**
**152 Maidstone Road, Ruxley Corner, Sidcup, Kent. Tel: 01-302 6426.**
Directors: P. M. & J. Hobcraft.
In business since 1970.
Member of ABTA; ATOL no. 806.
Holidays for 3,000 arranged annually.
Overland camping tours by bus to Greece, Morocco, Italy, Portugal and Turkey. Two and three week tours mainly in summer season except the trip to Morocco which departs from London throughout the year. Camping and budget accommodation throughout. Opportunity to go island-hopping in Greece on Tentrek's own boat. Prices from £249 inclusive.
Ages: 18-35 years.

**TRACKS AFRICA LTD.**
**12 Abingdon Road, London W8 6AF. Tel: 01-937 3028.**
Directors: D. Little, A. Toms.
In business since 1971.
Trans Africa expeditions, 18 weeks travelling by 4-wheel drive truck from London via Nairobi to Johannesburg. Price from £930 plus food kitty of £10 per week. Cairo to Nairobi also available, price from £620. All expeditions operate in reverse direction.
Ages: 18-35 years, but young at heart welcome.

**TRACKS EUROPE LTD.**
**12 Abingdon Road, London W8 6AF. Tel: 01-937 3028.**

**TRACKS**
Overland Adventure Travel Experts

**AFRICA**
**TRANS-AFRICAN EXPEDITIONS**
18 WEEKS LONDON–JO'BURG
15 WEEKS LONDON–NAIROBI
8 WEEKS CAIRO–NAIROBI
2 WEEK KENYA SAFARIS
2 WEEK TANZANIA SAFARIS
1 WEEK TURKANA
1 WEEK MT KILIMANJARO
1 WEEK ETHIOPIA

**EUROPE**
**CAMPING TOURS**
RUSSIA-SCANDI-CZECH     6¼ WEEKS
RUSSIA-SCANDINAVIA      3½ WEEKS
CENTRAL EUROPE          6 WEEKS
SCANDINAVIA             4½ WEEKS
ODYSSEY                 4½ WEEKS
GRAND EUROPE            10 WEEKS
SEND FOR COLOUR BROCHURE AND FULL DETAILS
WORLD TRACKS LIMITED
12 ABINGDON ROAD, LONDON W8 6AF, U.K.
TELEPHONE
01-937 3028
**TRACKS**

Holidays for 3,000 arranged annually. Overland camping tours to Europe and Scandinavia, Russia and Poland. Holidays usually last 3 or 4 weeks departing from London April-November. Destinations include the Greek Islands, Moscow, the "Running of the Bulls" in Pamplona, Spain and Florence. Tours pass through most European centres of interest. New for 1986 is the "Odyssey" tour covering southern Europe and the Greek Islands. Tented accommodation throughout. Prices range from £95 for 10 day trip to Pamplona, to £855 for 10 week tour of Italy, Greece and Bulgaria. Sleeping bag and air mattress needed.
Ages: 18-35 years.

## TRAILFINDERS
**42-48 Earls Court Road, London W8 6EJ. Tel: 01-937 9631.**
Directors: M Gooley, R Greenhill.
In business since 1970.
Member of ABTA; ATOL no. 1458.
Overland and air tour of north east Asia; 22 days commencing in Japan visiting South Korea and Taiwan ending in Hong Kong. Travel is by public transport. Price around £600 plus £20 per day for food and accommodation.
Overland tour of Thailand using public transports; 12 days visiting Bangkok, Chiang Mai, Khao Yai National Park and other places of interest. Price around £200 plus £110-£130 for meals and accommodation.
Overland and air tour of south east Asia; 20 days commencing in Bangkok and travelling through Malaysia, Singapore and Indonesia, terminating in Bali. Travel is by public transport. Price around £300 plus £12-£20 per day for meals and accommodation.

Air travel to departure point and from termination point is not included in these prices, but low fares can be arranged through Trailfinders. Alternatively, these three tours can be preceded by a Trans Siberian railway tour from London to Japan to form a complete journey from London to Bali.

## TREK AMERICA/TREK EUROPA
**62 Kenway Road, London SW5. Tel: 01-373 5083.**
Director: W M Fulton.
In business since 1971.
Member of ABTA.
Adventure camping tours to USA and Canada and Europe for the 18-35 age group. Operating fleet of over 150 Maxi-wagons and over 200 staff.
Trekamerica: 12 North American itineraries with prices from £265 for 2 weeks. 3, 4, 6 and 9 week treks from £430.
Trek Europa: itineraries ranging from 1 to 10 weeks with prices from £119. Also 5 week trek to North Africa and 4 week trek in Eastern Europe sampling life in the Communist bloc.
Groups are limited to 13-14 plus a qualified leader/driver and travel is in sturdy high specification converted minibuses. Tour costs are inclusive of all group transportation, modern camping and cooking equipment, admissions to national parks, specified attractions and campsite fees.

## UPSTAIRS DOWNSTAIRS TRAVEL LTD.
**90a Percy St, Oxford OX4 3AD. Tel: (0865) 241806.**
Directors: Julian and Jeremy Atiyah.
In business since 1985.
Double-decker bus tours of Europe. Mainly 21 day tours April-October, visiting some combination of France, Italy, Switzerland, Austria, Germany, Holland, Luxembourg and Belgium. Price around £295 plus £45 food kitty. Some help with cooking and cleaning is expected. Price includes accommodation in bunks on the upper deck. "One of the unusual features of these tours is their flexibility: the group can change the route or spend an extra day here or there."

## WESTCAN TREKS ADVENTURE TRAVEL
**3415 West Broadway, Vancouver, British Columbia, Canada V6R 2B4. Tel: (+1) 604-734 1066.**
Manager: Russell Jennings.
In business since 1979.
Camping and overland tours in North

America, Africa, South America, Asia and Europe. Departures year round for individuals and groups of up to 15. Participants erect tents and share the cooking. Average price of $40 per day. Ages: 18-70 years.

## WEXAS
**45 Brompton Road, London SW3 1DE. Tel: 01-589-0500/3315.**
Driving and camping tours from Tunis to Lomé, from Nairobi to Johannesburg, in Algeria, Morocco, North Yemen, Scandinavia, the Middle East, Kenya, Tanzania, Zaire, Rwanda and Botswana. Prices from £295 for 15 days in Morocco to £1,369 for 20 days in Botswana, including air fare. Food kitty is extra on some tours.

Overland to Kathmandu, 14 weeks departing March-September. Camping all the way. Price £1,290 plus US$12 per week kitty. Flights home or on to the Far East/ Australia can be arranged.

Overland to Johannesburg, 18 weeks, departing throughout the year. Price from £2,060.

Train journey from London to Istanbul. 15 days with sightseeing stops *en route*. April-September, price £1,750.

Train and plane from Cairo to Cape Town with extensive sightseeing, October-March. Price £3,495 including flights from and to London.

Russia, Mongolia and China by air, rail, road and river, using sleepers and good hotels. 40 days departing April-September. Price £2,950 including flight home from Hong Kong.

Overland budget hotel tours in Yugoslavia, Mexico, Sri Lanka, Russia, India, Czechoslovakia, Mali, Crete, Egypt and Malaysia. Prices from £285 for 16 days in Crete to £2,500 for 23 days in Mali including air fare. Food kitty extra in some cases.

Railway tour around India with private carriage. 28 days departing August-February. Price £450; air fare not included.

Driving and hotel tours in Turkey. 16 days (departing April-October) in western area from £375 plus £85 kitty. 22 days (departing May-October) tour of eastern area (including Black Sea cruise) from £580 plus £8 per day kitty.

Freestyle exploration of Madagascar. 25 days departing June-September. From £900 including air fare.

# Riding and Trekking

Although dressage and trekking are very different activities, enthusiasts of both activities are united by their love of and respect for the horse, and by their desire to learn to ride well. Throughout the world there are schools which run holiday courses, many of them residential. The standard of teaching and horses varies tremendously, as does the emphasis of each riding centre. Some specialise in family activities, others cater for unaccompanied children, and yet others welcome only experienced adult riders. For those interested in riding in Britain, further information can be obtained from the British Horse Society (BHS), British Equestrian Centre, Kenilworth, Warwickshire, which keeps a register of approved schools.

The full riding gear — boots, jodhpurs, jacket and hat — can be expensive (about £80). But the two essential pieces of equipment are an approved make of hard hat (about £10) and shoes or boots with a three-quarter inch heel to prevent slipping from the stirrup.

Trekking can be an exhilarating way of seeing the parts of the countryside not easily reached by road. It also has the great advantage of needing comparatively little exertion from the human participant. Generally the horses or ponies, often native to the locality, are tough yet gentle and the trek will be conducted at a walking pace. Some holidays are based at a single centre from which daily excursions are made. Others involve "post-trekking" which means moving on from place to place. This is usually meant for experienced riders. The organisation which inspects trekking centres for the benefit of both ponies and holiday-makers is Ponies of Britain. For a list of approved centres throughout Britain, send 85p to POB, Brookside Farm, Ascot, Berkshire SL5 TLU.

# England

## AM HOLIDAYS
**5 Eastfield, North Muskham, Newark, Notts NG23 6HE. Tel: (0636) 72488.**
Riding holidays in the Peak District at a BHS and POB approved Centre.
Riding, grooming, tacking up, stable management, full and half day trek, treasure hunt, games, competitions, instruction and visits. £130 for seven nights inclusive. Accommodation in adventure centre.
For unaccompanied children aged 10-16.

## ASHTREE RIDING SCHOOL AND CHILDREN'S HOLIDAY CENTRE
**Tamus Lodge, Purewell, Christchurch, Dorset BH23 1EH. Tel: (0202) 482642.**
Proprietor: Matthew Cook.
In business since 1959.
Recognised by BHS.
Holidays for 150 children arranged annually. Pony-club style riding and horse care holidays for children at Easter and from July to September. Prices in range £100-£120 including riding and full board. Hats provided.
Age limits: 7-16 years.

## CRABBET PARK EQUITATION CENTRE
**Worth, Crawley, Sussex RH10 4ST. Tel: (0293) 882601.**
Proprietor: T D Greenwood.
17 years in business.
Recognised by BHS, ABRS.
Riding holidays in Sussex for individuals and groups. Weekends or weeks throughout the year. Accommodation in small hotel in grounds of Equitation Centre. Bed and breakfast from around £16.50 per day. Instruction from £90 per week.
No experience needed.
Minimum age: 6 years.

## CRAG HOUSE FARM VENTURE CENTRE
**Crag House, Falstone, Hexham, Northumberland. Tel: (0660) 40259.**
Residential riding holidays for young people April-October. Dormitory accommodation and meals provided. Instruction to suit all abilities.
Ages: 8-16 years.

## EBBORLANDS FARM & RIDING CENTRE
**Ebborlands Farm, Wookey Hole, near Wells, Somerset. Tel: (0749) 72550.**
Proprietor: Mrs. E A Gibbs.
In business since 1975.
Approved by BHS.
Recognised by: ETB, West Country Tourist Board.
Riding holidays on the southern slopes of the Mendip Hills for individuals and groups of up to 8. Weekly from Easter to October. Self-catering caravan or camping available at Centre. Bed, breakfast and dinner at adjacent guest house; other types of accommodation available within $3\frac{1}{2}$ miles. Prices £36-£150 depending on type of accommodation and season.
Some experience preferable.
Minimum age: 7 years.

## ERA ADVENTURE HOLIDAYS LTD.
**18 Carr Field, Bamber Bridge, Preston, Lancs. PR5 8BS. Tel: (0772) 34998.**
Riding and pony trekking holidays for young people in the New Forest. One week in July or August. Dormitory accommodation and full board provided. Prices from £155.
Hard hats can be borrowed.
Ages: 8-16 years.

## EUROYOUTH
**301 Westborough Road, Westcliff on Sea, Essex SS0 9PT. Tel: (0702) 341434.**
Riding courses at BHS or ABRS approved centres. Two weeks by arrangement. Accommodation with families.
No experience needed.
Minimum age: 14 years.
Unaccompanied teenagers: 16 years+

## FLANDERS FARM RIDING CENTRE
**Silver St, Hordle, Lymington, Hants SO4 0DF.**
Directors: Frank and Mildred Rogers.
In business since 1975.
Recognised by ABRS, BHS, ETB, POB.
Horse riding instruction and forest rides

throughout the year. Price of £80-£100 per week includes instruction, farmhouse accommodation and all meals. Riding hats not included, but may be hired. Minimum age: 8 years. Unaccompanied children accepted. "Riding on well-mannered horses in ideal surroundings."

## HANBURIES RIDING CENTRE
**Hanburies, Bishops Frome, Worcestershire. Tel: (053 186) 312.**
Proprietor: Mrs C Hyett.
In business since 1974.
Approved by BHS.
Holidays for 300 arranged annually. Children's riding holidays in Worcestershire for individuals and groups of up to 25 throughout the year. Dormitory accommodation with full board. Price from around £80 (plus VAT) per week including instruction. The Centre has a heated swimming pool, trampoline and there are opportunities for fishing and archery.
No experience needed.
Ages: 7-17 years.

## HARROWAY HOUSE RIDING SCHOOL
**Harroway House, Penton Mewsey, Andover, Hants. SP11 0RA. Tel: (026 477) 2295.**
Proprietor: Mrs E C Skelton.
In business since 1943.
Recognised by ETB.
Instruction near Andover in all aspects of horsemanship for individuals all year round. Accommodation in large family house with all meals provided. Price from around £24 per day including accommodation, full board and instruction. Riding clothes are not provided.
No experience needed.
All ages.
Unaccompanied children: 9 years+.

## HAYNE BARN RIDING STABLES
**Saltwood, Hythe, Kent CT21 4QH. Tel: (0303) 65512.**
Partners: Ivor and Marie-Odile Record.
In business since 1978.
Riding, tennis and English language courses specifically for young foreign students. Holidays operate for four weeks at Easter and ten weeks in Summer. Price of £185 plus VAT per week. Includes all equipment, instruction, meals and accommodation. Age limits: 13-18.

## HF HOLIDAYS
**Dept 43, 142 Great North Way, London NW4 1EG. Tel: 01-203 3381.**
Pony trekking courses based at Penzance and Selworthy. Horse care, saddling and grooming instruction, plus riding in the local area. One week prices from around £190. Reduced rate rail travel available.

## KIDLANDLEE TRAIL RIDING
**Kidlandlee (AH), Harbottle, Morpeth, Northumberland NE65 7DA. Tel: (0669) 50254.**
Proprietors: Charles and Elspeth Davison.
In business since 1974.
Holidays for 150 people each year. Riding holidays through the Cheviot Hills, stopping at a different farmhouse or hotel each night. All meals provided. Luggage is carried by van. Three day trail ride £132 plus VAT; five day post trail ride £195 plus VAT. Participants must be able to ride a horse at all paces, but need not be experts. Ages: 16-70.
North American agent: Fits Equestrian, 2011 Alamo Pindado Road, Solvang CA 93463.

## LYDFORD HOUSE RIDING STABLES
**Lydford House Hotel, Lydford, Okehampton, Devon EX20 4AU. Tel: (082 282) 347.**
Principal: Claire Boulter, BHSAI.
In business since 1981.
Recognised by BHS, POB.
Riding holidays on Dartmoor. Prices from £195 per week include at least 18 hours of riding plus dinner, bed and breakfast. Reductions for children. Non-residential riding and instruction also available. Walking, golf and fishing opportunities for non-riders.
"Exceptional riding country with minimal road work. The ideal family holiday for non-horsey parents with horse-mad children."
Minimum age: 5 years.

**MATTHEW'S EQUESTRIAN CENTRE**
Walnut Tree Farm, Lower Rainham Road, Gillingham, Kent. Tel: (0634) 577131.
Directors: Antonio and Matteo Rocco.
In business since 1982.
Recognised by BHS.
Weekend breaks and one week courses for both beginners and advanced riders at the Centre and in Capstone Park. Accommodation (in Centre's hotel) and all meals included in price of £87 (weekend) or £210 (one week).
Age limits: 12-65 years.
Unaccompanied children accepted.

**MOAT HOUSE**
Benenden, Kent TN17 4EU. Tel: (0580) 240581.
Directors: P D & Mrs P Grindle.
In business since 1963.
Recognised by BHS.
Riding holidays in Kent for individuals and groups. One or more weeks throughout the year. Accommodation in private homes or farmhouses. Full instruction provided by qualified staff. During summer months visits arranged to horse shows, etc. £200 per week including accommodation, meals and instruction.
Some riding experience preferred.
Minimum age: 10 years.
Unaccompanied children accepted.

**NORTHERN EQUITATION CENTRE**
Brookfield Lane, Aughton, Ormskirk, Lancs. Tel: Aughton Green 423153.
Partners: Mr and Mrs H F Mackart.
In business for over 50 years.
Recognised by BHS, ABRS.
Holiday riding courses (including video sessions) for children or adults. Children's courses in April, July and August: five days for £75 inclusive of tuition and full board. Adults courses in June and September, four days for £90 inclusive. Accommodation with local landladies.
Professional courses for BHS examinations also arranged.
Minimum age: 9 years.
Hats required.

**NORTH HUMBERSIDE RIDING CENTRE**
Easington, near Hull, North Humberside HU12 0UA. Tel: (0964) 50250.
Proprietor: Mrs T Biglin.
In business since 1965.
Approved by BHS.
Riding holidays for unaccompanied children close to beach. Indoor school and cross country course. Price £90 including riding, accommodation, full board and instruction. Hard hats may be hired.
Ages: 7-16 years.

**NORTH WHEDDON FARM RIDING HOLIDAYS**
Wheddon Cross, Minehead, Somerset TA24 7EX. Tel: (064 384) 224.
Proprietors: Captain and Mrs J G Trouton.
In business since 1972.
Approved by POB.
Riding holidays on Exmoor for small groups. Weekly March to December; weekends and short breaks in March-April and October-December. Full board and accommodation in family farmhouse. Over 25 hours of riding per week. Adults from £185, children from £145 per week. Riding tours around Exmoor during April-June and September-October, staying in pubs and hotels, from £345 per week. Hunting holidays from October to March. Riding wear not provided.
Cantering experience needed.
Minimum age: 10 years.
Unaccompanied children: 11 years +.

**OUTOVERCOTT RIDING STABLES**
New Mill Farm, Lynton, North Devon EX35 6JR. Tel: (0598) 53341.
Proprietor: Mrs. Bingham.
In business since 1969 at above address.
Recognised by POB.
Member of ETB.
Riding on Exmoor for individuals and groups of up to 15. Self catering accommodation. Prices on application. Riding from £3.50 per hour and £15 per day. Reduced rates for parties of 8 or more. Hard hats provided. All rides accompanied. No experience needed.
All ages.

**PGL YOUNG ADVENTURE LTD.**
**128 Station Street, Ross-on-Wye, Herefordshire HR9 7AH. Tel: (0989) 64211.**
Riding and pony trekking in a choice of hill country locations. Instruction in riding technique and pony care.
No experience needed.
Ages: 8-18 years.

**RED HOUSE STABLES**
**Old Road, Darley Dale, Matlock, Derbyshire DE4 2ER. Tel: (0629) 733583.**
Proprietor: Caroline Dale.
In business since 1947.
Holidays for 1,000 arranged each year.
Riding and driving tuition for adults and unaccompanied children in the Peak District. Three day 'Introduction to Driving' course for around £100 plus VAT, excluding meals and accommodation. One week children's holiday (including riding, driving and full board) around £200 plus VAT. Individual and advanced courses available.
Minimum age: 8 years.
Unaccompanied children welcome.

**ROSEBROOK EQUESTRIAN CENTRE**
**South Lopham, Diss, Norfolk IP22 2JP. Tel: (0379 88) 278.**
Proprietors: John and Valerie Attenborough.
In business since 1979.
Dressage, show jumping and cross-country tuition for children and adults; beginners through to advanced riders. Two and six day holidays with two rides per day. Accommodation in bedrooms and Portakabin containing ten bunk beds. All meals provided. Two day price £45; six days £115.
Minimum age: 5 years.

**SKAIGH STABLES**
**Belstone, Okehampton, Devon EX20 1RD. Tel: (0837) 840429.**
Proprietors: Mrs R Hooley, Mr D Moore.
Holidays for 500 arranged annually.
Riding holidays on Dartmoor for individuals and groups of up to 9. Weekends or one week holidays May-September. Accommodation in chalets with full board.

Price from £150 all inclusive. Warm waterproof clothing and rubber boots must be taken.
No experience needed, but preferable.
Minimum age: 10 years.
Unaccompanied children accepted.

# Scotland

**ARDFERN RIDING CENTRE**
**The Galley of Lorne Inn, Ardfern by Lochgilphead, Argyll PA31 8QN. Tel: (085 25) 664.**
Approved by BHS.
Riding holidays for individuals and small groups year round. Western riding available. Unspoilt riding country with many miles of tracks, untarred roads and cross-country jumps. Accommodation at Inn or self-catering cottages.
No experience needed.

**AYRSHIRE EQUITATION CENTRE**
**Castlehill Stables, Hillfoot Road, Ayr. Tel: (0292) 266267.**
Partners: Kevin and John Galbraith.
In business since 1952.
Recognised by BHS, POB, SSC.
Riding holidays at Easter, summer and early winter. One week around £115 fully inclusive; about £65 without meals and accommodation. One day, student, cross-country and showjumping courses also available.
Age limits: 5-65 years.

**BAREND PROPERTIES LTD.**
**Barend, Sandyhills, Dalbeattie DG2 4NU. Tel: (0387 78) 663.**
Directors: F M G Gourlay, S D Gourlay.
Recognised by BHS.
Riding holidays throughout the year in Dumfries and Galloway. 5-day courses for adults and children covering all aspects of horsemanship. Special courses for beginners aged 6-10. Trekking in Dalbeattie Forest also available. Accommodation in self-catering chalets or bed and breakfast in local farmhouse.

**EQUI-VENTURE**
**Achinreir Farm, Barcaldine, Argyll PA37 1SF. Tel: (063 172) 320.**
Proprietor: Miss E M Whittome.
Long distance trail riding holidays in the West Highlands of Scotland for individuals and groups of up to 6. 3-10 days May-September. Varied accommodation including farmhouse bed and breakfast and self catering caravans. Price from £175 for 8 days all inclusive.
Some experience needed.
Minimum age: 12 years.
Unaccompanied children accepted.

**FERNIEHIRST MILL**
**Jedburgh, Roxburghshire TD8 6PQ. Tel: (0835) 63279.**
Proprietors: John and Beryl Tough.
In business since 1963.
Holidays for 350 arranged annually.
Riding tours in the Cheviot Hills for individuals and groups of up to 10. One week April-October. Accommodation and board provided. Price approximately £300 per week. Riding gear needed, though hard hats may be borrowed if necessary. "We move on each day with the horses on our tours, leaving them at hill farms overnight and bring riders back to comfort in our lodge".
Riding experience needed.
Minimum age: 16 years.

**HF HOLIDAYS**
**Dept 43, 142 Great North Way, London NW4 1EG.**
Pony trekking courses based on the Isle of Arran. Riding interspersed with training in grooming, horse care and saddling.

**LOCH NESS LOG CABINS**
**Drummond Farm, Dores, Inverness-shire IV1 2TX. Tel: (046 375) 251.**
Approved by BHS.
Proprietors: Mr & Mrs A I Cameron.
Riding holidays around Loch Ness for competent riders. Accommodation in self catering log cabins. Pony trekking available for novices.

**SCOTTISH YOUTH HOSTELS ASSOCIATION**
**7 Glebe Crescent, Stirling FK8 2JA. Tel: Stirling (0786) 72821.**
Pony trekking and riding holidays in a choice of hostels in the Trossach hills and the Borders. Prices from £69 per week.
Minimum age: 12 years.

**TOMINTOUL PONY TREKKING CENTRE**
**Tomintoul, Ballingdalloch, Banffshire AB3 9EX. Tel: (08074) 223.** ·
Proprietor: Jenny Herschell.
In business since 1975.
Recognised by BHS, POB.
Holidays for 200 arranged each year.
Pony trekking holidays based at the highest village in the Highlands. Treks on Highland, New Forest and Welsh ponies, April-October. Instruction as required. Price £150 per week, fully inclusive. Handicapped people catered for if possible, although no ground floor rooms are available.
Minimum age: 12 years.
Unaccompanied young people accepted.

# Wales

**BRYN GWYN FARM**
**Cwrtnewydd, Llanybydder, Dyfed SA40 9YR. Tel: (057 046) 263.**
Proprietors: Mr. & Mrs. N. Crank.
In business since 1983 at present address.
Riding, trekking, horse driving and trail riding holidays available throughout the year. Arrangements are made to suit individual requirements. Caravans are available at reasonable rates.
Minimum age: 7 years.
Unaccompanied children: 8 years+

**CRAEN RIDING CENTRE**
**Craen, Llanerfyl, Welshpool, Powys SY21 0JB. Tel: (093 888) 349.**
Proprietor: Mrs A V Wallace.
In business since 1973.
Pony trekking holidays and riding lessons for individuals and groups of up to 10. 1 week April-October. Full-board farmhouse

or self-catering accommodation. Camping space available. Riding hat can be provided. Riders are expected to help look after the ponies.
No experience needed.
Minimum age: 5 years.
Unaccompanied children: 8 years+.

## L & A HOLIDAY AND RIDING CENTRE

**Goytre, Port Talbot, West Glamorgan. Tel: (0639) 885509.**
Proprietors: Mr & Mrs A G Holden.
In business since 1968.
Holidays for 3,000 arranged annually.
Riding holidays amid mountain and woodland country in south Wales. One week throughout the year. Self-catering accommodation in log cabins. Treks accompanied by experienced leaders; opportunities to go cross-country jumping for experienced riders. Cabin rental from £60-£150 plus £45 for hire of horse or pony. Reductions for children.
No experience needed.
Minimum age: 8 years.

## MAESLLWYCH RIVER AND MOUNTAIN CENTRE

**Glasbury on Wye, Herefordshire. Tel: (04974) 226.**
Trail rides from ½ day to one week in the Welsh borders. Instruction is given on pony care and riding skills. Camping equipment provided for overnight trails. Prices up to £105 (plus VAT) for one week, including all meals. Trail rides may be combined with canoeing and/or caving.
Age limits: 7-70.
Minimum age (unaccompanied): 16 years.

## NORTH CARDIGANSHIRE TREKKING CENTRE

**Plas Cefn Gwyn, Bontgoch, Talybont, Aberystwyth, Dyfed SY24 5DP. Tel: (097 086) 413.**
Proprietor: D L Parry BSc.
In business since 1971.
Recognised by POB.
Holidays for 2,000 arranged annually.

Pony trekking in the Cambrian hills all year from two hours to one week. Novices are normally separated from experienced riders. Prices from £5 for two hours to £120 for one week (including full board and five days riding). Warm and waterproof clothing and sensible footwear required. Hard hats provided.
Minimum age: 3 years for two hour trek, 10 years for one week holiday.
Unaccompanied children welcome.

# Ireland

## THE CONNEMARA TRAIL

**Aille Cross, Loughrea, Co. Galway, Ireland. Tel: (+353) 91-412 16.**
Proprietor: William Leahy.
In business since 1970.
Holidays for 250 arranged annually.
Trail riding in the Connemara region of Co. Galway for individuals or groups of 4-25. One or two weeks May-October. High class hotel accommodation with full meals. Price from £500 includes hotels, meals, horses, tack, grooms and guide.
No experience needed.
All ages.
Unaccompanied children: 12 years +.

## ERRISLANNAN MANOR

**Clifden, County Galway, Ireland. Tel: (+353) 95-21134.**
Proprietors: Mr & Mrs Donal Brooks.
In business since 1965.
Riding holidays for individual children and young adults on Connemara ponies. Weekly during July and August. Supervised guest house accommodation with full board. Ponycraft days; lessons with qualified teachers. Price about £200 per week; hard hats can be bought.
"Mountain, moorland and seaside rides on surefooted and kind family ponies."
No experience needed.
Minimum age: 8 years; residential unaccompanied children welcome.

# Europe

**ACCUEIL DES JEUNES EN FRANCE**
**12 rue des Barres, 75004 Paris. Tel: (+33)**
**1-278 04 82.**
Six and seven day riding holidays in the
Alps and Pyrenees at Easter and from June-
September. Beginners and advanced tuition
available. Camping or youth hostel
accommodation and all meals included in
price of 1,400-1,800F (about £120-£175);
travel to site extra.
Minimum age: 16 years.
IYHF membership card required.

**ANTE**
**Associazione Nazionale per il Turismo**
**Equestre e l'Equitazione di Campagna**
**Largo Messico 13, 00198 Roma, Italy. Tel:**
**(+39) 6-864053.**
President: Avv. Vittorio de Sanctis.
In business since 1968.
Riding tours and holidays in all parts of
Italy for individuals and groups of up to 10.
Weekends or weeks all year round.
Accommodation in inns or small hotels.
Prices on application. Riding clothes and
hats must be taken.
Some riding experience needed.
Minimum age: 11 years.

**CLUB MEDITERRANEE**
**UK Office: 106-108 Brompton Road,**
**London SW3 1JJ. Tel: 01-581 1161.**
Riding instruction at a Club Med Village in
the Limousin countryside of France. 2, 5 or
7 days throughout the year. Meals and
accommodation at the Pompadour Centre.
Choice of riding lessons, manege work,
hacking and excursions as well as courses in
theory, stable management, dressage and
showing. There are horses for all degrees of
riding experience, a 4 km. bridle path on the
estate, a pony club for children 8-12 years
and two Olympic standard riding schools.
Minimum age: 4 years.

**YHA TRAVEL**
**14 Southampton Street, London WC2E**
**7HY. Tel: 01-240-5236.**
Riding holidays in Luxembourg for

individuals and groups of 15-20. 10 days
from March to October. Based at Beaufort
youth hostel and including 10 hours of
riding with instruction over 7 days. Full
board, use of horse and instruction plus
return transport from London are provided
but riding clothes are not.
No experience needed.
Minimum age: 16 years.

# Israel

**VERED HAGALIL GUEST FARM**
**M P Korozin, 12340 Israel. Tel: (+972)**
**67-35785.**
Directors: Yehude and Yonah Avni.
In business since 1961.
Trail riding in Galilee for individuals and
small groups of 4 to 8. 2-10 day holidays
March-November. Guided trekking along
various routes in northern Israel.
Accommodation in bunkhouse or cottages

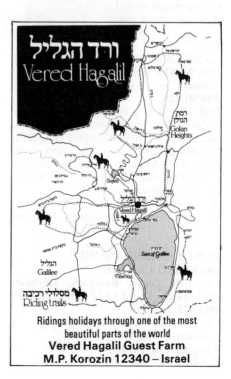

Ridings holidays through one of the most
beautiful parts of the world
**Vered Hagalil Guest Farm**
**M.P. Korozin 12340 – Israel**

overlooking the Sea of Galilee or camping under the stars when on the trail. Price from $42 a day plus varying charges for accommodation.
Minimum age: 14 years.

# Americas

## KINGSBERRY OUTFITTERS
Box 585, Salmon, ID 83467, USA. Tel: (+1) 208-756 2319.
Directors: S Millner, N Jones.
In business since 1980.
Holidays for 30 people arranged annually. Seven and ten day 'horsepack' trips to remote mountain lakes, with opportunities for fishing and photography. Horses, tents and meals provided. Holidays operate June-September: $800 for seven days, $1,000 for ten.

No experience necessary.
Age limits: 3-80 years.

# Australasia

## LOVICK'S MOUNTAIN TRAIL SAFARIS
Merrijig 3723, Victoria, Australia. Tel: (+61) 57-775510.
Directors: Jack Lovick, Charles Lovick.
In business since 1970.
Holidays for 1,000 arranged annually. Riding in the remote regions of the Great Divide. Weekends September-December and April-July; 8-day rides December-April. Price from A$60 per day including bush meals and tent or hut accommodation.
No experience needed.
All ages.

*Canadian Mountain Holidays Ltd*

# Sailing

The first boat to be used purely for recreation was the yacht which Charles II brought back from Holland in 1661. It was not until the Victorian era, however, that sailing and racing for pleasure became popular. The most important and longest established of all racing events is the America's Cup which was first sailed in 1851 (the oldest international trophy for any sport) and was consistently won by the USA until 1983 when the Australians managed to capture it. Their defence of the trophy in 1986 is sure to be a hard-fought battle.

Despite its venerable history, sailing is not necessarily a rich man's sport. Yachts are expensive to purchase, but residential sailing holidays and courses are often accessibly priced. Dinghy sailing holidays are available almost wherever there is a stretch of water. They can be ideal for a family with children old enough to swim and to endure what can be a fairly wet and cold experience (usually over 10 years of age). For unaccompanied young people, dinghy sailing features in many multi activity holidays.

Dinghies can be very fast and exhilarating, sacrificing stability for speed. Because a dinghy reacts more quickly than a larger boat to the slightest movement of wind and tide, a practical knowledge of seamanship is essential. Before setting out it is important to find out about local conditions, the direction and strength of currents, the times of high and low water and the weather forecast. In addition to life jackets, distress signals and a bailer, it is advisable to carry some means of propelling the boat if there is no wind.

Cruising means touring by boat. Originally cruising was always under sail, but nowadays almost all cruisers are equipped with an auxiliary engine. The yachts used for estuary, coastal and ocean cruising are usually capable of looking after themselves in rough seas because of their size and the electronic equipment they carry. People who are seeking a gentle introduction to sailing may choose to charter a skippered yacht, where the crew offer instruction as desired. Coping with the cooking and sanitary facilities in a small cabin may prove to be enough of an adventure for some. "Bare boat" charters are available only for skilled sailors who have the appropriate qualifications. In Britain the Yacht Charter Association Ltd. admits only those charterers who satisfy high standards of maintenance, service, safety equipment and insurance. A list of the approved charter members may be obtained from the YCA, c/o D R Howard, 60 Silverdale, New Milton, Hants.

Flotilla Cruising is gaining popularity from the Hebrides to the Sporades. The idea of sailing in a flotilla appeals to those who may not be confident enough sailors to set off on their own, or who are attracted by the social benefits. Usually about six yachts cruise together accompanied by the Captain's yacht, which is equipped with spare parts and acts as navigator for the group.

For all forms of sailing from centreboard dinghy racing to schooner sailing, good thick jerseys and a wind and waterproof anorak or oilskins are necessary. The required footwear is a pair of rubber soled canvas non-slip deck shoes or boots. Often some of the gear is included in the holiday cost.

The Royal Yachting Association, founded in 1875, is the governing body of the sport of sailing, and caters for all those who go afloat in small boats whether propelled by power or sail. It attempts to foster a sensible approach to safety and proficiency and runs a most successful coaching scheme. Details about RYA activities and recognised teaching establishments can be obtained from the Royal Yachting Association, Victoria Way, Woking, Surrey GU21 1EQ. Tel: (04862) 5022.

# England

## ANGLIAN YACHT SERVICES LTD.
The Hythe, Maldon, Essex CM9 7HN. Tel: (0621) 52290.
Directors: Roger and Christine Beckett.
In business since 1974.
Holidays for 400 arranged annually.
Cruising on traditional Thames sailing barges on the rivers, estuaries and creeks of the East Coast. Weeks and weekends April-October for parties of 12. 2 or 3 berth cabins with full 3 meals provided. The vessels are over 80 ft. long but of shallow draft. Although the barge carries a professional skipper, mate and cook, the passengers are encouraged to participate in the running of the vessel. Price from £75.
Minimum age: 10 years.

## ANVIL YACHTS LTD.
13 Harbour View Road, Parkstone, Poole, Dorset BH14 0PD. Tel: (0202) 741637.
Directors: R J & B Saunders, A J & A Claypole.
In business since 1968.
Holidays for 1,200 arranged annually.
Self-sail cruises from Poole for individuals and groups of up to 12. 1-2 weeks March-November. Choice of 10 or 12 berths; complete self-catering. Oilskins needed but can be hired. Price approximately £70 per person per week. Possible to sail to Norway and Spain.
Skippers available.

## BOSHAM SEA SCHOOL
1 High St, Bosham, West Sussex PO18 8HN.
Directors: B W Goodman, S P Goodman, M E Goodman.

In business since 1960.
Recognised by RYA.
Holidays for 300 arranged annually.
Sail training for individuals and groups of up to six. Courses run March-October: weekend (£75), 5 day (£180), 7 day (£220) and 12 day (£395).
No experience necessary.
Ages: 12-70. Unaccompanied children welcome.

**BOWLES OUTDOOR PURSUITS CENTRE (4)**
**Eridge Green, Tunbridge Wells, TN3 9LW. Tel: (089 26) 4127.**
Dinghy sailing courses on Bewlbridge Reservoir. RYA certificate courses in Otter dinghies. Staff/student ratio 1:2. All sailors must be able to swim 50 metres in light clothing. One week from about £82 non residential or £100 fully inclusive.
No experience needed.
Ages: 10-65 years.
Unaccompanied children: 10 years +.

**BRADWELL FIELD STUDIES & SAILING CENTRE**
**Bradwell Waterside, near Southminster, Essex CM0 7QY. Tel: (0621) 76256.**
Recognised by RYA.
Sailing instruction for individuals and groups of up to 40. Courses daily/weekend/mid-week/weekly April-October. Board and accommodation provided. Introductory and advanced instruction in dinghy sailing, off-shore sailing, practical navigation and keel boat handling. Sailing expeditions can be arranged in craft suitable for sleeping aboard. Price from around £7 per day.
Participants must be able to swim.
Minimum age: 13 years.

**CALSHOT ACTIVITIES CENTRE**
**Calshot Road, Calshot, Southampton SO4 1BR. Tel: (0703) 892077/891380.**
Recognised by RYA.
Dinghy and cruiser sailing courses take place in wayfarers, bosuns, lasers, toppers and 420's. All grades catered for from beginners to instructors. Weekends and weeks all year round. Cost from £44 for a weekend course (reductions for those under 19 years) including accommodation, food,

use of equipment and highly qualified instruction. Also evening courses for local residents.
No experience needed.
Minimum age: 11 years.
Unaccompanied children accepted.

**DOLPHIN SAILING SCHOOL**
**'The Foreshore' Woodside, Wootton, Isle of Wight PO33 4JR. Tel: (0983) 882246.**
Directors: R Fitchett, D Fitchett.
In business since 1967.
Approved by RYA.
Holidays for 200-300 arranged annually.
Sailing holiday with dinghy and cruising courses around the Isle of Wight for individuals, families and groups of up to 16. March-October. Prices from £175 per week with hotel accommodation and meals. All equipment provided.
No experience needed.
Minimum age: 12 years.
Unaccompanied children: 14 years+.
Disabled sailors accepted.

**EAST ANGLIAN SCHOOL OF SAILING**
**PO Box 64, The Strand, Ipswich, Suffolk IP2 8NN. Tel: (0473 84) 246.**
Proprietor: William Smith.
In business since 1973.
Recognised by RYA.
Holidays for 300 arranged annually.
Offshore and coastal sailing based at Ipswich and sailing to Belgium and Holland. Weekends, 1 week and 2 week trips April-October. Weekend prices from around £50. Accommodation aboard modern cruising yachts with access to shore-based marina facilities at most stops.
No experience needed.
Ages: 2-75 years.
No unaccompanied people under 17.

**EASTBOURNE SAILING AND WINDSURFING SCHOOL**
**11 Wrestwood Avenue, Willingdon, Eastbourne, East Sussex. Tel: (0323) 502674.**
Partners: Peter and Caroline Towner.
In business since 1980.
Recognised by RYA.
Courses for 300 arranged annually.

Sailing courses from April to October. Price for five tuition sessions (including all equipment) £35; with bed, breakfast and evening meal, £95.
All ages; unaccompanied children welcome.

**EMSWORTH SAILING SCHOOL**
**Northney Marina, Hayling Island, Hants, PO11 0NH. Tel: (0705) 468925.**
Sailing instruction in Chichester Harbour for individuals and groups of up to 30. 2 days — 3 weeks March-October. Many types of accommodation available. Price from £67 for 6 days. Also 2-3 week multiwatersport courses including canoeing and windsurfing.
Boats used are Wayfarers, 420s, X4s, Toppers and Optimists.
No experience needed.
Minimum age: 6 years.
Unaccompanied children: 10 years+.

**EUROYOUTH**
**301 Westborough Road, Westcliff on Sea, Essex SS0 9PT. Tel: (0702) 341434.**

**Emsworth Sailing School**
(Established 1954)

Situated in beautiful Chichester Harbour.
R.Y.A. elementary, intermediate, advanced and racing sailing courses for children and adults in a wide range of dinghies including Wayfarers, 420s, X4s, Toppers and Optimists.
Also windsurfing, canoeing, Camp and Sail holidays (see Young People's holidays).
Special Adult All In budget holiday accommodation and Junior Residential holidays.

*For colour brochure and details*
**telephone (0705) 468925** *or write:*
**Emsworth Sailing School, Northney Marina Hayling Island, Hants. PO11 0NH**

Sailing courses at Thorpe Bay for individuals and groups. Accommodation arranged with families.
No experience needed.
Minimum age: 14 years.
Unaccompanied teenagers: 16 years+

**FOWEY CRUISING SCHOOL**
**9 North Street, Fowey, Cornwall PL23 1DD. Tel: (072 683) 2129.**
Principal: John Myatt.
In business since 1972.
Recognised by RYA.
Cruiser sailing from base on Cornish riviera to Western Channel, Scilly Isles, Channel Islands and Britany. 5-14 day cruises throughout the year (except for four week break December/January). Prices from £190 for six nights inclusive of meals and accommodation ashore and afloat.
"Close-quarter spectating at international sailing races. Visits to islands, coves and little used harbours."
No experience necessary for beginners courses and family cruises.
Age limits: 5-75.

**FRIGATE "FOUDROYANT"**
**The Foudroyant Trust, c/o GPO, High Street, Gosport, Hants PO12 1EH. Tel: (0705) 582696.**
A company limited by guarantee; charity no. 51221.
Holidays for 2,000 arranged annually.
Sailing, seamanship and offshore courses in Portsmouth Harbour, the Solent and Channel for individuals and groups of up to 60. One week holidays April-September. Accommodation in hammocks on board and four meals per day provided. Price from £105 per week. Waterproof gear should be taken.
No experience needed.
Minimum age: 11 years.
Unaccompanied children accepted.
Book through the Captain Superintendent, Frigate "Foudroyant."

**HOLME PIERREPONT NATIONAL WATERSPORTS CENTRE**
**Adbolton Lane, Holme Pierrepont, Nottingham NG12 2LU. Tel: (0602) 821212.**

Sailing holidays at large purpose built watersports centre for individuals and groups of up to 60. Available April-September. Water skiing, boardsailing, canoeing and fishing available.
Ages: 12-60 years.

**INSTOW SAILING TUITION CENTRE**
**The Quay, Instow, Nr. Bideford, North Devon. Tel: (0271) 860475.**
Proprietors: J and M Bowers.
In business since 1975.
Holidays for 150 arranged annually.
Sailing tuition holidays on the Torridge and Taw Estuaries, individuals and groups of up to 15. Weekly courses March-October. Bed and breakfast or self-catering accommodation available. All equipment provided except soft shoes.
Ages: 10-66 years.

**JIB-SET SAIL SCHOOL AND YACHT CHARTER**
**Beacon Quay, Torquay, Devon TQ1 2BG. Tel: (0803) 25414.**
Partners: Gordon and Rosemary Hutley.
In business since 1979 under present ownership.
Recognised by RYA.
Dinghy and yacht sailing courses from April to October. Private tuition, holiday courses and RYA Certificate instruction. Prices from £10 per hour to £155 for five days yachting (including food and accommodation aboard). Shore accommodation not included but can be arranged locally.
Minimum age: 8 years.
Unaccompanied children: 14 years+.

**KENT SAILING SCHOOL**
**68 Grange Road, Ramsgate, Kent CT11 9QB. Tel: (0843) 584477.**
Partners: Neill and Susan Hunter.
In business since 1975.
Recognised by RYA.
Offshore sailing instruction cruises. All cruises visit Belgium and France. Weekend, six day and two week courses from March to October. Price including accommodation

# FOUDROYANT

## Adventure Sailing Holidays

Weekly Sailing/Seamanship holidays on board
Frigate Foudroyant moored in Portsmouth Harbour

For boys and girls aged 11 years-17 years, individually or in groups, an exciting week is guaranteed learning to sail and handle boats, visiting the naval dockyard, HMS Victory and the submarine base, sailing to the Isle of Wight. All carried out each week with the pleasure of plenty of young company.

For full details write to:
**Captain Superintendent, Frigate Foudroyant,**
**c/o GPO, Gosport, Hants. PO12 1EH.**
**Telephone: (0705) 582696**

afloat and all meals: £195 for six days.
Special menus on request.
"We believe that crew enjoyment is just as important as careful coaching."
No experience necessary.
Minimum age (unaccompanied): 14.

## MARITIME STUDIES LTD.
**Shaftesbury House, 20/22 Tylney Road, Bromley, Kent BR1 2RL. Tel: 01-290 0385.**
Directors: C J and E A Corcoran.
Established in 1971 as Llanelli Marine Ltd.
Recognised by RYA.
Motor cruising and sportsboat certificate courses on the Bristol Channel for individuals and groups of up to 12. 3 or 6 day courses in summer, and theory courses in winter. Prices from £45 per day on board training vessel 'Good Shepherd'. Bunk accommodation and 2 meals a day are provided. Students are in charge of vessel operation including catering. "The Bristol Channel has the second highest tidal range in the world, which together with emphasis on passage planning and pilotage in and out of small ports by day and night, results in exciting and exacting training."
Minimum age: 17 years.

## MEDINA VALLEY CENTRE
**Dodnor Lane, Newport, Isle of Wight PO30 5TE. Tel: (0983) 522195.**
Non-profit making company.
Executive Director: P E Lee.
In business since 1953 (since 1977 under present name).
Holidays for over 1,000 arranged annually.
Member of NFSS.
Recognised by RYA.
Sailing holidays ranging from elementary dinghy sailing to Channel cruising for individuals and groups of up to 60. 7 days April-October. Prices from £100 for 1 week dinghy sailing, with accommodation and meals. Life jackets provided on deposit. The Medina Valley Centre organises a programme of talks, discussions and films designed to stimulate thought about the Christian faith.
All ages.
Unaccompanied children: 14 years +.

## NEWTON FERRERS SAILING SCHOOL
**Westerly, Yealm Road, Newton Ferrers, Plymouth, Devon PL8 1BJ. Tel: (0752) 872375.**
Directors: A P & A E Thomson.
In business since 1958.
Recognised by RYA, NFSS.
Member of West Country Tourist Board.
Sailing tuition for individuals and groups of up to 12. One or two week courses from April-October. Accommodation and meals available at school headquarters. Prices on application. Oilskins can be hired.
No experience needed.
Minimum age: 8 years.
Unaccompanied children welcome.

## NORFOLK SCHOOL OF SAILING & SEAMANSHIP
**34 Riverside, Martham, Great Yarmouth, Norfolk. Tel: (0493) 748045.**
Principal: Erick J Manners.
In business since 1954.
Sailing and boatbuilding courses on the

# Medina Valley Centre

**The way to Fellowship and Fun**
Learn to sail in the attractive waters of Wight

RYA dinghy sailing courses up to instructor

Leisure sailing
Channel yacht cruising

**Learn and explore this beautiful Isle**

Rambling and Natural History holidays
Drawing and Painting holidays
*Multi activity weeks combining several of the activities and including canoeing and sailboarding.*
*Why not use us just as a holiday base to visit the Isle of Wight (accommodation-only rates).*
*Come and join us for a stimulating holiday and enjoy Christian Fellowship, there is something for every member of the family.*

Write or phone for comprehensive brochure:
**MEDINA VALLEY CENTRE**
Dodnor Lane, Newport, Isle of Wight PO30 5TE.
Telephone: 0983 522195

lakes and rivers of the Norfolk Broads for individuals and groups. 2 hours — 2 weeks from May to October. Self catering accommodation in chalets on the riverside. Prices on application. Slightly handicapped people catered for. Minimum age: 12 years.

## OCEAN YOUTH CLUB
**South Street, Gosport, Hampshire PO12 1EP. Tel: (0705) 528421.**
Registered as an Educational Charity.
Director: T R Jones, MBE.
In business since 1950.
Holidays for over 4,000 arranged annually. Adventure sailing holidays with "the finest sailing fleet in the British Isles". Weekends, weeks or longer for individuals and groups of 12, March-November. The OYC aims "to give young people the opportunity to go to sea offshore under sail, to foster the spirit of adventure, to inculcate a sense of responsibility towards themselves and others and to encourage a wider outlook and understanding of other people". Vessels are based in Ipswich, Gosport, and Plymouth, as well as in Wales, Scotland and Northern Ireland. Prices range from £42 to £147 per week including meals, safety equipment and oilskins.
No experience needed.
Ages: 12-24; adult cruises also available from £175.

## OYSTERWORLD SAILING HOLIDAYS LTD.
**No. 1 Wherry Lane, Wherry Quay, Ipswich, Suffolk. Tel: (0473) 58900.**
Director: P J Abbott.
In business since 1980.
Recognised by RYA.
Instructional sailing holidays leading to RYA certificate standards for individuals and groups of up to 15. Beginners courses on the East coast of England and more advanced Coastal Skipper/Yachtmaster offshore courses to France, Belgium and Holland. 1 week from April to November. Accommodation on board yachts. Price around £165 per week not including food. Oilskins and bedding can be hired. Bareboat and crewed charters and flotilla cruises also available.

No experience needed.
All ages.
Unaccompanied children: 14 years+.

## PARKSTONE SAILING
**Lilliput Yacht Station, 324 Sandbanks Road, Poole, Dorset BH14 8HY. Tel: (0202) 709707.**
Directors: R C and B L Pain.
In business since 1975.
Recognised by RYA.
Sailing on 26 to 35 foot cruisers from Poole and Lymington. Two days to two weeks, April-November. Instruction given on marina-based or coastal cruising. RYA certificates awarded. Some cruises to France and Channel Islands. Price around £170 for five days, all found.
Minimum age: 8 years.
Minimum age (unaccompanied): 17 years.

## PGL YOUNG ADVENTURE LTD.
**128 Station Street, Ross-on-Wye, Herefordshire HR9 7AH. Tel: (0989) 64211.**
Yachting and cruising holidays for teenagers during July and August. Instruction, accommodation, all specialist equipment and clothing provided.
No experience needed.
Ages: 12-18 years.

## POOLE SCHOOL OF SAILING
**43 Panorama Road, Sandbanks, Poole, Dorset BH13 7RA. Tel: (0202) 709231.**
Proprietor: H Poole.
In business since 1958.
Recognised by RYA.
Yachting instruction and yacht cruising courses. Daily or weekly for individuals and groups of up to 6. Open throughout the year. All types of accommodation available locally. Price £20 per day, £120 per week (plus VAT). Rubber soled shoes essential. Waterproof clothing can be hired. Safety equipment provided.
Windsurfing also available.
No experience needed.
Minimum age: 14 years.

## ROCKLEY POINT SAILING SCHOOL
**Rockley Sands, Hamworthy, Poole, Dorset. Tel: (0202) 677272.**

Principal: J C Gordon.
In business since 1977.
Member of NFSS.
Approved and recognised by RYA.
Holidays for 2,000 arranged annually.
Dinghy sailing in Poole Harbour for individuals and groups of up to 30 from March to November. 6 and 12 day courses at all levels. Fees from £70. Race training courses using advanced performance dinghies. Also multi watersport courses including sailing, windsurfing and canoeing. Residential courses include meals. Tent, caravan and bed and breakfast accommodation available. Four main classes of dinghies: Wayfarer and Laser for adults, 420' for experienced sailors. Topper for 13-18 year olds and International Optimists for 8-12 year olds.
Beginners welcome.
All ages.
Unaccompanied children: 10 years+.

**┌RPSs┐ ROCKLEY POINT**
(RYA Approved)

**Sailing School**

**19 Rockley Sands, Poole, Dorset**
**(0202) 677272**

**ENJOY LEARNING TO SAIL**
**IN**
**BEAUTIFUL POOLE HARBOUR**
★

Multi-watersport courses
including windsurfing
and canoeing
★
Separate Adult, Teenager
and Children's Fleets
★
**Various types of accommodation**
**can be arranged**

Well supervised residential
accommodation for unaccompanied
children from the age of 10-17

*R.Y.A. Sailing courses for Adults and*
*Teenagers. International Optimist Badge*
*scheme for Children*

**SEASCOPE SAILING SCHOOL**
**162 Lake Road, Hamworthy, Poole, Dorset**
**BH15 4LW. Tel: (0202) 672442.**
Principal: J Chapman.
Recognised by RYA, NFSS.
Sailing and seamanship tuition April-October. 5-day beginners' dinghy sailing courses and daily tuition for all grades of RYA requirements. Accommodation can be arranged. Oilskins can be hired.
Ages: 14-70 years.

**JOHN SHARP SAILING (FOWEY)**
**Brockles Quay, St Veep, Lostwithiel,**
**Cornwall PL22 0NT. Tel: (0208) 872470.**
Proprietor: John Sharp.
In business since 1972.
Recognised by RYA.
Weekly RYA dinghy sailing training in the Fowey Estuary and along the adjacent coast. Courses operate April-October. Prices from £33-£82.50 per week including instruction, use of boat and personal bouyancy. Accommodation not included, camping, self-catering and hotels nearby. Wet weather gear required.
No experience necessary.
Minimum age: 8 years.
Unaccompanied children accepted.
"We like pupils to learn to sail — not to sit in a boat and go for a ride."

**SOLENT SCHOOL OF YACHTING**
**The Quay, Warsash, Southampton, Hants**
**SO3 6FR. Tel: (048 95) 83066/7.**
Directors: David Olley, Juliet Olley.
In business since 1947.
Recognised by RYA, NFSS.
Holidays for 2,000 arranged annually.
Sailing holidays and practical instruction afloat from Novice Competent Crew to Yachtmaster Offshore. Weekends or longer February-November. Accommodation and all meals on board. Chance to sail to the Channel Islands and France. Prices in range £58-£68 per weekend and £140-£175 per 5 day course.
No experience needed.
Instruction in all RYA Shorebased Theory Courses also available.
Minimum age: 16 years.

**WELLINGTON WATERSPORTS**
**Reeds, Three Stiles Road, Farnham, Surrey GU9 7DE. Tel: (0252) 724433 or (0734) 884438.**
Dinghy sailing courses on country park lake for individuals in groups of 5 per instructor. One day starter and five day RYA National Dinghy Sailing Certificate April-October. Prices from £20 per day. Dinghies available for hire by the hour, day or week.
Minimum age: 8 years.

**YHA TRAVEL**
**14 Southampton Street, London WC2E 7HY. Tel: 01-240-5236.**
Dinghy sailing holidays on the River Dart for individuals and groups. 7 days July-August. Price from £150 inclusive. Tuition in Wayfarer sailing dinghies approved by RYA. Lifejackets are supplied and must be worn at all times when sailing.
Sailors must be able to swim 50 metres.
Minimum age: 11 years.
Unaccompanied children accepted.

# Scotland

**ABERNETHY OUTDOOR CENTRE**
**Nethy Bridge, Inverness-shire PH25 3ED. Tel: (047 982) 279.**
Recognised by RYA.
Dinghy sailing courses on Loch Morlich for individuals and groups of up to 16. 1 week June-September. Prices from £99 including accommodation, meals, equipment and instruction. RYA instruction in Wayfarer and Mirror dinghies by experienced staff. "The staff are committed Christians and enjoy sharing their faith with visitors to the Centre".
Ability to swim 50 metres required.
All ages.
Unaccompanied children: 12 years +.

**ARDFERN SEA SCHOOL**
**The Galley of Lorne Inn, Ardfern by Lochgilphead, Argyll PA31 8QN. Tel: (085 25) 664.**
Dinghy sailing instruction for beginners and advanced sailors in the Sound of Jura and Mull off the west coast of Scotland. Local accommodation at Inn, holiday cottage or campsite. Skippered yacht charter also available.

**CARNOCH OUTDOOR CENTRE**
**Carnoch House, Glencoe, Argyll PA39 4HS. Tel: (08552) 350/374.**
Dinghy sailing courses at National Dinghy Sailing, Seamanship 1 and Seamanship 2 levels beginning on the sea loch Leven and progressing through the Strait of Ballachulish to the open sea, for individuals and groups of up to 36. 7 days from May to October. Accommodation and full board at the Centre. Price from £103 per week. Opportunities to obtain RYA certificates. Cruising courses also available.
Handicapped people catered for.
No experience needed.
Minimum age: 10 years.

**CROFT NA CABER WATERSPORTS CENTRE**
**Kenmore on Loch Tay, Perthshire PH15 2HW. Tel: (08873) 236.**
Dinghy sailing courses from May to September. All equipment and instruction included in price of around £80 for five day Wayfarer course following RYA syllabus. Around £40 for two day Topper course, intended mainly for younger people. Accommodation not included in price, but various alternatives available locally.
Minimum age: 8 years.
Unaccompanied children welcome.

**CUILLINS YACHT CHARTERS**
**The Flat-a-Float, Ardlui, Arrochar, Dunbartonshire. Tel: (03014) 244.**
Proprietor: E Wallace.
In business since 1969.
Holidays for 1,000 arranged annually.
Sailing, cruising and houseboat holidays on Loch Lomond for individuals and groups of up to 10. 1-2 weeks Easter-October. Prices begin at £35 per week. Hotel, caravan and camping accommodation available.
All ages.

**EAST NEUK CHARTERS**
**Dunstaffnage Yacht Haven, near Oban, Scotland.**
Proprietor: W Sturrock.
In business since 1978.
Recognised by RYA.
Instructional offshore cruising holidays around the West Coast of Scotland and the Hebridean Islands for individuals and groups of up to 12 in two boats. Courses for RYA Day Skipper/Watch Leader and Coastal Skipper/Yachtmaster certificates. 5, 6 or 10 days from April to September. Accommodation and meals aboard yacht. Oilskins and wellington boots required.
No experience needed.
Minimum age: 15 years.

**LOCH INSH WATERSPORTS AND SKIING CENTRE**
**Insh Hall, Kincraig, by Kingussie, Inverness-shire, PH21 1NU. Tel: (054 04) 272.**
Dinghy sailing and canoeing and windsurfing holidays for individuals and groups of up to 30. 1-3 weeks May-September. Price £140-£154 per week including accommodation, all meals and 5-day course. Beginners and advanced courses available. Good waterproof anorak and trousers and several changes of clothing required. Anorak and trousers available for hire including wetsuits. Students are expected to keep their own room tidy, prepare packed lunch and help in turn to serve and clear meals in the dining room. Self-catering terms on request.
No experience needed.
Minimum age: 12 years.
Unaccompanied children accepted.

**OCEAN YOUTH CLUB**
**South Street, Gosport, Hampshire PO12 1EP. Tel: (0705) 528421/2.**
Offshore sailing adventure holidays for individuals and groups of up to 12. Weekends, weeks or longer March-October. Prices from £126 for 6 days including meals. Expeditions to the Outer Hebrides and St. Kilda. Vessel based at Inverkip (Clyde) and Oban.
No experience needed.
Ages: 12-24 years. Adult cruises also available.

**SCOTTISH YOUTH HOSTELS ASSOCIATION**
**7 Glebe Crescent, Stirling FK8 2JA. Tel: (0786) 72821.**
Choice of 6 sailing courses at Tighnabruaich youth hostel to suit all standards. Price from £67 for 6-day course. Minimum age: 12 years.

**TIGHNABRUAICH SAILING SCHOOL**
**Tighnabruaich, Argyll, PA21 2BD. Tel: (0700) 811396.**
Partners: D R Stephens, K M Stephens.
In business since 1965.
Approved by RYA.
Holidays for 500 arranged annually.
Sailing tuition holidays with RYA Basic, Intermediate, Advanced, racing and cruising courses. Individuals and groups of up to 20. 1 or more weeks May-September. Buoyancy aids are provided, sailing clothing can be hired or bought.
No experience needed.
Minimum age: 8 years.
Unaccompanied children: 12 years +.

**TIGHNABRUAICH SAILING SCHOOL**

Tighnabruaich is long established as one of Britain's leading Sailing Schools. Six-day Basic, Intermediate, Advanced, Racing and Junior courses from £60 per week. Also boardsailing, and combined boardsailing and dinghy sailing, and cruising courses, living on board. There is a wide range of accommodation including a Youth Hostel, self catering flats and seven Hotels.

Complete details of all courses in our brochure.

*To arrange a wonderful holiday, write to:*

**The Secretary,**
**Tighnabruaich Sailing School,**
**Tighnabruaich, Argyll.**
Tel: Tighnabruaich 811396
(STD 0700 811396)

# Wales

## OCEAN YOUTH CLUB
**South Street, Gosport, Hampshire PO12 1EP. Tel: (0705) 528421/2.**
Adventure cruising from Holyhead. 2, 7 or more days March-November. Inclusive prices in range £42-£147.
No experience needed.
Ages: 12-24 years. Adult cruises also available.

## PGL YOUNG ADVENTURE LTD.
**110 Station Street, Ross-on-Wye, Herefordshire HR9 7AH. Tel: (0989) 64211.**
Sailing courses in the Brecon Beacons. June-September. Elementary, intermediate and advanced tuition. All specialist equipment and clothing provided.
Ages: 12-18 years.

## YHA TRAVEL
**14 Southampton Street, London WC2E 7HY. Tel: 01-240 5236.**
Dinghy sailing on Lake Bala for individuals, families and groups. 7 days June-September. Price from £120 inclusive. Tuition in Wayfarer sailing dinghies approved by RYA. Life jackets are supplied and must be worn at all times when sailing. Sailors must be able to swim 50 metres.
Minimum age: 11 years.
Unaccompanied children accepted.

# Europe

## ACCUEIL DES JEUNES EN FRANCE
**12 rue des Barres, 75004 Paris. Tel: (+33) 1-278 04 82.**
Sailing and windsurfing courses on the Atlantic and Mediterranean at Easter, Whitsun and June-September. Six days from 1,050-1,700F (£85-£150) including equipment, instruction and hostel accommodation.
Minimum age: 15 years.
Unaccompanied young people welcome.

## CENTRO VELICO CAPRERA
**Corso Italia 10, 20122 Milan, Italy. Tel: (+39) 2-808428.**
In business since 1964.
Member of International Sailing Schools Association.
Holidays for 1,600 arranged annually.
Sailing courses for individuals, whether beginners or more experienced sailors, on the Island of Caprera near Sardinia April-November. Hostel accommodation with meals. "Caprera is located in an area very rich of wind: beautiful, colourful and wild at the same time. Courses take place in complete isolation from the world of TV, radio, newspapers and automobiles."
No experience needed.
Minimum age: 17 years.

## FALCON SAILING
**4 Dell Court, Salcombe, Devon TQ8 8BW. Tel: (054 884) 3451.**
Directors: J C K & G M Baerselman.
In business since 1978.
Holidays for 3,500 arranged annually.
Dinghy sailing, board sailing, sailing cruiser instruction and dinghy hire in the Ionian Sea west of the Greek mainland and near Bodrum in Turkey. 2 weeks April to mid-October. RYA instruction available for beginners and experts. Accommodation in villas at two Greek centres (on Paxos and Levkas); meals are taken at local tavernas. Flotilla sailing living aboard small sailing cruisers and independent cruising. Racing, long sailing expeditions and crazy regattas are arranged. Price from £220-£450 for 2 weeks including flight.
No experience needed.
Bookings through: Falcon Sailing, 190(V) Campden Hill Road, London W8 7TH. Tel: 01-727 0232.

## LENZERHEIDE — VALBELLA
**Tourist Office, 7078 Lenzerheide, Switzerland. Tel: (+41) 81-34 15 89 or 34 19 59.**
Sailing instruction on Heidsee in the Graübunden Alps. SFr 40 (about £12) for a single lesson, SFr 220 for a complete course. Equipment hire also available.

**MINORCA SAILING HOLIDAYS LTD.**
**287 Green Lanes, The Triangle, London N13 4XT. Tel: 01-886 7193.**
Directors: H Hooper, C Hamblin.
In business since 1973 (since 1978 under present name).
Holidays for 1,000 arranged annually.
Dinghy sailing and windsurfing in Minorca. 45 types of sailboard and 10 types of dinghy available. Self-catering apartments and hotel accommodation with breakfast. Prices from £205-£495.
All ages.

**DISTRICT OF NEUCHATEL TOURIST OFFICE**
**9 rue du Trésor (Place des Halles), Neuchâtel 2001, Switzerland. Tel: (+41) 38-251789.**
Sailing holidays on Lake Neuchâtel, Switzerland. Hotel accommodation with half board. Prices from £65 per weekend including 8 hours of lessons; £117 to £140 for 4-6 days with 10 hours of lessons.

**NSTS — STUDENT & YOUTH TRAVEL MALTA**
**220 St Paul Street, Valletta, Malta. Tel: (+356) 624 983.**
Sailing holidays for individuals and groups of 10-30. One week June-September. Accommodation in lower category hotels with half-board. 8 hours of accompanied sailing in "Marauder" class boats for beginners and experienced sailors. Visits to Comino and Valletta. Price about £90. Opportunities to go windsurfing, scuba diving, etc.
Ages: 14-29 years.

**OCEAN YOUTH CLUB**
**South Street, Gosport, Hampshire PO12 1EP. Tel: (0705) 528421/2.**
Cruising in North European waters for individuals and groups of 12, March-November. Vessels based in Holyhead, Belfast, Glasgow and Southern England. Prices in range £42-£147, including meals, safety equipment and oilskins.
No experience needed.
Ages: 12-24 years. Adult cruises also organised.

**RIVIERA SAILING HOLIDAYS**
**45 Bath Road, Emsworth, Hants PO10 7ER. Tel: (02434) 4376.**
Organiser: M V Coop.
In business since 1968.
Self-sail yachting holidays on the French Atlantic and Mediterranean Coasts and in Greece. Attended craft also available. Apartment accommodation for up to 7 people. Travel by air or road can be arranged through Riviera Sailing Holidays. All ages.

**SEGELSCHULE MONDSEE**
**5310 Mondsee, Austria. Tel: (+43) 6232-2175.**
Director: Dr Brand Stötter.
In business since 1969.
Recognised by Union of Austrian Sailing Schools.
Holidays for 3,000 arranged annually. One week sailing courses on Mondsee, near Salzburg, in July and August. Price around AS1,700 (£90) per week for sailing (including equipment); full board available for an additional AS1,800 per week.
Minimum age: 6 years.
Unaccompanied children accepted.

**THOMAS COOK HOLIDAYS — MARLBORO ADVENTURE TRAVEL**
**Thorpe Wood, PO Box 36, Peterborough, Cambs PE3 8LB. Tel: (0733) 64200.**
Flotilla sailing in the Ionian Sea around Corfu on board Comet 850s, from May to October. Prices from £250 include flights, 14 nights accommodation on board, starter food pack and services of lead boat crew. Some experience required by at least one member of crew.

**YACHT CRUISING ASSOCIATION**
**Old Stone House, Judges Terrace, Ship Street, East Grinstead, West Sussex RH19 1AQ. Tel: (0342) 311366.**

Partners: E B Richardson, M Cox.
In business since 1974.
Recognised by RYA.
Holidays for 6,000 arranged annually.
Flotilla sailing holidays in the Greek islands, the Dalmatian islands of Yugoslavia and the coast of Turkey. Two weeks April-October. Accommodation on board yachts. Skipper of boat must have at least dinghy sailing experience. Day boat sailing in Marmaris fjord, Turkey, staying in villa. Villa/flotilla holidays staying one week in a villa in Parga, Greece and one week sailing the Ionian islands. Also dinghy sailing and board sailing holidays in Marmaris, Turkey, staying in clubhouse. Prices from £205.
All ages.

**WEXAS**
**45 Brompton Road, London SW3 1DE.**
**Tel: 01-589 0500.**
Cruising in small vessel around the Greek islands and Turkish coast. 15 days, May-October. Price around £750 including air fare.
Membership required.

# Americas

**OCEAN VOYAGES INC.**
**1709 Bridgeway, Sausalito, CA 94965, USA. Tel: (+1) 415-332 4681.**
Director: Mary T Crowley.
In business since 1979.
Holidays for over 2,000 arranged annually. Adventure sailing holidays on all types of vessels in the Caribbean, around North and South America and also in the Pacific Basin, the Galapagos Islands, Tahiti, the Cook Islands, Vanuatu, Singapore, Thailand, New Zealand, the Red Sea, Indian Ocean and the Aegean. Individuals and groups of 2-50, 1-10 weeks all year round. Prices from $550 per person per week all inclusive. Long ocean passage trips available from $350 per week. Opportunities to study wildlife such as sea lions, whales and porpoises and to go scuba diving and snorkelling.
Handicapped people catered for.
No experience needed.
All ages.

# Scuba Diving
## and Snorkelling

Since the introduction of a relatively simple, low-cost diving lung by Emile Gagnan and Jacques-Yves Cousteau in 1943, scuba diving has become available to more and more people throughout the world. Previously untouched areas such as the Red Sea and the South Pacific are opening up as excellent sites for diving holidays.

Some holidays require experience which can be gained by attending a course at a British Sub-Aqua Club (BS-AC) school. These offer two levels of training: Elementary Training Certificate and Sport Diving Certificate. The instruction takes place in a swimming pool at first while you learn the principles and how to use the equipment and then progresses to open water diving. It is not necessary to become a member of the BS-AC to obtain these certificates. If you simply wish to sample the sport these standards are sufficient for you to continue diving under the supervision of a qualified diving instructor.

To go further you should join the BS-AC through one of its branches. These offer regular diving programmes, progression to more advanced diving qualifications and all the benefits of an active social group. Membership also gives liability insurance, a monthly magazine (*Diver,* price 90p) and the opportunity to take part in courses and events. The address is 16 Upper Woburn Place, London WC1H 0QW; Tel: 01-387 9302.

The term scuba is an abbreviation of Self-Contained Underwater Breathing Apparatus and involves the wearing of a wet suit, weight belt, breathing regulator and air cylinder. The suit not only keeps the diver warm but acts as a protector against cuts and grazes from sharp coral reefs. Aqualung equipment starts about £250 but can often be hired.

Snorkelling provides a good introduction to underwater swimming especially for those who are too young to be able to cope with the equipment for scuba diving. Only a mask, fins and snorkel are required. Information about snorkelling can be obtained from the National Snorkellers Club (see entry in chapter), which is the young people's section of the BS-AC. Some multi activity centres provide opportunities for sub-aqua activities; these may be found in the first chapter.

# England

## BRITISH SUB-AQUA CLUB
**16 Upper Woburn Place, London WC1H 0QW. Tel: 01-387 9302.**
Manager: D D Robertson.
In business since 1953.
A members' club offering diving instruction through its many branches. BS-AC Schools provide instruction during holiday courses. There are also many BS-AC schools throughout the world which offer diving holidays to the experienced diver.
The Club also provides a diving holidays information service.

## BROMFORD BOATS
**Arwenack Barton, Grove Place, Falmouth, Cornwall TR11 4AU. Tel: (0326) 319124.**
Proprietor: K S Roberts.
In business since 1969.
Recognised by RYA.
Holidays for 500 arranged annually.
Sub aqua holidays around the wrecks and reefs off the Channel Islands and the Isles of Scilly. Individuals and groups of up to 12. 1 week May-October and weekends October-May. Accommodation aboard cruiser. Price from £40 for a weekend and from £165 per week. Sleeping bags and diving gear should be taken.
Experience needed.
Ages: 16-60 years.

## DIVER TRAINING SCHOOL
**The Quayside, Exmouth Harbour, Devon EX8 1ER. Tel: (0395) 266300.**
Partners: D W and G Lea.
In business since 1975.
Recognised by BS-AC; founder member of Professional Association of Scuba Schools.
Beginners to advanced courses in sports diving of one to three weeks to gain BS-AC or PADI qualifications. Prices from £65 (three day introductory course) to £504

(three week BS-AC advanced diver course).
Accommodation in guest house approximately £10 per night extra.
"Learn a fascinating new sport safely, quickly and easily."
Minimum age: 12 years (14 years if unaccompanied).

## ISLES OF SCILLY UNDERWATER CENTRE
**"Warleggan", St. Mary's, Isles of Scilly. Tel: (0720) 22563.**
Subsidiary of Scillonian Diving Services Ltd.
Directors: T J Hiron, C F Hiron, J R Heslin.
In business since 1970.
Holidays for 700 arranged annually.
Diving holidays exploring wrecks from 17th century galleons to 20th century steamers and the underwater canyons off the Scilly Isles, for individuals and groups Easter-October. Price £180 per week for divers, £125 per week for non-divers including accommodation, breakfast and evening meal. Wet suits, equipment and one cylinder needed; full bottles for further dives supplied.
3rd class BS-AC qualification needed.

## SEAWAYS
**38 Lemon St, Truro, Cornwall TR1 2NS. Tel: (0872) 77652.**
Partners: J R and S J Elliss.
In business since 1979.
Recognised by BS-AC.
Diver training throughout the year in Cornwall. Prices for five day course from around £115; meals and accommodation not included.
Short introductory courses and dive boat charter also available.
Minimum age: 14 years.
Unaccompanied young people accepted.

## YHA TRAVEL
**14 Southampton Street, London WC2E 7HY. Tel: 01-240 5236.**

Underwater swimming holidays at Salcombe for individuals and groups. 7 days June-August. Price from £150 inclusive. Qualified members of the BS-AC instruct beginners progressively from their first underwater session to aqua-lung diving to depths of 30 feet.
Participants must be able to swim 200 metres and be medically fit.
Minimum age: 16 years.

# Wales

## DALE FORT FIELD CENTRE
Haverfordwest, Dyfed SA62 3RD. Tel: (064 65) 205.
Warden and Director of Studies: D C Emerson.
Administered by the Field Studies Council. Marine biology courses for divers. 7 days in the summer. Prices from around £125 including tuition, board and accommodation.
Minimum age: 18 years.

# Ireland

## ASSOCIATION FOR ADVENTURE SPORTS
Tiglin Adventure Centre, Ashford, Co. Wicklow, Ireland. Tel: (+353) 404-4169.
Snorkelling instruction at the Tiglin Adventure Centre. Weekly courses June-August. Dormitory accommodation with meals provided. Instruction by experienced and qualified staff. Part of sea sport holidays including surfing, canoeing and windsurfing.
Price about IR£117.
No experience needed.
Minimum age: 16 years.

# Europe

## CLUB MEDITERRANEE
U.K. Office: 106-108 Brompton Road, London SW3 1JJ. Tel: 01-581 1161.
Scuba diving and snorkelling at many resorts in Europe and Worldwide, from Elenthera (Bahamas) to Hurghede (Egypt).

## CYDIVE LTD.
1 Poseidon Avenue, Kato Paphos 419, Cyprus. Tel: (+357) 61-34271.
Recognised by: Cyprus Tourist Organisation, BS-AC.
Scuba diving and snorkelling holidays around Paphos and the west of Cyprus for individuals and groups of up to 25. Open all year. Price from £75 for 5 days including equipment, dives and instruction. Accommodation can be arranged locally. Wet suits are provided.
Diving experience not necessary as instruction will be given but ability to swim essential.
Minimum age: 12 years.

## MALTAQUA
Triton Court, Mosta Road, St Paul's Bay, Malta. Tel: (+356) 571873.
Directors: Agnes and Michael Upton.
In business since 1970.
Recognised by BS-AC, PADI.
A range of diving courses from taster session (half day £M18), through BS-AC Novice Diver (one week, £M80) to Advanced Diver (ten days, £M110), equipment and instruction included. Flights and accommodation packages available from around £170 sterling; course fees extra. Equipment hire also available. Medical examination (£M2) required.
Minimum age: 14 years.
Book through Exchange Travel or Thomas Cook.

## NATIONAL SNORKELLERS CLUB
13 Langham Gardens, Wembley, Middlesex HA0 3RG. Tel: 01-904 7850 or 907 1131.
Director: Lionel F Blandford.
Children's section of the British Sub-Aqua Club.

In business since 1970.
Snorkel diving in Yugoslavia for individual young people, during the Easter school vacation. Hotel accommodation and full board provided. 12-day course leading to a National Snorkellers Club award. Also advanced courses for proficient snorkellers. School and youth groups catered for May-October. Basic snorkelling equipment required. Price about £200 including flight. No snorkelling experience needed. Participants must be reasonable swimmers. Ages: 11-16 years.

**THOMAS COOK HOLIDAYS — MARLBORO ADVENTURE TRAVEL**
**Thorpe Wood, P.O. Box 36, Peterborough, Cambs. PE3 8LB. Tel: (0733) 63200.**
Scuba diving packages in Malta and Cyprus. 1-2 weeks year round. Hotel accommodation and car hire arranged. BS-AC and PADI approved instruction for beginners and advanced divers. Basic price from £300 plus supplements for diving facilities.

---

# Americas

---

**ALOHA DIVE SHOP**
**Koko Marina, Hawaii Kai, Honolulu, HI 96825, USA. Tel: (+1) 808-395-5922/ 8882.**
President: Jacqueline James.
In business since 1973.
Member of PADI.
Scuba and skin diving, snorkelling and charter rentals available throughout the year. Beginners, inexperienced and experienced divers courses, prices from $45 for half morning or afternoon instruction.
No experience needed.
Minimum age: 9 years.
Unaccompanied children: 10 years+

**OCEAN VOYAGES INC.**
**1709 Bridgeway, Sausalito, CA 94965, USA. Tel: (+1) 415-332 4681.**
Special scuba programmes to Cocos Island off the coast of Costa Rica. Individuals and groups of 2-12, one or more weeks all year round. Prices from $525 per person per week all inclusive except travel. Scuba in the Virgin Islands: groups of six, $775 per person.
Handicapped people catered for.
No experience needed.
All ages.

**SEE AND SEA TRAVEL**
**680 Beach Street, San Francisco, CA 94109, USA. Tel: (+1) 415-771-0077. Toll-free (within USA): 1-800-DIVXPRT.**
Director: Carl Roessler.
In business since 1965.
Recognised by IATA.
Holidays for 3,500 arranged annually.
Diving holidays for avid divers and especially underwater photographers in the Cayman Islands, Belize, Guadeloupe, Thailand, Philippines, Galapagos Islands, Australia, New Guinea, Fiji, Micronesia and the Red Sea. Individuals and groups of up to 12. 1 week throughout the year. A chance to see coral reefs, rays, barracuda, turtles, brilliantly coloured sponges and many other forms of marine life found only in these areas. Unlimited diving including night dives well out of the range of hotel based operations. Accommodation is aboard luxury vessels with full meals provided. Prices from $895 not including flight. Personal diving gear must be taken.
Some experience necessary.

**WILDERNESS SOUTHEAST**
**711 Sandtown Road, Savannah, GA 31410, USA. Tel: (+1) 912-897 5108.**
Naturalist-led expeditions to the Florida Keys and the Bahamas. 7 days August-September. Opportunities to go snorkelling and hiking on uninhabited islands and beaches. Price from $600.
No experience needed.
Minimum age: 15 years.

---

# Israel

---

**JABALIYA TREKKING**
**36 Keren Hayesod Street, Jerusalem, Israel. Tel: (+972) 2-699385.**

Red Sea diving tours along the Sinai coast. Scuba diving at the coral reefs and visits to some of the nearby canyons and oases. Night diving possible. Nights spent camping out with dinners eaten around a campfire. 6 day tour costs $425 including transport, guide, equipment and meals. Price for non-diving participants $385.
Divers must be licenced.

**TWICKENHAM TRAVEL**
**33 Notting Hill Gate, London W11 3JQ.**
**Tel: 01-894 5500.**
Diving in the Red Sea for individuals and groups. One or two weeks October-April. Accommodation on board motor yacht and at diving centres. Price from around £400 for one week camping includes flight, tanks, air, vehicle and camping equipment. Non divers and families welcome. Learn to dive and snorkelling courses available. Qualified divers require log books for some courses.

# Africa

**SEE AND SEA TRAVEL**
**680 Beach Street, San Francisco, CA 94109. USA. Tel: (+1) 415-771-0077.**
Diving holidays off the barren coasts of the Sinai desert in the reefs of the Red Sea. Cairo programme with 10 days diving for 2-6 divers aboard 60 foot motor sailer Colonna II. Unlimited diving. Prices from $2,250 not including flights. Personal diving gear must be taken.
Experience needed.

# Asia

**UNDERWATER SAFARIS LTD.**
**25 Barnes Place, Colombo 7, Sri Lanka.**
**Tel: (+94) 1-94012.**
Director: H Ekanayake.
In business since 1968.

Recognised by Ceylon Tourist Board.
Scuba diving and underwater photography trips in Sri Lanka for individuals and groups. Qualified instructors/divers conduct reef and wreck diving expeditions at Hikkaduwa (south-west coast) October-April and Trincomalee (east coast) March-September. Accommodation available. All equipment can be hired. Prices on application.
International Diving Certificate required. Minimum age: 12 years.

# Australasia

**SEE AND SEA TRAVEL**
**680 Beach Street, San Francisco, CA 94109, USA. Tel: (+1) 415-771-0077.**
Diving holidays to the oceanic reefs of the Coral Sea north-east of Australia, to see sharks, huge tuna and sea snakes. 12 days cruising and diving in October and November. Accommodation aboard a luxury dive boat with full meals provided. Prices from $2,950 not including flight.

Diving holidays in the Maldives (Indian Ocean), Fiji, Papua New Guinea and the Philippines. 16-17 days March-October. Accommodation in hotels at beginning and end of holidays and on luxury dive boats for duration of dive trips. Full meals provided. Unlimited diving to see lagoons of tropical marine life plus deep water dives with sightings of barracuda, turtles, manta rays, caverns and prolific fields of coral. Prices from $1,900 not including flights.

Diving holidays in the Islands of Palau in the Pacific. 14 days February/March, May, July, August and October. Accommodation in modern hotel with fast speedboat to dive areas. Price from $2,050 not including flights.
Personal diving gear must be taken.
Some experience needed.

# Skiing

Second only to sunning oneself on the Mediterranean, skiing is the most popular type of holiday. Because so many travel companies organise ski-packages abroad and information about such holidays is so easily obtainable from travel agents or the media, we have tried to include those holidays which are more unusual or adventurous: such as being transported by helicopter to ski down remote mountains and glaciers in the Rockies of Canada and the USA.

Cross-country skiing, sometimes called *langlauf*, does not have the glamour of downhill skiing or slalom skiing; but it offers much pleasure to the adventurous, especially those who wish to see more of the countryside and its wildlife. It is not necessary to travel to Lapland or the Rockies to participate in the sport. There are opportunities in Snowdonia and in Scotland for ski-touring during the winter. Skis with sealskins are often used to prevent slipping backwards when ascending a slope. Ski-trekking can be very strenuous and at an advanced level overlaps with winter mountaineering. Essential clothing for snow skiing is a warm and waterproof suit of jacket and trousers (often these are one-piece saloupettes), strong leather or plastic gloves, a woollen hat, goggles and of course ski boots. Skis, sticks, fastenings and boots can usually be hired.

Helicopter skiing or heli-skiing allows the skier who has had at least three years of skiing experience the chance to descend thousands of feet of deep powder snow on untouched mountainsides. It is not without its risks, since avalanches and sudden blizzards are ever-present hazards. But accidents are rare, partly because of the guides trained to spot crevasses, and because skiers are equipped with an electronic bleeper for signalling in an emergency.

Further information and details of centres and race meetings in Britain can be obtained from the national organiser: The Ski Club of Great Britain, 118 Eaton Square, London SW1W 9AF. Some multi activity holidays include skiing, especially at mountain centres which remain open throughout the winter; see the first chapter for details.

A valuable preliminary to any skiing holiday is to train for a spell on a dry ski slope before starting on the snow. Complete novices are able to get the feel of boots, sticks and skis, and reduce the aching muscles from which many beginners suffer. Intermediate and advanced skiers find that they regain their skills after a year's lapse very quickly, which enables them to pick up immediately on the piste. Many skiing holiday operators offer cut-price sessions at artificial ski slopes to their clients.

Snow skiing is familiar to everyone, but grass skiing is a lesser known derivative sport. It was started in Germany 19 years ago, but was not recognised by the National Ski Federation of Great Britain as a separate discipline until 1979. Grass skis are very short with rollers or a caterpillar track and can be attached to ordinary ski boots. A good grass skier can move up to 50 mph and race around slalom posts.

# England

**BOWLES OUTDOOR PURSUITS CENTRE (4)**
**Eridge Green, Tunbridge Wells, TN3 9LW. Tel: (089 26) 4127.**
Skiing courses for beginners, intermediate and advanced skiers. Instruction given on a 250 ft. long artificial ski slope with ski tow. Also 150 ft. long nursery slope available. Winter courses in the Alps also offered. Courses from £24.
No experience needed.
Ages: 7-65 years.
Unaccompanied children: 10 years+.

**CALSHOT ACTIVITIES CENTRE**
**Calshot Road, Calshot, Southampton SO4 1BR. Tel: (0703) 892077/891380.**
Recognised by: English Ski Council.
Skiing courses for beginners, intermediate and advanced skiers. Instruction given on the largest indoor ski slope in Britain (100ft. long with ski tow). Ski party organisers, pre-ski and preliminary courses are held frequently for training purposes. Weekend and evening courses. Weekends from £48 including accommodation, food, instruction and equipment. Reductions for those under 19 years.
Minimum age: 9 years.

**YMCA HIGH PLAINS LODGE**
**Alston, Cumbria. Tel: (0498) 81886.**
Skiing courses for groups at England's highest ski centre in the North Pennines. Weekend, mid week and week courses January-March. Prices from £18 including accommodation and meals.
Minimum age: 8 years.
Unaccompanied children accepted.

# Scotland

**ABERNETHY OUTDOOR CENTRE**
**Nethy Bridge, Inverness-shire PH25 3ED. Tel: (047 982) 279.**
Skiing courses in the Cairngorm Mountains, for individuals and groups of up to 80. 7 nights January-May. Prices from £115 including accommodation, meals, instruction, equipment, ski pass and transport; £112 for 18 year-olds and under. "The staff are committed Christians and enjoy sharing their faith with visitors to the Centre". No experience needed.
All ages.
Unaccompanied children: 12 years+.

**ARGYLL GUEST HOUSE**
**Tomintoul, Ballindalloch, Banffshire AB3 9EX. Tel: (08074) 223.**

Proprietor: Jenny Herschell.
In business since 1975.
Skiing holidays based at the Lecht Ski Centre with accommodation at Tomintoul, the highest village in the Highlands. One week price £140 including ski hire, lift pass and full accommodation. "Good intermediate and novice skiing — very suitable for learners or families."

## CAIRDSPORT SKI SCHOOLS LTD.
**Aviemore Centre, Inverness-shire PH22 1PL. Tel: (0479) 810310.**
Member of Association of Ski Schools in Great Britain.
Ski schools in Aviemore and Glenshee mid-December to mid-April. Accommodation can be arranged in local hotels, self-catering units or youth hostels. Price for 5 days instruction and unlimited lift pass from £59; skis and boots can be hired. Dry slope skiing available in the summer.
No experience needed.
Minimum age: 7 years.
Unaccompanied children: 16 years +.

## CARNOCH OUTDOOR CENTRE
**Carnoch House, Glencoe, Argyll PA39 4HS. Tel: (08552) 350/374.**
Skiing holidays at White Corries, Glencoe for individuals and groups of up to 36. 2-6 days from late December to early May. Full board and accommodation at the Centre. Price from around £31 for a weekend. All equipment included.
No experience needed.
Minimum age: 6 years.
Unaccompanied children: 10 years+.

## COMPASS SKI CLUB LTD.
**Glenshee Lodge, by Blairgowrie, Perthshire PH10 7QD. Tel: (025 085) 209.**
Skiing in the Grampian Mountains. 5 or more days January-April. Prices from around £80 including Ski Rescue Service insurance, ski hire and instruction. Dormitory accommodation and half board provided. All equipment supplied. The Centre is run as a Christian home and short morning and evening prayers are held daily.
No experience needed.
Minimum age (unaccompanied): 16 years.

## HIGHLAND ADVENTURE NORDIC SKI SCHOOL
**Knockshannoch Lodge, Glenisla, By Alyth, Perthshire PH11 8PE. Tel: (057 582) 207/238.**
Nordic and Alpine skiing instruction at Glenisla and Glenshee for individuals and groups. Weekends, 5 and 7 days December-April. Prices from £36 for weekend to £120 for 7 days including instruction, equipment hire, meals and accommodation. Over 50 km of marked sheltered forest trails.
No experience needed.
Minimum age: 5 years.
Unaccompanied children: 10 years+

## HIGHLAND GUIDES (VW)
**Inverdruie, Aviemore, Inverness-shire PH22 1QH. Tel: (0479) 810729.**
Nordic and downhill skiing at Aviemore and in the Cairngorms. 2-6 days from December to early May. Various types of accommodation can be arranged locally. Price £27-£120 depending on age and duration (less for those under 16) including instruction, equipment, transport and accommodation. Reductions for use of own equipment.
No experience needed.
Age limits: 6-70 years.
Minimum age (unaccompanied): 14 years.

## HILLEND SKI CENTRE
**Biggar Road, Edinburgh EH10 7DU. Tel: 031-445 4433.**
Administered by Lothian Regional Council.
In business since 1968.
130,000 visitors annually.
Instruction available for individuals, groups and special courses for adults and young people on Europe's largest artificial ski complex. Grass skiing facilities May-September. Equipment can be hired.
No experience needed.
All ages.

## LOCH INSH WATERSPORTS & SKIING CENTRE
**Insh Hall, Kincraig, By Kingussie, Inverness-shire. Tel: (054 04) 272.**
Skiing instruction in the Cairngorms at all standards. Weekends and 5 nights December-April. Prices from £39 for

weekend and from £130 for 5 nights, including ski hire, instruction, lift passes, accommodation and meals. An alternative programme of walking, swimming or skating arranged if skiing is not possible. No experience needed. Minimum age: 12 years. Unaccompanied young people welcome.

# Wales

## PLAS Y BRENIN
The National Centre for Mountain Activities, Capel Curig, Betws-y-coed, Gwynedd. Tel: (069 04) 280 or 214.
Ski training in Snowdonia. Weekends November-February and some longer courses. Board and accommodation provided in Centre. Equipment can be hired. Skills are learnt on an artificial slope, but snow skiing is arranged if conditions allow. Coaching with the Centre's video system where appropriate. Graded courses from novice to coach. Multi activity holidays also available.
Minimum age: 16 years.

# Europe

## BERGSTEIGERSCHULE PONTRESINA
7504 Pontresina, Switzerland. Tel: (+41) 82-66444.
Ski touring each spring in the Alps at altitudes of up to 4,000m/13,000ft. One, four and seven day programmes.
Minimum age: 16 years.

## BERGSTEIGERSCHULE ROSENLAUI
3860 Meiringen, Bernese Oberland, Switzerland. Tel: (+41) 36-711653.
Ski touring for beginners and advanced skiers. One week holidays throughout the winter. Hotel accommodation with meals at Meiringen. Instructor-guide with every 8 participants. Equipment may be hired.

Prices from SFr 635 (about £200) plus travel.
No experience needed.
Age limits: 14-70 years.

## FIELD STUDIES COUNCIL
Overseas Expeditions, Flatford Mill Field Centre, East Bergholt, Colchester C07 6UL. Tel: (0206) 298283.
Cross-country skiing, with photography tuition, in the French Alps. Further details from Miss Ros Evans, Flatford Mill Field Centre.

## JUGI TOURS
Wildhainweg 19, PO Box 2332, 3001 Berne, Switzerland. Tel: (+41) 31-23 26 21.
Travel section of Swiss Youth Hostel Association.
In business since 1965.
Ski camps for young people at 12 resorts in Switzerland and Liechtenstein. Accommodation in youth hostels: prices from around SFr420 (about £140) plus travel. Cross country skiing camps at Le

Celebrate the 25th year of

# BERGSTEIGERSCHULE PONTRESINA
(Swiss Mountain School)

*Join us in the Alps for ski touring, mountaineering expeditions with expert guides . . . or travel with us to the great mountains of Africa and the Americas*

**BERGSTEIGERSCHULE PONTRESINA**
CH-7504 Pontresina
Switzerland
**Tel: (010 41) 82-66444**

Bemont and Maloja, around SFr300 including full board.
Membership of a national youth hostel association required.
Age limits: 16-27 for ski camps, 18-35 for cross country.

## KVITAVATN FJELLSTOGE
**3660 Rjukan, Norway. Tel: (+47) 36-91174.**
Directors: R Tuck, R Lorentzen, L Bergsagel.
In business since 1971.
Holidays for 2,400 arranged annually.
Cross-country skiing and ski-orienteering in the mountains of southern Norway from early November to late April. Bunkhouse accommodation and full board provided. 100 km of ski tracks and 600m and 1,400m slalom hill. Equipment can be hired. Maps provided for ski-orienteering courses set in nearby forest. Fishing, canoeing and mountain hiking available in summer.
Book through Kvitåvatn Fjellstoge, or Waymark Holidays, 295 Lillie Road, London SW6 7LL. Tel: 01-385 5015.

## NORSKE TURISTFORENING
**(Norwegian Mountain Touring Association)**
**Boks 1963, Vika N-0125, Oslo 1, Norway. Tel: (+47) 2-41 80 20.**
In business since 1870.
Holidays for 4,000 arranged annually.
Cross-country skiing holidays in the mountains of Norway for individuals and groups of 10-20 from end of February to mid-April. Dormitory accommodation in huts and all meals provided.
Sleeping bag must be taken.
Some experience needed.
All ages.

## PGL YOUNG ADVENTURE LTD.
**128 Station Street, Ross-on-Wye, Herefordshire HR9 7AH. Tel: (0989) 64211.**
Skiing holidays for teenagers at Laterns in Austria, Soldeu in Andorra, Cerler in Spain, and family holidays at Werfenweng, Austria. December-March. All instruction, equipment, accommodation meals provided.

No experience needed.
Ages: 11-18 years and families.

## PSOM/MGS INC.
**PO Box 694, Bishop, CA 93514, USA. Tel: (+1) 619-873 5037.**
Alpine ski touring/mountaineering in Austria, Switzerland and Italy. Price $1,600-$2,000 (plus travel to Alps) depending on numbers taking part.
Some experience necessary.
Minimum age 16 years.

## RAMBLERS HOLIDAYS
**Longcroft House, Fretherne Road, Welwyn Garden City, Herts AL8 6PQ. Tel: (0707) 331133.**
Cross-country skiing in Austria and Switzerland. 7-10 nights December-March. Hotel meals and accommodation. Many grades of maintained runs for beginners and advanced skiers. Chairlifts are often available to give access to higher level tracks. Other activities such as ice skating, curling and tobogganing may also be arranged.
Experience needed for some tours.

## RIEDERALP VERKEHRSBURO
**CH-3981 Riederalp, Switzerland. Tel: (+41) 28 27 1365.**
Ski weeks in the Aletsch Glacier area of Switzerland, in December, January and part of March. Instruction given at local ski school and winter sports season ticket included in the price which is from S Fr.489-S Fr.720 for 7 days half board. For more experienced skiers there are opportunities to learn ski-acrobatics.

## SSR-REISEN
**Bäckerstrasse 52, CH-8026 Zurich, Switzerland. Tel: (+41) 1-242 3000.**
Intensive cross-country ski courses in St. Moritz. One week January-March. Half board and hotel accommodation provided. Instruction available for beginners and experts along 50 km of unkept ski trails. Price of S.Fr.480 (about £150) including 6 days of 4-hour lessons, films and ski waxing instruction. Good preparation for cross-country skiers wishing to take part in the Engadine Ski Marathon in March.

No experience needed.
Ages: 16-35 years.

**SUOMEN LATU**
**Finnish Ski Track Association**
**Fabianinkatu 7, 00130 Helsinki, Finland.**
**Tel: (+358) 0-170101.**
In business since 1938.
Holidays for 3,000 arranged each year.
Guided ski treks and ski weeks in Lapland and central Eastern Finland, February-April. Ski treks are for experienced skiers; ski weeks cater for beginners as well. Prices in range 2,061-2907FIM (about £250-£360) plus air fare to Helsinki.
Minimum age for ski treks: 15 years.
Book through Finnair offices.

**THOMAS COOK HOLIDAYS —**
**MARLBORO ADVENTURE TRAVEL**
**Thorpe Wood, PO Box 36, Peterborough, Cambs PE3 8LB. Tel: (0733) 64200.**
Summer skiing based at the Hintertux glacier in the Austrian Alps. One or two weeks in July and August. Prices from £310 include scheduled flight, half board accommodation, lift pass and instruction; equipment not included but may be hired locally. Participants must be intermediate skiers.

**WAYMARK HOLIDAYS**
**295 Lillie Road, London SW6 7LL. Tel: 01-385 5015.**
Cross-country skiing in Austria, France, Germany, Italy, Norway and Switzerland. 8-12 days throughout the winter. Accommodation varies with terrain and type of ski touring.
Experience required on more challenging routes.
Minimum age (unaccompanied): 16 years.

# Americas

**CMH HELI-SKIING**
**P.O. Box 1660, Banff, Alberta, Canada T0L 0C0. Tel: (+1) 403-762-4531.**
Heli-skiing in the Canadian Rockies for individuals throughout the winter. 5 or 7 day itineraries to suit participants' levels of expertise. Novice heli-skiers can join an introductory week at an easy pace with instruction. Accommodation in comfortable lodges and all meals provided. Guides are internationally qualified. Prices from C$1,460.
Participants must have skied regularly for at least 3 years.
U.K. agent: David & Tessa Brooksbank, Powder Skiing in North America, 61 Doneraile Street, London SW6 6EW. Tel: 01-736 8191.

**LIBERTY BELL ALPINE TOURS**
**Star Route, Mazama, WA 98833, USA.**
**Tel: (+1) 509-996 2250.**
Heli-skiing and ski touring in the North Cascades National Park, Washington State, January-May. All instruction (one guide for five participants) and equipment included in heli-skiing prices from around $200 per day for 13,000ft of vertical lift; higher skiing at $12 per thousand feet. One day 'Supertour' at lower heights, $55. Accommodation available at Mazama Country Inn. All-inclusive 'Ultimate Powder Week' (January), about $1,600. Cross-country and ski mountaineering courses also available.

**NORTHERN LIGHTS ALPINE RECREATION**
**Box 399, Invermere, British Columbia V0A 1K0, Canada. Tel: (+1) 604-342 6042.**
Glacier skiing in the Rocky Mountains of British Columbia for groups of 2-6. One week May-June. Base camp set up after 6 mile hike. Skiing on open runs some in untouched terrain, dropping 2,000 vertical feet over distances up to 2 miles. Afternoon instruction in knots, prussiking, self arrest, crevasse rescue, etc. Alpine skis with bindings that allow heel lift are needed, as well as most camping and mountaineering equipment. Some equipment such as camp stoves and tents may be hired. Prices from $400 per week exclusive of transportation. Participants must be very fit and at least intermediate skiers, with camping and hiking experience.

Mountain ski touring in the Rockies. One week December-April. Accommodation in

a small log cabin called the Hermitage, set high in the mountains near the tree-line.
Prices from $385 per week.
Skiing experience needed.

Ski touring based in Invermere, BC. 2, 5 or 7 days throughout the winter. Hotel accommodation with full board. Expert guides. Prices from C$475 per week.
Minimum age: 14 years.

### ROCKY MOUNTAIN SKI TOURS
**165 E Elkhorn Ave, Box 2868, Estes Park, CO 80517, USA. Tel: (+1) 303-586-2065.**
Proprietor: W C Bill Evans.
In business since 1970.
Recognised by: Professional Ski Instructors of America.
Holidays for 4,000 arranged annually.

Cross country skiing holidays, courses and equipment rental in the Rocky Mountains National Park for groups of up to 20.
No experience needed.
Minimum age: 7 years.

### WOLF RIVER LODGE, INC.
**White Lake, Wisconsin 54491, USA. Tel: (+1) 715 882 2182.**
Ski touring holidays in Wisconsin for individuals and groups of 10-12. Weekends and five days December-March. Accommodation and full board provided at the lodge. Price from $125 for weekend and $250 for 5 days all inclusive. All equipment provided. Good physical fitness required.
No experience needed.
Ages: 12-65 years.

*Heli-skiing*                                   *Canadian Mountain Holidays Ltd*

# Wildlife

One of the fortunate consequences of the increasingly urban lifestyle of modern man is his new awareness of the threats to the environment. Organisations such as the World Wildlife Fund have encouraged the designation of many areas of the world as particularly worthy of preservation. Flora and fauna are protected not only for their varied beauty and interest but also to maintain the ecological balance.

There are now seven National Parks in England — Peak District, Lake District, North York Moors, Yorkshire Dales, Northumberland, Dartmoor and Exmoor; and three in Wales — Brecon Beacons, Pembrokeshire Coast and Snowdonia (see map in Hiking chapter). There are also several Nature Reserves and extensive Forestry Commission areas; and wildlife lovers will also find a great deal to interest them in their local hedgerows and fields.

Details of Britain's National Parks are available from the Countryside Commission, John Dower House, Crescent Place, Cheltenham, Gloucestershire GL50 3RA; tel (0242) 521381. For information on National Trust properties, write to the Trust at 42 Queen Anne's Gate, London SW1; tel 01-222 9251. The Young Ornithologists' Club — part of the Royal Society for the Protection of Birds — organises residential birdwatching courses for those aged 9 to 16. Membership costs £9 from the Club at The Lodge, Sandy, Bedfordshire SG19 2DL; tel (0767) 80551.

The first section of this chapter deals with general and miscellaneous wildlife holidays which range from identifying fungi in Sussex to tracking gorillas in Zaire. There are separate sections for birdwatching and botanical holidays and finally one for safaris.

# General

**FIELD STUDIES COUNCIL**
**Information Office (AHF), Preston Montford, Montford Bridge, Shrewsbury SY4 1HW. Tel: (0743) 850674.**
Director: A D Thomas, BA, CertEd, Acad DipEd.
Birdwatching, botany, photography and plant and animal ecology studies at 9 residential centres in England and Wales. The localities of the centres have been chosen for the diversity and richness of their surroundings. There are short courses at every level, from introductory to specialised, in a wide range of field study topics, as well as painting, drawing and photographing country subjects. The resident teaching staff are all fully qualified naturalists and there are visiting tutors for some specialised courses. The fee is approximately £125 per week, £50 per weekend inclusive of accommodation, meals and tuition, with reductions for children (on courses available to them). The nine centres (see index for names) are entered individually below. Details of these holidays may be obtained from the Information Office at the address above, or from the Warden of any of the Centres.
Handicapped people catered for.
Minimum age: 16 years, except on courses especially organised for families.

## England

**BODMIN MOOR NATURE OBSERVATORY**
**Ninestones Farm, Liskeard, Cornwall PL14 6SD. Tel: (0549) 20455.**
Partners: John and Pamela Miller.
In business since 1983.
Conducted field trips throughout the year to interesting habitats to look for birds, plants, insects etc. or explore on your own. Help given to beginners. Accommodation provided: prices from £40 (bed and breakfast, October-March), to £96 (full

board, April-September); supplement for single rooms. Petrol costs and washing up are shared. Binoculars and walking gear required.
Minimum age (unaccompanied): 16 years.
"The peace and quiet of the Moor is a revelation and tonic to most people."

**BRADWELL FIELD STUDIES & SAILING CENTRE**
**Bradwell Waterside, near Southminster, Essex CM0 7QY. Tel: (0621) 76256.**
Field studies courses for individuals and groups of up to 40 throughout the winter. Full board and accommodation provided. Instruction by qualified biologist and geographer in biology, geography, environmental studies, etc. The Centre is equipped with laboratory and observation room, two trawling boats and equipment. Note books and Wellington boots must be brought. Price from £5 per day.

Field Studies Council

## Courses for All

A course at one of our nine Centres (listed in the Index) provides a really enjoyable short holiday. All are in lovely countryside – in Devon, Suffolk, Surrey, Somerset, Shropshire, Yorkshire, Dyfed and Gwynedd where people of all ages and abilities are welcome. Learning more about Birds, Wild Flowers, Local History, Photography, Landscape Painting (and much more) makes a short break really worthwhile. The residential fee is around £125 a week. Find out more by writing, with a first-class stamp, to:

**The Information Office (AHF)**
**Field Studies Council**
**Montford Bridge**
**Shrewsbury SY4 1HW**

Minimum age: 13 years.
Bookings through: The Warden, Bradwell Centre.

## CASTLE HEAD FIELD CENTRE
**Grange-over-Sands, Cumbria LA11 6QT. Tel: (04484) 4300.**
General wildlife observation in South Lakeland and/or Scotland for young naturalists. One week during the Easter holidays and bank holidays. Heated accommodation and meals in field centre which is equipped with a laboratory and includes a nature reserve and a small working farm. Wide range of habitats will be visited including the seashore to see creatures in rock pools and sea cliffs and high fells to see Golden Eagle, Peregrine and Buzzards and the limestone hills to see spring flowers. Price from £115 including all tuition, course transport and the use of specialist maps and equipment.
No experience needed, but course members should have a genuine interest in the natural world.
Minimum age: 13 years.

## CHURCHTOWN FARM FIELD CENTRE
**Lanlivery, Bodmin, Cornwall PL30 5BT. Tel: (0208) 872148.**
Field study holidays in Cornwall for the disabled, regardless of degree or type of disability. Prices for one week range from £72 to £130; reductions for accompanying helpers.
All ages.

## DORSET COAST STUDY CENTRE
**Sunnydown, Gallows Gore, Worth Matravers, Dorset BH19 3JP. Tel: (092 943) 394.**
Proprietors: Buck and Julie Buckhurst.
In business since 1978.
Holidays for 350-400 arranged annually.
Wildlife walking holidays mainly for individuals. 4-8 days throughout the year. Prices: 4 days £55 and 8 days £115 including accommodation and all meals. Country house, church and pub walks also arranged.
Minimum age: 16 years.

## THE DORSET NATURALIST
**19 Cromwell Road, Dorchester, Dorset. Tel: (0305) 67994.**
Natural history and birdwatching holidays around Dorset. From two days to one week, April-October. Prices from £45 (weekend) include full board and minibus transport. Special courses such as 'Hardy Dorset' also available.
"A superb variety of wildlife in some of England's most attractive scenery."
Minimum age: 14 years.

## THE EARNLEY CONCOURSE
**Earnley, Chichester, Sussex PO20 7JL. Tel: (0243) 670392 or 670326.**
Administered by: The Earnley Trust Ltd.
In business since 1952 (Earnley Concourse since 1975).
Recognised by ETB.
Holidays for 4,000 arranged annually.
Wildlife courses for individuals and groups with tuition and full board accommodation. Instruction given in birdwatching, wildflower studies and wildlife photography.
Minimum age: 16 years.

## FLATFORD MILL FIELD CENTRE
**East Bergholt, Colchester, Essex CO7 6UL. Tel: (0206) 298283.**
Wildlife study courses on the banks of the River Stour. 7 days throughout the year. Sample courses include "Spring in Suffolk" and "Small Mammals". Price around £125 per week, £50 per weekend including tuition, accommodation and meals.
No experience needed.
Minimum age: 16 years.

## JUNIPER HALL FIELD CENTRE
**Dorking, Surrey RH5 6DA. Tel: (0306) 883849.**
Administered by the Field Studies Council.
Warden and Director of Studies: J E Bebbington BSc, ARPS.
Nature conservation and natural history study courses on the North Downs around Box Hill. 7 days, 5 days and weekends February-November. For those interested in butterflies an opportunity to see a wide variety including the Chalkhill and Adonis Blues and the Silver-spotted Skipper. Price from around £125 per week, £50 per

weekend including tuition, accommodation and meals.
No experience needed.
Minimum age: 16 years except on family courses.

## THE LEONARD WILLS FIELD CENTRE
**Nettlecombe Court, Williton, Taunton, Somerset TA4 4HT. Tel: (0984) 40320.**
Administered by the Field Studies Council.
Warden and Director of Studies: J H Crothers MA, TD, CertEd.
Mammals and aquatic animals study courses centred on the edge of Exmoor, with the opportunity to explore nearby rocky sea shores as well as open moorland and sheltered combes in the National Park. Some evenings will be spent watching badger, fox, deer and rabbits. Weeks and weekends, February-October. Price from £125 per week, £50 per weekend including tuition, accommodation and meals. Waterproof clothing needed. Wellington boots can be hired.
No experience needed.
Minimum age: 16 years.

## MALHAM TARN FIELD CENTRE
**Settle, North Yorkshire BD24 9PU. Tel: (072 93) 331.**
Administered by the Field Studies Council.
Warden and Director of Studies: K Iball, BSc, CertEd.
Courses in natural history, landscape painting, landform and scenery at all levels of knowledge and experience, in the heart of the Yorkshire Dales. Weeks and weekends, March-October. Price from around £125 per week, £50 per weekend including tuition, meals and accommodation.
Families welcome.

## MEDINA VALLEY CENTRE
**Dodnor Lane, Newport, Isle of Wight PO30 5TE. Tel: (0983) 522195.**
Ecology and geography courses and expeditions on the Isle of Wight for individuals and groups of up to 60. Weekend, one week and 5 day courses throughout the year. Meals and accommodation in the Centre. Studies are conducted in the fauna of rocky and sandy shores, ecology and genetics, structure and scenery of the Isle of Wight and conservation of estuaries. Boat trips will be arranged to collect plankton and fish. The Centre organises a programme which is designed to provoke thought about the Christian faith. Prices from £75 for 5 days.
Unaccompanied children: 14 years +.

## PRESTON MONTFORD FIELD CENTRE
**Montford Bridge, Shrewsbury SY4 1DX. Tel: (0743) 850380.**
Administered by the Field Studies Council.
Warden and Director of Studies: J A Bayley BSc, DipEd.
Wildlife courses near the River Severn in the north Shropshire lowland. Farmland and coverts, meres, mosses and canals contrast with the neighbouring wild and varied hills of the Welsh border. 2, 5 or 7 days March-October. Price from £125 per week, £50 per weekend including tuition, meals and accommodation.
No experience needed for most courses.
Minimum age: 16 years, except on family courses.

## SLAPTON LEY FIELD CENTRE
**Slapton, Kingsbridge, Devon TQ7 2QP. Tel: (0548) 580466.**
Administered by the Field Studies Council.
Warden and Director of Studies: Keith Chell, BSc.
Wildlife studies in south Devon from March to October. For example there will be courses on mammals and their habitats, butterflies and moths and others which generally explore Dartmoor. Price from around £125 per week, £50 per weekend including tuition, board and lodging.
No experience needed on most courses.
All ages.
Unaccompanied children: 16 years +.

# Scotland

## AIGAS FIELD CENTRES LTD.
**Beauly, Inverness-shire IV4 7AD. Tel: (0463) 782443.**

132

Run by The Aigas Trust, a registered conservation charity.
In business since 1970.
Holiday courses for 700 arranged each year.
Wildlife courses in the Highlands for individuals and groups of up to 26. One or more weeks April-October. Prices from around £200 per week including accommodation and meals. 'Economy weeks' (in self catering accommodation) for about £160. Reductions for school parties. Stout and well worn boots, anorak, haversack and thermos flask needed. Field glasses can be hired. Group rates available.
Minimum age: 10 years.
Unaccompanied children: 12 years+.

**BRIAN BURNETT**
**14 Allington Place, Chester CH4 7DX. Tel: (0244) 6755295.**
In business since 1977.
Offshore, coastal or canal sailing cruises with special emphasis on wildlife watching and photography, painting and sketching, mainly off the north and west coasts of Scotland but also in Europe and England and in the Mediterranean in the winter. Individuals and groups of up to 5 all year round. Prices from £100 per week with discounts for groups, children and out of season periods. Accommodation is on board ship and all meals are vegetarian.
No experience needed.
All ages.

**COUL HOUSE HOTEL**
**Contin, by Strathpeffer, Ross-shire IV14 9EY. Tel: (0997) 21487.**
Proprietor: Martyn Hill.
In business since 1977.
Guided rambling in the Highlands geared to birdwatching and other interests. Holidays are based on the hotel and daily trips are made by minibus to places of interest within 75 miles. One week April-October from £200 including full board, excursions and guide.
"Flora and fauna which you are unlikely otherwise to discover."
Minimum age: 13 years.

**ISLE OF COLONSAY HOTEL AND CHALETS**
**Isle of Colonsay, Argyll PA61 7YP. Tel: (09512) 316.**
Partners: Kevin & Christa Byrne.
In business since 1977.
Holidays for 7,000 guests annually.
Wildlife holidays on a remote island off the west coast. Hotel or chalet accommodation available throughout the year. The island is home to wild goat, otters, 150 types of British bird and 500 species of flora. Other activities available include sailing, cycling and golf.
Book through Isle of Colonsay Hotel or ABTA agents.

**ORKNEY FIELD CENTRE**
**Aigas Field Centres Ltd, Beauly, Inverness-shire IV4 7AD. Tel: (0463) 782443.**
Birdwatching and wild flower study holidays around the Orkneys, May-September. Prices (not including travel) around £180 per week, including full board, instruction and evening talks and films. Special seal week in September/October for around £125.
Minimum age: 10 years; 12 years if unaccompanied.

**ST MAGNUS BAY HOTEL**
**Hillswick, Shetland ZE2 9RW. Tel: (080623) 372.**
Proprietor: Mrs L A Calland.
In business since 1971.
Natural history holidays to Shetland, studying the archaeology, botany, marine biology and ornithology of the islands.
"Sightings of rare birds such as Snowy Owl or Albatross."

**UIST WILDLIFE HOLIDAYS**
**Old School, Lochcarnan, Isle of South Uist, Outer Hebrides PA81 5PD. Tel: (08704) 278.**
Proprietor: Jane Twelves.
In business since 1980.
Holidays for 60 arranged each year. One week holidays, May-August, walking and observing birds, plants, animals and scenery on Uist and St Kilda. Uist holidays include full board at Grogarry Lodge, boat trips, minibus transport, evening talks and fishing

in price of £265. St Kilda holidays require a tent and sleeping bag (not provided); price of £250 includes boat fare, food and camping fees.
Minimum age: 14 years.

# Wales

**DALE FORT FIELD CENTRE**
Haverfordwest, Dyfed SA62 3RD. Tel: (064 65) 205.
Administered by the Field Studies Council.
Warden and Director of Studies: D C Emerson.
Small mammals and marine biology courses on the Pembrokeshire coast throughout the year. Exploring the wildlife which inhabits sandy and rocky shores. Price from around £125 per week, £50 per weekend including tuition, meals and accommodation.
No experience needed on most courses.
Minimum age: 16 years.

**THE DRAPERS' FIELD CENTRE**
Rhyd-y-creuau, Betws-y-coed, Gwynedd LL24 0HB. Tel: (06902) 494.
Administered by the Field Studies Council.
Warden and Director of Studies: A J Schärer BA.
A wide variety of wildlife courses during spring, summer and autumn in Snowdonia. "Mountain Walking" weeks provide the opportunity to find out more about the mountains while learning about the wildlife of the National Park. Price around £125 per week, £50 per weekend including tuition, meals and accommodation.
Beginners welcome.
Minimum age: 16 years, except on family courses.

**ORIELTON FIELD CENTRE**
Pembroke, Dyfed SA71 5EZ. Tel: (064 681) 225.
Administered by the Field Studies Council.
Warden and Director of Studies: R J Crump BA, PhD.
Wildlife courses on many topics, for example "Exploring Rocky Shores". A relaxed introduction to the wealth of

animals and plants found between tidemarks. March-October. Price from around £125 per week, £50 per weekend including tuition, meals and accommodation.
No experience needed for most courses.
Minimum age: 16 years.

# Europe

**LENZERHEIDE — VALBELLA**
Tourist Office, 7078 Lenzerheide, Switzerland. Tel: (+41) 81-34 15 89 or 34 19 59.
Guided flora and fauna tours in the Graübunden Alps. No charge except for local travelling expenses.

**RAMBLERS HOLIDAYS**
Longcroft House, Fretherne Road, Welwyn Garden City, Herts. AL8 6PQ. Tel: (0707) 331133.
Walking holidays near Cape Trafalgar, Spain, for those interested in flowers and bird life. 2 weeks April-May and September-October. Hotel accommodation provided. Walking over the sierras, through the pine forests and along the rugged cliffs of South West Spain. Excursions are also made to the salt pans at Chiclana and Vejer de la Frontera. Jerez may also be visited and an excursion by hydrofoil to Tangier on the north coast of Africa can be arranged. Maximum of 5 hours walking per day.

# Arctic

**CAMP DENALI**
PO Box 67, Denali Park, Alaska 99755, USA. Tel: (+1) 907-683 2290 (summer), (+1) 907-683 2302 (winter).
Proprietors: Wally and Jerryne Cole.
In business since 1949.
Holidays for 600-700 arranged annually.
Wilderness holidays which focus on plant, bird and animal life of the tundra world.
Four or more days June-September.
Accommodation in log cabins with centrally

served meals. Chances to see caribou, grizzly bear, moose, wolf, beaver and lynx. Price $650 for 4 nights and $800 for 5 nights. Transportation, guides and equipment are available for excursions. All ages.

## ERSKINE EXPEDITIONS
**14 Inverleith Place, Edinburgh EH3 5PZ. Tel: 031-552 2673.**
Wildlife holidays cruising around fjords in Spitsbergen, 80°N, in converted fishing vessel. Vessel lands each day for walks with opportunities to see rare Arctic wildlife such as walrus, Sabine's Gull and the "Spider Plant". 2 weeks in July, flying to Spitsbergen and back. Price around £1,200 all inclusive from London. Also wildlife treks to Greenland and the Canadian Arctic. No experience needed.
Minimum age: 16 years.

# Americas

## CANYONLAND TOURS
**PO Box 460, Dept. V, Flagstaff, AZ 86002 USA. Tel: (+1) 602-774-7343.**
Four-wheel drive vehicle tours into Arches and Canyonlands National Parks in Utah, and into Navajo and Hopi Indian lands. Other National Park tours of Zion, Bryce, Grand Canyon also available on charter basis. 1-12 days, year round. Prices average $85-100 per person per day. All ages. Photography field expeditions with professional photographer, 4-7 days, from $595 per person, April-October.

## ECOSUMMER CANADA EXPEDITIONS
**1516 Duranleau St, Vancouver, BC V6H 3S4. Tel: (+1) 604-669 7741.**
President: Jim Allan.
Expeditions in the British Columbian wilderness and elsewhere: opportunities for kayaking, canoeing, skiing, photography and sailing. 8-14 days, mainly June-September.
Tents and meals included in prices of

C$700-C$2,000 plus air travel; sleeping bag required.
"A unique opportunity to experience Canada's wilderness, with a small group of like-minded people led by experienced naturalist/guides."
Minimum age: about 14 years with parent.

## INTERNATIONAL ZOOLOGICAL EXPEDITIONS
**210 Washington St, Sherborn MA 01770. Tel: (+1) 617-655 1461.**
Director: Frederick Dodd.
In business since 1970.
Recognised by Belize Tourist Association.
Holidays for 300-500 arranged annually.
Educational natural history tours in Belize and Guatemala. Two or three week expeditions from January to August. Birdwatching, tropical ecology and coral reef biology with expert naturalist guides. Cost around $50 per day (all inclusive) plus air travel to Central America.
"Experience the tremendous diversity of life in the rain forest".

## SOUTHWEST SAFARIS
**PO Box 945, Santa Fe, NM 87504-0945, USA. Tel: (+1) 505-988 4246.**
Proprietor: Bruce Adams.
In business since 1973.
Holidays for 100-200 arranged annually.
Natural history expeditions in New Mexico, Colorado, Utah and Arizona. 1-5 days May-October. Travelling by air and raft. Prices from $299 for one day to $1,695 for 5 days. Opportunities to explore the geology, archaeology, botany and history of the canyonlands of southwestern USA. Sleeping bag for camping trips required. Members help set up and break camp and assist with cooking.
Minimum age: 8 years.

## WHITEWATER ADVENTURES LTD.
**1616 Duranleau St, Vancouver, British Columbia, Canada V6H 3RJ. Tel: (+1) 604-669-1100.**
Whale watching trips along the coast of Vancouver Island. Three day Gray Whale trips off the west coast April-June. Cost approximately $250. Ten day Killer Whale trips along the Inside Passage June-August.

Also opportunities to see porpoises which gather to feed on salmon. Price $1,300. No experience needed. All ages.

# Africa

**ABERCROMBIE & KENT TRAVEL**
**Sloane Square House, Holbein Place, London SW1W 8NS. Tel: 01-730 9600.**
Gorilla tracking in Rwanda. 4 days. Hotel accommodation. Stalking the silverback mountain gorillas (Beringer) on foot in the Volcanoes National Park.
Minimum age: 12 years.
North American headquarters: 1000 Oak Brook Road, Oak Brook, IL 60521, USA.

**BRATHAY EXPLORATION GROUP**
**Brathay Hall, Ambleside, Cumbria LA22 0HN. Tel: (0966) 33042.**
Wildlife expedition in Zimbabwe in July-August. Price £1,050. Travelling extensively in the hot dry areas of the Chete Gorge recording animal populations, working along the shores of Lake Kariba and from boats counting fish-eating birds and contributing to wildlife conservation and management plans with the Zimbabwe National Parks organisation.
Ages: 16-22 years.

**EXPLORE WORLDWIDE LTD.**
**7 High Street, Aldershot, Hampshire GU11 1BH. Tel: (0252) 319448/9.**
Tracking gorillas in Virunga National Park and game spotting with Pygmy guides in the Ituri Forest of Zaire. Camping accommodation. 24 days from about £900. Price includes flight from London, accommodation, equipment, etc.
Minimum age: 18 years.

**SOBEK EXPEDITIONS, INC.**
**One Sobek Tower, Angels Camp, CA 95222, USA. Tel: (+1) 209-736 4524.**
Gorilla tracking in Rwanda in December and January. "The great apes live secluded, high on the forested slopes of Ruwenzori mountains and Virunga volcanoes in the border regions of Rwanda, Uganda and Zaire." Accommodation, all meals, local transport and visit to Akagera National Park included in price of $1,920 plus air fare to Rwanda.

Wildlife circuit visiting the national parks of Kenya plus Lake Kamba and the Victoria Falls. Price of $999 includes accommodation, all meals and transport in Kenya; air fare to Nairobi extra. Zambezi wildlife safari in Zimbabwe and Zambia including tracking of lions and visit to Victoria Falls. Price from around $2,000 includes air travel from New York.

# Asia

**ABERCROMBIE & KENT TRAVEL**
**Sloane Square House, Holbein Place, London SW1W 8NS. Tel: 01-730 9600.**
Wildlife tour in the jungles and foothills of Nepal. 16 days October-November, March-April. Accommodation in luxury tented camps and hotels, with meals. 4 days rafting down the Trisuli River. Other transport is by Land-Rover, dugout canoe, elephant and by foot. Opportunities to see tropical fauna as well as poinsettia and rhododendrons. Visit to Chitwan National Park includes 2-day trek into the remote areas of the park accompanied by Chikari guides, cook and porters. Activities include swimming and fishing for mahseer (Indian salmon). Optional extra week's tour of the remote Himalayan kingdom of Bhutan, as well as 5 or 6 day treks, fishing trips and river rafting in the Himalayas. Prices from $2,800 including return flight New York-Kathmandu.
Minimum age: 12 years.
North American headquarters: 1000 Oak Brook Road, Oak Brook, IL 60521, USA.

**PEREGRINE HOLIDAYS**
**Town and Gown Travel, 40/41 South Parade, Summertown, Oxford OX2 7JP. Tel: (0865) 511341.**
Wildlife, bird and flower observation tours

to India and Nepal. Various itineraries available; 2 to 3 weeks. Price from £1,900.

**SHERPA EXPEDITIONS**
**Link Travel Ltd.**
**131A Heston Road, Hounslow, Middlesex TW5 0RD. Tel: 01-577 2717.**
Wildlife excursion included in hiking holidays in Nepal. 3 days in the Chitwan National Park. Opportunities to see deer, monkeys, wild boar, bears and the one-horned rhinoceros while travelling through the jungle on an elephant.
Minimum age: 18 years.

## Australasia

**VENTURE TREKS**
**PO Box 37610, Auckland, New Zealand. Tel: 799-855.**
Guided field trips based in central North Island. 6 days January-March. Subjects include natural history, nature photography, volcanoes and landscape painting. Price NZ$459 including accommodation and meals. All trips are hosted by an expert in the particular activity.
All ages.

# Birdwatching

## England

**BARN OWL TRAVEL**
**27 Seaview Road, Gillingham, Kent ME7 4NL. Tel: (0634) 56759.**
Proprietor: D Tutt.
In business since 1973.
Holidays for 100 arranged annually.
Birdwatching and naturalist holidays in selected areas for individuals and groups of up to 8. 1-14 days throughout the year, led by Derek Tutt whose main interests are birds and butterflies. Binoculars and rucksack not provided. Warm waterproof clothing needed. Transportation in mini-bus provided.
Minimum age: 14 years.

**CASTLE HEAD FIELD CENTRE**
**Grange-over-Sands, Cumbria LA11 6QT. Tel: (04484) 4300.**
Winter birds and winter walking around Morecambe Bay, or winter mountain walking in the Lake District on Centre-led excursions. Accommodation in centrally-heated rooms in field centre; full board provided. Huge flocks of wintering waders alight on the inter-tidal mud of the bay; peak counts reach 140,000 birds. Price from £45 per weekend.
No experience needed but must be able to walk 4 or 5 miles and must bring suitable clothing and footwear for severe winter walking.

**THE EARNLEY CONCOURSE**
**Earnley, Chichester, Sussex PO20 7JL. Tel: (0243) 670392 or 670326.**
Birdwatching courses for individuals and groups. Accommodation available. Field trips arranged to explore the bird life in the variety of habitats in West Sussex, including wetlands and estuaries, woods and downland.
No experience needed.
Minimum age: 16 years.

**FLATFORD MILL FIELD CENTRE**
**East Bergholt, Colchester, CO7 6UL. Tel: (0206) 298283.**
Seasonal bird study courses in East Anglia in spring, autumn and winter. Instruction in bird identification, breeding, behaviour, song, migration and conservation. Prices from around £125 per week, £50 per weekend including tuition, accommodation and meals.
No experience needed.
Minimum age: 16 years.

**HF HOLIDAYS**
**Dept 43, 142 Great North Way, London NW4 1EG. Tel: 01-203 3381.**
Bird studies in Alnmouth on the Northumberland Coast and Derwentwater in the Lake District. 1 week May-June and September. Board and lodging provided. Daily expeditions to wide range of bird habitats with slides, recordings and lectures in the evenings. Opportunities to see ringed ouzels in the Cheviot valleys, and peregrines and pied fly catchers in the Lakes. Participants are asked to bring binoculars, strong footwear, Wellingtons, waterproofs, notebook and pocket field guide. Prices from £99. Reduced rate rail travel available. No experience needed.
Unaccompanied children: 16 years +.

**JUNIPER HALL FIELD CENTRE**
**Dorking, Surrey RH5 6DA. Tel: (0306) 883849.**
Bird study courses on the North Downs of Surrey. One week, sometimes less, throughout the year. Dartford Warblers and Woodlarks are usually seen. Price from £125 per week, £50 per weekend including tuition, accommodation and meals. No experience needed.
Minimum age: 16 years.

**THE LEONARD WILLS FIELD CENTRE**
**Nettlecombe Court, Williton, Taunton, Somerset TA4 4HT. Tel: (0984) 40320.**
Bird study courses centred on the edge of Exmoor. 7 days and weekends February-October. Prices from around £125 per week, £50 per weekend including tuition, accommodation and meals. Instruction on bird recognition and song. Warm waterproof clothing needed. No experience needed.
Minimum age: 16 years.

**MALHAM TARN FIELD CENTRE**
**Settle, North Yorkshire BD24 9PU. Tel: (072 93) 331.**
Bird study courses in the Yorkshire Dales in summer and autumn, with upland birds a speciality. Prices from £125 per week, £50 per weekend including tuition, accommodation and meals. Warm waterproof clothing needed.
No experience needed.
Families with older children welcome.

**PRESTON MONTFORD FIELD CENTRE**
**Montford Bridge, Shrewsbury SY4 1DX. Tel: (0743) 850380.**
Bird study courses in interesting Borderland country throughout the year. Prices from around £125 for 7 days, £50 for a weekend, tuition, accommodation and meals included. Beginners welcome.
Minimum age: 16 years, except on courses arranged specifically for young ornithologists.

**SLAPTON LEY FIELD CENTRE**
**Slapton, Kingsbridge, Devon TQ7 2QP. Tel: (0548) 580466.**
Bird study courses throughout the year. Varying habitats are investigated and bird songs are studied. Price from around £125 per week, £50 per weekend including tuition, accommodation and meals. Warm waterproof clothes needed.
No experience required.
All ages (accompanied children only).

# Scotland

**HF HOLIDAYS**
**Dept 43, 142 Great North Way, London NW4 1EG. Tel: 01-203 3381.**
Birdwatching holidays in Arran and Loch Awe in the Western Highlands. 1 week May or September. Food and lodging provided. Hiking excursions led by expert naturalists. Possibilities of seeing golden eagle, osprey, goosander and great northern diver. Participants are asked to bring binoculars, strong footwear and pocket field guide for identification. Prices from £99. Reduced rate rail travel available.
No experience needed.
Unaccompanied children: 16 years+.

**HIGHLAND SAFARIS**
**Kyle and Glen, Muir of Ord, Ross-shire IV6 7UQ. Tel: (0463) 870363.**

Partners: D Hulme, A Brebner.
In business since 1963.
Holidays for 250 arranged annually.
Birdwatching and wildlife holidays in the Highlands for individuals and groups of up to 12. One or two weeks Easter-August. Prices from £260 to £280 per week including boat trips, ferries, travel from Inverness, hotel accommodation and meals. Choice of 6 centres for holidays in: Isle of Skye; Morar and Rhum; Wester Ross; Sutherland border and Summer Isles; north west Sutherland, Handa and Cape Wrath; and Easter and Wester Ross.
No experience needed.
Minimum age: 14 years.
Unaccompanied children accepted.

# Wales

**DALE FORT FIELD CENTRE**
**Haverfordwest, Dyfed SA62 3RD. Tel: (064 65) 205.**
Bird study courses on the Pembrokeshire coast throughout the year. Prices from around £125 per week, £50 per weekend including tuition, board and accommodation. Courses in seabird ecology with visits to offshore islands (weather permitting) in the Centre's own vessel. The magnificent colony of gannets on Grassholm may be explored.
No experience needed.
Minimum age: 16 years.

**THE DRAPERS' FIELD CENTRE**
**Rhyd-y-creuau, Betws-y-coed, Gwynedd LL24 0HB. Tel: (069 02) 494.**
Bird study — especially song recognition — in the Conway Valley and Snowdonia throughout the year. The oakwoods around the Centre are the home of summer migrants, and nearby there are mountain birds and birds of prey. On the cliffs of Anglesey, there are colonies of seabirds including Puffins. Prices from around £125 per week, £50 per weekend including tuition, board and accommodation.
No experience needed.
Minimum age: 16 years.

**ORIELTON FIELD CENTRE**
**Pembroke, Dyfed SA71 5EZ. Tel: (064 681) 225.**
A "Spring Bird Course" for 7 days in May. Price from around £125 including tuition, accommodation and meals. Waterproof warm clothing needed.
No experience needed.
Minimum age: 16 years.

# Europe

**FIELD STUDIES COUNCIL**
**Overseas Expeditions, Flatford Mill Field Centre, East Bergholt, Colchester CO7 6UL. Tel: (0206) 298283.**
Birdwatching holidays in Europe, including two weeks in Andalucia in spring, and one week in Majorca in spring and autumn.
Bookings through: Miss Ros Evans, Flatford Mill Field Centre.

**ORNITHOLIDAYS**
**1-3 Victoria Drive, Bognor Regis, Sussex PO21 2PW. Tel: (0243) 821230.**
In business since 1967.
Member of ABTA; ATOL no. 743; recognised by IATA.
Birdwatching holidays throughout Europe including Lake Neusiedl and the High Alps of Austria; France's Camargue; north east Greece, the Spanish Pyrenees, south west Spain, Majorca, Andorra, Turkey, Arctic Norway, Bulgaria, Czechoslovakia and Yugoslavia. 15 day tours in the spring and autumn. Full board and accommodation in hotels. Visits by minibus or on foot to lagoons, salt pans, coastlines, meadows and mountains to see a wide range of birdlife. All tours are escorted by experienced British ornithologists. Binoculars are needed.
Minimum age: 17 years.

**PEREGRINE HOLIDAYS**
**Town and Gown Travel, 40/41 South Parade, Summertown, Oxford OX2 7JP. Tel: (0865) 511341.**
Birdwatching and botanising holidays in Greece during different seasons. Tours led by specialists. 14 days from £500.

**RAMBLERS HOLIDAYS LTD.**
Longcroft House, Fretherne Road, Welwyn Garden City, Herts AL8 6PQ. Tel: (0707) 331133.
Walking holidays near Cape Trafalgar, Spain for those interested in birdwatching. 2 weeks April-May and September-October. Hotel accommodation provided. Minimum age: 16 years.

## Arctic

**WEXAS**
45 Brompton Road, London SW3 1DE. Tel: 01-589 0500/3315.
Birdwatching, camping and driving in the Iceland Highlands. 15 days June-August. Travelling by mountain bus into the interior, bathing in thermal springs and exploring fascinating areas of glaciers, volcanoes and waterfalls. Abundant and tame birds. Price from £632 including return air fare. Membership required.

## Americas

**WONDER BIRD TOURS**
500 Fifth Avenue, New York, NY 10036, USA. Tel: (+1) 212-840 5961.
Partners: Manny Arias, Ben Galperin. In business since 1970. Members of: IATA, ASTA. Holidays for around 500 arranged annually. Birdwatching and natural history holidays in Trinidad and Tobago for individuals and groups of up to 16. Most tours last nine days all year round. Hotel accommodation. Prices from $545 not including air fare. Binoculars should be taken. No experience needed. Minimum age: 14 years.

## Asia

**ORNITHOLIDAYS**
1-3 Victoria Drive, Bognor Regis, Sussex PO21 2PW. Tel: (0243) 821230.
Birdwatching in southern India during January; northern India and Nepal in March; Sikkim/Assam in December. Tours also planned for Kashmir in August-September; New Zealand in October; Thailand in November-December. Guided by experienced British ornithologist and local experts. Binoculars needed. Minimum age: 17 years.

## Israel

**SOCIETY FOR THE PROTECTION OF NATURE IN ISRAEL**
13 Helene Hamalka Street, PO Box 930, Jerusalem 91008, Israel. Tel: (+972) 2-249567.
Birdwatching tours of Israel. Tailor-made for individuals, groups from abroad. 7-12 days throughout the year. Accommodation includes youth hostels, Field Study Centres, camping or hotels with full board. Expert guides accompany the coach tours. Opportunities to see some of Israel's 350 species of birds.

## Africa

**FIELD STUDIES COUNCIL**
Overseas Expeditions, Flatford Mill Field Centre, East Bergholt, Colchester C07 6UL. Tel: (0206) 298283.
Two weeks birdwatching in the Gambia, West Africa, March. Further details from: Miss Ros Evans, Flatford Mill Field Centre.

**ORNITHOLIDAYS**
**1-3 Victoria Drive, Bognor Regis, Sussex**
**PO21 2PW. Tel: (0243) 821230.**
Birdwatching tours throughout the year to
Morocco, Kenya (including Mount Kenya),
Botswana (Okavango), Zambia, Zimbabwe,
the Seychelles and Madagascar. Hotel and
lodge accommodation with meals.
Transport by minibus. Groups are led by
experienced British ornithologist. Gorilla
tour to Rwanda also arranged.
Binoculars needed.
Minimum age: 17 years.

# Botanical

## England

**THE EARNLEY CONCOURSE**
**Earnley, Chichester, Sussex PO20 7JL. Tel:**
**(0243) 670392 or 670326.**
Field trips to the Sussex coast and the
woodlands and chalk downlands of the
South Downs to examine the wild flowers of
the area. Help is given with identification,
and there are talks and slides of rare and
common wild flowers. Price for weekend
about £70 including accommodation,
meals, tuition and use of facilities.

**FLATFORD MILL FIELD CENTRE**
**East Bergholt, Colchester, CO7 6UL. Tel:**
**(0206) 298283.**
Wild flower study courses in East Anglia in
spring and summer. 'Fungi' in autumn.
Prices from around £125 per week, £50 per
weekend including tuition, accommodation
and meals. Woodlands, marshes,
riverbanks, hedgerows and coastal sites
provide a wide variety of habitat.
No experience needed.
Minimum age: 16 years.

**JUNIPER HALL FIELD CENTRE**
**Dorking, Surrey RH5 6DA. Tel: (0306)**
**883849.**
Wild flowers and tree study courses,
February-November. There is a wide range
of orchids in the area and some weekends
are devoted to this flower. There are also
'Lichens near London' and 'Fungus'
weekends. Prices from around £125 per
week, £50 per weekend, including tuition,
accommodation and meals.

No experience needed. Beginners may
expect much help with identification.
Minimum age: 16 years.

**THE LEONARD WILLS FIELD**
**CENTRE**
**Nettlecombe Court, Williton, Taunton,**
**Somerset TA4 4HT. Tel: (0984) 40320.**
Flower study courses centred on the edge of
Exmoor. Weekends and one week courses
February-October. Prices from £125 per
week, £50 per weekend, including tuition,
accommodation and meals. Waterproof
clothes needed.
Beginners welcome.

**MALHAM TARN FIELD CENTRE**
**Settle, North Yorkshire BD24 9PU. Tel:**
**(07293) 331.**
Flower study courses in the Dales lasting
one week, June-August. The Centre, with its
acid fen amid the limestone hills, offers ideal
habitats for a variety of flowers. Prices from
around £125 per week, including tuition,
accommodation and meals.
No experience needed.
Minimum age: 16 years.

**PRESTON MONTFORD FIELD**
**CENTRE**
**Montford Bridge, Shrewsbury SY4 1DX.**
**Tel: (0743) 850380.**
Wild flower study courses. 7 days, or less,
throughout the year. Prices from around
£125 per week, £50 per weekend, including
tuition, accommodation and meals. Warm
waterproof clothing needed.
No experience needed.
Minimum age: 16 years.

**SLAPTON LEY FIELD CENTRE**
**Slapton, Kingsbridge, Devon TQ7 2QP.**
**Tel: (0548) 580466.**
Wild flower study courses in a typical Devonian village. Prices from around £125 per week, including tuition, accommodation and meals. Warm waterproof clothing needed.
No experience needed.
All ages.
Unaccompanied children: 16 years+.

## Scotland

**HF HOLIDAYS**
**Dept 43, 142-144 Great North Way, London NW4 1EG. Tel: 01-203 3381.**
Wild flower holidays on the Isle of Arran. Food and lodging provided. Visits made to a wide range of habitats: mountains, moorlands, dunes, woodlands and wetlands. Price from £99; reduced rate rail travel available.
No experience needed.
Unaccompanied children: 16 years+.

**HIGHLAND SAFARIS**
**Kyle and Glen, Muir of Ord, Ross-shire IV6 7UQ. Tel: (0463) 870363.**
Botanical and wildlife holidays in the Highlands for individuals and groups of up to 12. One or two weeks Easter-August. Prices from £260-£280 per week including boat trips, ferries, travel from Inverness, hotel accommodation and meals. Choice of six centres for holidays.
No experience needed.
Minimum age: 14 years.
Unaccompanied children accepted.

## Wales

**DALE FORT FIELD CENTRE**
**Haverfordwest, Dyfed SA62 3RD. Tel: (064 65) 205.**
Flower study courses on the Pembrokeshire Coast. 7 days in spring and summer. Price

around £125 per week, including tuition, board and accommodation.
No experience needed.
Minimum age: 16 years.

**THE DRAPERS' FIELD CENTRE**
**Rhyd-y-creuau, Betws-y-coed, Gwynedd LL24 0HB. Tel: (069 02) 494.**
Flower and plant courses in North West Wales. 7 days or less May-August. Price from around £125 per week including tuition, accommodation and meals. Courses are available on 'Houses and Gardens of North Wales' and 'Practical Tree-Planting'.
No experience needed.
Minimum age: 16 years.

**ORIELTON FIELD CENTRE**
**Pembroke, Dyfed SA71 5EZ. Tel: Castlemartin (064 681) 225.**
Wild plant study course on coastal vegetation. Price from around £125 per week, including tuition, accommodation and meals. Waterproof and warm clothing needed.
No experience needed.
Minimum age: 16 years.

## Europe

**FIELD STUDIES COUNCIL**
**Overseas Expeditions, Flatford Mill Field Centre, East Bergholt, Colchester CO7 6UL. Tel: (0206) 298283.**
Wild flower holidays, with opportunities to study butterflies as well, in the Pyrenees, Andalucia, Majorca, the Dordogne, the Burren in Eire and Mount Olympus in northern Greece.
Bookings through: Miss Ros Evans, Flatford Mill Field Centre.

**RAMBLERS HOLIDAYS**
**Longcroft House, Fretherne Road, Welwyn Garden City, Herts. AL8 6PQ. Tel: (0707) 331133.**
Alpine flowers and photography holidays in the Pyrenees, the Dolomites, Pindos and Olympus areas of Greece and Crete. 2 weeks May-July. Hotel accommodation.

Average of 5-6 hours of hiking daily to upper slopes, ridges, meadows and valleys. As the snow melts, the meadows are covered with narcissi and other alpine flowers. Holidays arranged with ample time for photography. Boots or shoes with moulded rubber soles needed. Minimum age: 16 years.

# Israel

## SOCIETY FOR THE PROTECTION OF NATURE IN ISRAEL
**13 Helene Hamalka Street, PO Box 930, Jerusalem 91008, Israel. Tel: (+972) 2-249567.**
Botany tours with several hours of hiking each day in Israel. Tailor-made for groups from abroad. 7-12 days throughout the year. Accommodation includes youth hostels, hotels, Field Study Centres and hotels with full board. Expert guides

accompany the tours. Israel has over 3,000 different species of plant including many wild flowers which cannot be seen outside Israel.

# Asia

## FIELD STUDIES COUNCIL
**Overseas Expeditions, Flatford Mill Field Centre, East Bergholt, Colchester CO7 6UL. Tel: (0206) 298283.**
Two week wild flower holiday with opportunities for birdwatching in Nepal. Bookings through: Miss Ros Evans, Flatford Mill Field Centre.

## TRAVELLERS
**Waterside, Kendal, Cumbria LA9 4HE. Tel: (0539) 28334.**
Botanical journeys and expeditions in the Himalayas. Travelling with well known naturalists in Nepal, Sikkim and India.

# Safari

# Arctic

## SPECIAL ODYSSEYS
**PO Box 37, Medina, Washington 98039, USA. Tel: (+1) 206-455-1960.**
Wildlife treks in the Canadian arctic. 6 or 8 days in May. Camping in tents or igloos. Travel by snowmobile across the ice-floes. Chances to see caribour, seal, wolves, arctic hare and snowy owls. Groups led by Eskimo guide.

## TWICKENHAM TRAVEL
**33 Notting Hill Gate, London W11 3JQ. Tel: 01-221 7278.**
Camping expeditions through the deserts, mountains and volcanoes of Iceland in June,

July and August. Transport is in high-clearance bus over rugged terrain. All food and tents provided; sleeping bags may be hired. Participation expected in erecting tents and (preferably) washing-up. Prices of around £620 includes flight from London or Glasgow. Additional extensions and tours available.

## YHA TRAVEL
**14 Southampton Street, London WC2E 7HY. Tel: 01-240 5236.**
Iceland Safari. 8 days July-August. Travelling by bus or landrover, camping overnight. Price from £418. Highlights include visits to Gullfors, Llandmannalangar Eldgin and the Skaftafell National Parks. 2 and 3 week safaris also available.
Minimum age: 16 years.

# Americas

## COLONEL SAM HOGAN'S SAFARIS
Casilla A-122, Quito, Ecuador. Tel: (+593) 2-450242.
Proprietor: Colonel S. M. Hogan.
In business since 1968.
Member of Ecuadorean North American Chamber of Commerce.
Holidays for 60 arranged annually.
Safaris by 4-wheel drive vehicle, speedboat and dugout canoe in the upper Amazon basin for small parties. 7 days all year round. Tented accommodation and American style camp cooking. Emphasis on photography and fishing with some hunting and anthropology. Opportunities for jungle walks and night trips to see varied animals and reptiles on sand bars. Price per person in group of 4 is $815.
Minimum age: 10 years.

## SOBEK EXPEDITIONS, INC.
One Sobek Tower, Angels Camp, CA 95222, USA. Tel: (+1) 209-736 4524.
Wildlife tours in June and July along the length of the Rio Tambopata in the south eastern Andes. Overland travel from Lima (5 days) followed by 10 days of rafting downstream through the Tambopata Reserve. Price around $1,500 plus air travel to Lima.

Jungle exploration of the Amazon based at the confluence with Rio Napa. Six days, originating at Lima, throughout the year. Price around $600 plus air travel to Lima.

Expedition by motorised canoe from Manaus (central Amazon) up the Rio Negro, "moving without schedule or physical goal, at the pace of surroundings." 15 days in March. Price around $2,000 plus air travel to Manaus.

Cruise around the Galapagos Islands studying the vast number of species of flora and fauna. 8 days throughout the year. Price around $1,000 plus air travel to Lima.

# Israel

## PROJECT EXPEDITIONS LTD.
36 Great Russell Street, London WC1B 3PP. Tel: 01-636 1262/3.
Directors: A. Jones, D. Mezzetti.
In business since 1963 (since 1973 under present name).
Holidays for 2,000 arranged annually.
Desert safari tours in Sinai. 6, 5 or 3 days throughout the year. Travelling by command car "in the footsteps of Moses", visiting Eilat, Wadi Nasib, St. Catherine's Plateau and Mount Sinai. Prices from £290 for 6 days including return air fare.

# Africa

## ABERCROMBIE & KENT TRAVEL
Sloane Square House, Holbein Place, London SW1W 8N5. Tel: 01-730 9600.
Camel and walking safari in the northen frontier district of Kenya. 4 days. Tent accommodation. Trekking to see giraffes, zebras, gazelles, etc. while camels carry the load. Opportunities to ride the camels, to fish and to birdwatch. Prices from $850 per person in groups of 4 including return charter flight from Nairobi. Mountaineering and horse riding safaris also available.

Wildlife safari in the Masai Mara Game Reserve of Kenya. 16 days throughout the year. Accommodation in luxury tents and hotels with all meals. Last 4 days of holiday spent at Malindi for swimming, underwater diving and marlin or shark fishing. Walking safaris are also available from the Kichwa Tembo Camp. Other safaris in Zambia, Tanzania, Zimbabwe, Malawi, Botswana, Namibia and Rwanda available with visits to a variety of game parks, Mount Kilimanjaro, Mount Kenya, etc. Prices from $2,500 including return flight New York-Nairobi.
Minimum age: 12 years.
North American headquarters: 1000 Oak Brook Road, Oak Brook, IL 60521, USA.

**ADVENTURE AFRICA**
**9 The Square, Ramsbury, Marlborough,**
**Wiltshire SN8 2PE. Tel: (0672) 20569.**
Directors: Ben & Carole Satterthwaite.
In business since 1974.
Personally escorted, small group, tented
wildlife safaris ideal for photographers, bird-
watchers, etc. In Kenya during January,
August and December visiting Masai Mara,
Amboseli, Mount Kenya, Samburu and Rift
Valley Lakes with the Indian Ocean. 14
days — £985, or 28 days — £1,570, all
inclusive. Special safari within Namibia: 21
days visiting the Kalahari, Etosha Pan,
Namib, Fish River Canyon, Ai-Ais Hot
Springs. Departing May, all inclusive,
£1,325. Day-by-day safari itineraries
available.

**AFRO VENTURES (PTY) LTD.**
**PO Box 10848, Johannesburg 2000, South**
**Africa. Tel: (+27) 11-29 7601.**
Directors: Mr & Mrs A Simpson.
In business since 1972.

Member of: Association of South African
Travel Agents, South African Tour and
Safari Association.
Holidays for 1,000 arranged annually.
Camping and hotel safaris in Southern
Africa for individuals in groups of 8 or 16
with guides with in-depth knowledge of
Africa. Transport by Land-Rovers which
have been modified to cope with the
toughest territory. 8-25 days throughout the
year. Safaris arranged in South Africa,
Botswana, Namibia, Victoria Falls and the
Cape, with many well-stocked game
reserves. Activities include exploring
swamps by dugout canoe, ostrich-riding,
sleeping in authentic Kalahari Desert, Fish
River Canyon, Victoria Falls and Zulu
kraals, visits to the wilderness of the cave
paintings. Opportunities to see wildebeest,
kudu, giraffe and fish eagles. Full camping
participation expected. All equipment is
provided except sleeping bags. Prices from
£350-£880 from Johannesburg; food kitty
from £23.

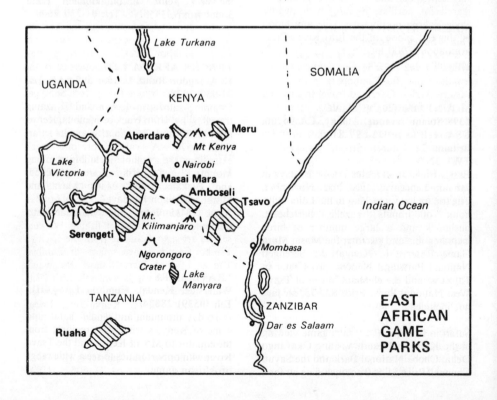

Minimum age: 12 years.
UK agent: Tempo Travel, 337 Bowes Road, London N11 1BA. Tel: 01-361 1131.
North American agent: Adventure Center, 5540 College Avenue, Oakland, CA 94618.

## EXODUS EXPEDITIONS LTD.
**All Saints Passage, 100 Wandsworth High Street, London SW18 4LE. Tel: 01-870 0151.**
Safaris in Kenya and Tanzania lasting 17 days throughout the year. Camping accommodation and truck transport. Cost from £350 (excluding air travel) plus food kitty from £60. Mombasa, Mount Kenya and Kilimanjaro available as extensions.

## EXPLORE WORLDWIDE LTD.
**7 High Street, Aldershot, Hampshire GU11 1BH. Tel: (0252) 319448/9.**
24 day safari in Zaire in the region of the Ruwenzori Mountains, January, February, July-September and December. Hiking to search for gorillas, hunting with pygmy guides, photospotting crocodile and hippo by dug-out canoe on the Ituri River. Price from about £900 inclusive.
Minimum age: 18 years.

## MOUNTAIN TRAVEL INC.
**1398 Solano Avenue, Albany, CA 94706, USA. Tel: (+1) 415-527 8100.**
**Britain: 22 Church Street, Twickenham TW1 3NW.**
East African trekking safari for 20 days in January-February, July and November. The trip includes trekking in the Loita Hills, home of impala, gazelle, hartebeest, bushbuck and a large number of birds including ibis and parrots; the Masai Mara Game Reserve in Kenya; the Serengeti National Park and Ngorongoro Crater in Tanzania and the elephant haven of Tsavo West National Park. Price $2,375, air fare not included.

Safari in Botswana. 18 days game viewing in the Kalahari Desert. Visiting Okavango Delta, Chobe National Park and the Savuti Channel. Price $1,650 not including air fare.

## SOBEK EXPEDITIONS, INC.
**One Sobek Tower, Angels Camp, CA 95222, USA. Tel: (+1) 209-736 4524.**
Zambezi wildlife safari taking in the Bumi Hills, Hwange National Park and the Victoria Falls, plus whitewater rafting or boating on the Zambezi. Price from around $2,000 for 12 days, including flights on KLM from New York via Amsterdam. Three other safaris may be added as optional extras to the main expedition: Kenya Wildlife Circuit (about $1,200). Parks of Botswana ($1,600) and Wilderness Waters and Trails ($1,000).
"The classic African adventure."

## THOMAS COOK HOLIDAYS — MARLBORO ADVENTURE TRAVEL
**Thorpe Wood, PO Box 36, Peterborough PE3 8LB. Tel: (0733) 63200.**
Wildlife safaris in Tanzania, Kenya and Rwanda. 14-23 days departing throughout the year. Tented accommodation. Land prices from £345.

## TRACKS AFRICA LTD.
**12 Abingdon Road, London W8 6AF. Tel: 01-937 3028.**
Camping safaris in Kenya and Tanzania travelling by safari truck or minibus. Kenya price £370 and Tanzania Serengeti safari price £570. A variety of one week extensions are available including climbing Mounts Kenya or Kilimanjaro price £255, and Turkana truck, Masai Mara and Mombasa beach holidays.
Ages: 18-35 years, but young at heart welcome.

## TRAVELLERS
**Waterside, Kendal, Cumbria LA9 4HE. Tel: (0539) 28334.**
A 16 day mountain and wildlife safari into some of Kenya's wilderness regions, from the equator to Mount Kenya and the Tsavo River with opportunities to see a wide range of African game.

# Asia

**EXPLORE WORLDWIDE LTD.**
**7 High Street, Aldershot, Hampshire GU11**
**1BH. Tel: (0252) 319448/9.**
15 or 22 days in Rajasthan State, India,
including a 5-day camel safari through the
Great Thar Desert to Jaisalmer. Travel in
small groups, maximum 16 persons. Tented
accommodation during safari, hotels and
resthouses elsewhere. All equipment (except
sleeping bag) provided. Price including flight
from London from £925 November-
February.
Minimum age: 18 years.

# Australasia

**AMESZ ADVENTURE CHARTERS**
**223 Collier Road, Bayswater, Western**
**Australia 6053. Tel: (+61) 9-271 2696.**
Safaris across Western Australia, the
Northern Territory and the Great Sandy
Desert for individuals and groups of up to
20. 7-35 days throughout the year. Travel in
four wheel drive safari wagons and coaches.
Price around A$55 to A$85 per day
including transport, equipment and meals.
Opportunities for photography, swimming,
walking, riding and visiting early historical
settlements, rugged mountains, tropical
waterholes and uninhabited deserts.
No experience needed.
All ages.
Bookings through: Amesz Charters, PO
Box 232, Morley, WA 6062.

**TRANSCONTINENTAL SAFARIS**
**'The Ravine' Wildlife Park, PMB 251,**
**Kingscote, Kangaroo Island, South**
**Australia 5223. Tel: (+61) 848-93256.**
Directors: M R and P H Ellis.
In business since 1965.
Outback safaris by four wheel drive
vehicles, camel and boat throughout the
year. Short safaris around Kangaroo Island
by vehicle and camel. Typical price for a 14
day camel trek and vehicle safari: A$980 all
inclusive.
"Travelling with camels where no white man
has been before."

# Windsurfing and Surfing

WINDSURFING, also known as boardsailing and sailboarding, became popular about 15 years ago in California by attaching a mast and sail to a surf-board; it has since become a very widespread participant sport. There are now more than 100,000 windsurfers on European waters alone, and it was accepted as a new sport for the 1984 Olympic Games. In Hawaii, a new freestyle has evolved which requires that the windsurfer sail fast into the surf and use the wave as a ramp from which to take off.

In the UK there are around 60 approved International Windsurfer Schools which offer courses for beginners. Instruction progresses from a dry land simulator which is a windsurfer mounted on springs, to a moored windsurfer to learn about balance and control and finally to freesailing and the principles of tacking and gybing. Most people can learn to stand and experience the thrill after just an hour or two of practice. The schools provide the equipment: you only need to be able to swim. If you enjoy the sport you may wish to purchase your own board. A basic board costs from around £400 although you can find some kits from £250; a top racer can cost £800. A list of schools can be obtained from International Windsurfer Schools UK, Unit 10, Stort Valley Industrial Park, Bishops Stortford, Herts.

SURFING: It's one thing to grow up in Southern California or Australia and become a surfer, but quite another to take up the activity in Britain. To acquire some experience and improve your technique requires many winter weekends of clambering into a cold wet suit and braving the waters. But enthusiastic surfers forget the occasions when their hands turned blue, and remember only the sunshine and the 7 foot breakers. It is possible to surf intuitively and try to ride whatever wave is available. But it also appeals to the more scientifically minded who weigh such factors as the tidal position, the wind direction, underwater shelves, etc. The experienced surfer develops a fairly acute meteorological eye.

The only equipment needed is a wet suit for North European waters and the board. The advanced surfer may have a custom-built board made. However the average surfer can obtain a reasonable board for around £75. The beginner may want to hire a board before committing himself.

Many multi activity holidays offer windsurfing or surfing as part of their adventure weeks. See the first chapter for details.

# England

## BRADWELL FIELD STUDIES & SAILING CENTRE
Bradwell Waterside, near Southminster, Essex CM0 7QY. Tel: (0621) 76256.
Recognised by RYA.
Windsurfing instruction for individuals and groups of up to 40. Courses daily/weekends/mid-week/weekly April-October. Board and accommodation provided. Price from £8.30 per day.
Participants must be able to swim.
Minimum age: 13 years.

## CALSHOT ACTIVITIES CENTRE
Calshot Road, Calshot, Southampton SO4 1BR. Tel: (0703) 892077/891380.
The Centre has two boardsailing fleets with immediate access to the water. It also has the use of a large water tank canoe training pool where preliminary steps can be taken after training on the dry land simulators. Courses then progress to a sheltered creek and eventually to deeper water. RYA certificates issued. Prices from £44 (less for those under 19 years) per weekend including accommodation, food, equipment and instruction.
No experience needed.
Minimum age: 13 years.
Unaccompanied children accepted.

## EASTBOURNE SAILING AND WINDSURFING SCHOOL
11 Wrestwood Avenue, Willingdon, Eastbourne, East Sussex. Tel: (0223) 502674.
Windsurfing courses from April to October.
Price for five tuition sessions (including all equipment) £35; with bed, breakfast and evening meal, £95.
No age limits: unaccompanied children welcome.

## EUROYOUTH
301 Westborough Road, Westcliff on Sea, Essex SS0 9PT. Tel: (0702) 341434.
Windsurfing courses at International Windsurfing School, Thorpe Bay. 5 hours instruction over 2 weeks June-September. Paying guest accommodation arranged.
No experience needed.
Minimum age: 14 years.
Unaccompanied teenagers: 16 years+.

## HARBOUR SPORTS
The Harbour, Paignton, Devon TQ4 6DT. Tel: (0803) 550 180.
Proprietors: F Sobey, J Smith.
In business since 1980.
Approved by RYA.
Holidays for 500 arranged annually.
Windsurfing tuition and hire in Paignton Harbour on the South Devon Coast. 1 or more days throughout the year. Accommodation organised locally. Instructors are fully qualified and issue IWS and RYA Certificates. Half day lesson costs £15 including wet suit and other equipment.
Minimum age: 10 years.

## HOLME PIERREPONT NATIONAL WATERSPORTS CENTRE
Ardbolton Lane, Holme Pierrepont, Nottingham NG12 2LU. Tel: (0602) 821212.
Windsurfing courses and hire at large purpose built watersports centre for individuals and groups of up to 60. Open April-September. Water skiing, canoeing, sailing and fishing also available.
Ages: 12-60 years.
Unaccompanied children: 14 years.

## JIB-SET SAIL SCHOOL AND YACHT CHARTER
**Beacon Quay, Torquay, Devon TQ1 2BG. Tel: (0803) 25414.**
Windsurfing starter courses from April to October. Weekend or one week courses for RYA National Boardsailing Award, both with 12 hours of tuition, costing around £45. Accommodation not included but can be arranged locally.
All equipment except plimsolls provided.
Minimum age: 8 years (14 unaccompanied).

## OUTDOOR ADVENTURE
**Atlantic Court, Widemouth Bay, near Bude, Cornwall EX23 0DF. Tel: (028 885) 312.**
Sea and lake windsurfing for individuals and groups. Price for 1 week self catering £115 and for full board £157. RYA Certificate (beginners), Advanced Regatta and Fun Board Courses can be booked on a daily basis. Beach and lake locations provide a large variety of conditions.
No experience needed.
Minimum age: 16 years.

## PRINCES CLUB
**Clockhouse Lane, Bedfont, Middlesex TW14 8QA. Tel: (07842) 56153.**
Recognised by RYA.
Windsurfing and waterskiing courses for beginners. Full tuition given, first on dry land then later on water. Equipment can be hired by qualified windsurfers; intermediate and advanced courses available for waterskiers. Windsurfer beginners course around £35 for a full day including all equipment.
Minimum age: 8 years.

## SANDBANKS BOARDSAILING SCHOOL
**43 Panorama Road, Sandbanks, Poole, Dorset BH13 7RA. Tel: (0202) 709231.**
Proprietors: H Poole, J Speigal.
Windsurfing courses at Sandbanks in sheltered harbour or open sea for individuals and groups of 5-20. Short or weekly courses throughout the year. All types of accommodation available locally. Courses including tuition and use of wetsuits from £10. Rubber soled shoes

essential. Board hire available to competent windsurfers.
No experience needed.
Minimum age: 10 years.

## SKEWJACK SURF VILLAGE
**Porthcurno, Penzance, Cornwall TR19 6NB. Tel: (073 687) 287.**
**Nationwide Holidays Ltd.**
Directors: A D Hemley, C D South.
In business since 1973.
Holidays for 3,000 arranged annually.
Surfing and windsurfing holidays at Land's End. Short breaks or long stays from Easter to October. Prices from £35 per week including accommodation in tents, self-catering chalets or cabins, surfing and tuition. All equipment provided. Evening activities include coastal boat trips, barbeques and discos. Fishing, surf skiing, rock-climbing and horse riding also available.
Swimming ability needed.
Minimum age: 16 years.

## TOP MARK WINDSURFING
**110 Greengate Street, Barrow-in-Furness, Cumbria. Tel: (0229) 24740.**
Proprietor: Bill Nickson.
In business since 1974.
Windsurfing on Lake Windermere for beginners. Courses run April-September. Prices: £12 for 2½ hours or £24 for 5 hours, all equipment provided. Special rates for groups.
Participants must be able to swim.

## WELLINGTON WATERSPORTS
**Reeds, Three Stiles Road, Farnham, Surrey GU9 7DE. Tel: (0252) 724433 or (0734) 884438.**
Sailboarding courses on country park lake April-October. RYA starter courses, and National Boardsailing Award training. Advanced training also available. Prices from £20 for 6 hour RYA boardsailing award including all equipment.
Minimum age: 8 years.

## WENTWORTH SPORT AND LEISURE
**Tallington Lake Leisure Park, Tallington, Stamford, Lincs. Tel: (0778) 346342.**
Partners: H Strenge, J Cant.

In business since 1973 (since 1977 under present name).
Windsurfing tuition and hire for individuals and youth groups. One or more days May-September. Prices from £16.50 for three hour course. All equipment provided. Accommodation on caravan and camping site. Waterskiing, sailing and fishing also available.
No experience needed.
Minimum age: 11 years.

# Scotland

### ARDFERN SEA SCHOOL
**The Galley of Lorne Inn, Ardfern by Lochgilphead, Argyll PA31 8QN. Tel: (085 25) 664.**
Board sailing holidays for one or more days. Two day course of instruction available as well as hourly instruction. Participants learn on simulator and then may hire boards from the school. Wet suits and buoyancy aids may be hired.
No experience needed.

### CROFT NA CABER WATERSPORTS CENTRE
**Kenmore on Loch Tay, Perthshire PH15 2HW. Tel: (08873) 236.**
One, two and three day board sailing courses. Prices around £25, £40 and £55 respectively including tuition and equipment.
"Most participants can reach standard required for RYA Certificate within two days."
Accommodation not included in price, but various alternatives available locally.
Minimum age: 8 years.
Unaccompanied children welcome.

### LOCH INSH WATERSPORTS & SKIING CENTRE
**Insh Hall, Kincraig, By Kingussie, Inverness-shire. Tel: (054 04) 272.**
Windsurfing instruction and sail board hire May-September. 3-5 day courses midweek following RYA syllabus. Price £140-£154 for 5 days including accommodation and meals.

No experience needed.
Minimum age: 12 years.
Unaccompanied children: 12 years+

### TIGHNABRUAICH SAILING SCHOOL
**Tignabruaich, Argyll, PA21 2BD. Tel: (0700) 811396.**
Windsurfing holidays for individuals and groups of up to 20. 1 or more weeks from May to September. All equipment provided. Wide range of accommodation available locally. Courses from £67 per week.
No experience needed.
All ages.

# Wales

### ABERSOCH LAND & SEA LTD.
**Abersoch, Gwynedd. Tel: (075 881) 2957/2941/2408.**
Directors: Harry and Patricia Dodd.
In business since 1976.
Recognised by: RYA, IWS.
Windsurfing and waterskiing holidays for individuals and groups of up to 6. Daily courses available May-September. Price £25. No accommodation or meals available.
No experience needed.
Minimum age: 10 years.

### PGL YOUNG ADVENTURE LTD.
**128 Station Street, Ross-on-Wye, Herefordshire HR9 7AH. Tel: (0989) 64211.**
Windsurfing on Lake Llangorse in the Brecon Beacons National Park. Instruction, all equipment and specialist clothing provided.
No experience needed.
Ages: 12-18 years.

# Europe

### ACCUEIL DES JEUNES EN FRANCE
**12 rue des Barres, 75004 Paris. Tel: (+33) 1-278 04 82.**

Atlantic surfing holidays near Biarritz in the south west of France, six days from May to September. Price of 1,300F (about £110) including equipment, instruction, all meals and youth hostel accommodation. Travel to Biarritz extra.
Minimum age: 16 years.
IYHF membership card required.

**FALCON SAILING**
**4 Dell Court, Salcombe, Devon TQ8 8BW.**
**Tel: (054 884) 3451.**
Board sailing in the Ionian Sea west of the Greek mainland and near Bodrum in Turkey. 2 weeks April to mid-October. RYA instruction available for beginners and experts. Accommodation in villas at two Greek centres (on Paxos and Levkas); meals are taken at local tavernas. Half-board hotel at Bitez, Bodrum. Price from £220-£450 for 2 weeks including flight.
No experience needed.
Minimum age: 14 years.
Book through Falcon Sailing, 190(V) Campden Hill Road, London W8 7TH. Tel: 01-727 0232.

**MINORCA SAILING HOLIDAYS LTD.**
**287 Green Lanes, The Triangle, London N13 4XT. Tel: 01-886 7193.**
Windsurfing and dinghy sailing off the island of Minorca. 45 types of sailboard and 10 types of dinghy. Self-catering apartments or hotel accommodation with breakfast. Prices from £205-£495 depending on time of departure and length of holiday.
All ages.

**MULTITOURS**
**21 Sussex St, London SW1V 4RR. Tel: 01-821 7000 or Linkline 0345-01-0345.**
Maltatours UK Ltd.
Director: A G Zahra.
In business since 1973.
Member of ABTA.
Windsurfing in Malta available as option on inclusive tours. Holidays from around £150 per week self catering; sailboard rental £55 per week. Instruction available at £7.50 per hour or £55 for seven hours. All prices in sterling.
Book direct or through ABTA agents.

**DISTRICT OF NEUCHATEL TOURIST OFFICE**
**9 rue du Trésor (Place des Halles), Neuchâtel 2001, Switzerland. Tel: (+41) 38-25 17 89.**
Windsurfing holidays for beginners on Lake Neuchâtel. 2-6 days June-September. Hotel accommodation with half board. Prices from £54 per weekend including six hours of instruction; £110-£135 for 4-6 days with ten hours of lessons.
Some swimming experience needed.

**NSTS-STUDENT & YOUTH TRAVEL MALTA**
**220 St. Paul Street, Valletta, Malta. Tel: (+356) 624 983.**
Windsurfing holidays for individuals or groups of 10-30. One week June-September. Accommodation in lower category hotels with half board. 8 hours of accompanied windsurfing on "Hifly" boards for beginners and experienced persons. Visits to Comino and Valletta. Price about £90. Opportunities to go waterskiing, scuba diving, etc.
Ages: 14-29 years.

**PGL YOUNG ADVENTURE LTD.**
**128 Station Street, Ross-on-Wye, Herefordshire HR9 7AH. Tel: (0989) 64211.**
Windsurfing holidays for teenagers in the South of France. 5 days windsurfing with instruction followed by canoeing on the Ardeche River. Variety of rigs available for all levels of ability. Boards and specialist clothing provided.
No experience needed.
Ages: 12 years+.

# Israel

**TWICKENHAM TRAVEL**
**33 Notting Hill Gate, London W11 3JQ.**
**Tel: 01-221 7278.**
Windsurfing courses at Eilat on the Red Sea for individuals and groups. Price from around £350 for one week to £650 for two weeks including flights, hotel accommodation and Israeli breakfast.
All ages.

# Other Activities

## Archaeology

### Britain

**ANGLO-AMERICAN ARCHAEOLOGY**
35 Lapwing Lane, West Didsbury, Manchester M20. Tel: 061-445 3732.
Director: C J Crowe, MA.
In operation since 1981.
An archaeological research project in co-operation with Dumfries Museum. Exploring the vestiges of ancient chapels in Dumfries and Galloway, southern Scotland. Digging plus visits to local historic monuments. Each holiday is for one or two weeks in July/August. Adults: £105 (one week)/£180 (two weeks); under 18s: £81/£140; lower rates for school parties of up to five students plus a teacher. Transport from Manchester available for additional charge. Accommodation in large farmhouse near Castle Douglas. All meals provided. Minimum age: 10 years if accompanied by a parent or an older brother or sister, otherwise 13.

**COUNCIL FOR BRITISH ARCHAEOLOGY**
112 Kennington Road, London, SE11 6RE. Tel: 01-582 0494.
Director: H F Cleere, PhD, FSA, MBIM.
Established 1945.
Information on archaeological excavations throughout Britain advertised in Council's Newsletter/Calendar. Most excavations take place from March to September. 7-8 hours per day. Generally camping. Experience preferred but not essential.

**FIELD STUDIES COUNCIL**
**Information Office (AHF), Preston Montford, Montford Bridge, Shrewsbury SY4 1HW. Tel: (0743) 850674.**
Mediaeval, industrial and rural archaeology studies at several of nine residential centres throughout the year. Price from £125 per

### Anglo-American
# Archaeology

Join us in July or August for purposeful exploration in Dumfries and Galloway.

*Experience the reward of participation and achievement.*

Prices from £105 per week including tuition, full board and transport from Manchester.

*Beginners welcome.*

### Anglo-American
### Archaeology
35 Lapwing Lane, West Didsbury,
Manchester 20
**Tel: 061-445 3732**

week, £50 per weekend, including tuition, meals and accommodation.
No experience needed.
Minimum age: 16 years, except on courses arranged for families.

**FRESCO**
**23 Chilworth St, London W2 3HA. Tel: 01-258 3643.**
Partners: Jim Black and John Manley.
In business since 1984.
Archeological tours led by professionals currently working in the UK. One week in Normandy (commencing May 11 1986) based in Caen and Rouen, featuring sites associated with William the Conqueror. Price of around £290 includes travel from London, local transport, site visits, meals (except lunch) and accommodation. Ten days in Campania, southern Italy in autumn 1986; exploring Greek and Roman antiquities of the Bay of Naples, including Pompeii.
"The emphasis is on a low number of participants, the involvement of local archaeologists and a relaxing holiday."

## Arctic

**ERSKINE EXPEDITIONS**
**14 Inverleith Place, Edinburgh EH3 5PZ. Tel: (031) 552 2673.**
Expeditions to study the Vikings in the Arctic with an expert escort. Fly out via Copenhagen and spend 11 days in Greenland in August viewing sites, staying at small hotels. Opportunities also to see Eskimo villages, glaciers and scenic fjords. Price about £950.
No experience needed.
Minimum age: 16 years.

## Israel

**PROJECT EXPEDITIONS LTD.**
**36 Great Russell Street, London WC1B 3PP. Tel: 01-636 1262/3.**
Archaeological digs in Israel for 2 weeks at Jerusalem, at Tel Yoqne'am in the Jezreel Valley, July-August and at Dor on the Mediterranean. Prices from £260. 2 week digs are also organised at Lachish (southwest of Jerusalem) which was captured by Joshua, destroyed first by Sennacherib and later by the Babylonians.

# Camel Caravanning

## Africa

**JABALIYA TREKKING LTD.**
**36 Keren Hayesod Street, Jerusalem, Israel. Tel: (+972) 2-699385.**
Camel trekking in the Sandstone region and the desert mountains of Sinai in Egypt for individuals and small groups. 4-15 days throughout the year. Camping accommodation with meals cooked on campfire. All equipment provided and carried by camels. Trips accompanied by guides knowledgeable about the area including the archaeology, geology, history and biology.
Ages: 18-75 years.

**MOUNTAIN TRAVEL INC**
**1398 Solano Avenue, Albany, CA 94706, USA. Tel: (+1) 415-527 8100.**
**Britain: 22 Church Street, Twickenham TW1 3NW.**
Camel expedition in the Sahara. 19 days in December and January. Travelling by camel and on foot in the Hoggar Mountains of the central Sahara, an area of basalt gorges and volcanic spires. Guided by Touaregs, desert nomads, with the opportunity of sampling their way of life. Nights are spent around blazing fires being entertained by the dances, songs and drumming of the guides and sleeping under the stars, as there is no need for tents. Price $2,100, air fare not included.

# Asia

**MOUNTAIN TRAVEL INDIA PVT. LTD.**
**1/1 Rani Jhansi Road, New Delhi 110055, India. Tel: (+91) 11-523057.**
Camel safaris in the Great Indian Desert of Rajasthan. Tours begin in Jaisalmer near the border with Pakistan.
Bookings through: Mountain Travel India, c/o ExplorAsia, 13 Chapter Street, London S.W.1. Tel: 01-630 7102.
North American agent: Tiger Tops International Inc., 2627 Lombard Street, San Francisco, California 94123. Tel: 415-346-3402.

**SITA WORLD TRAVEL (INDIA) PVT. LTD.**
**F-12 Connaught Place, New Delhi 110001, India. Tel: (+91) 11-3311133.**
Camel safaris in the Thar Desert of India. Tented and hotel accommodation.

**THOMAS COOK HOLIDAYS — MARLBORO ADVENTURE TRAVEL**
**Thorpe Wood, PO Box 36, Peterborough, Cambs PE3 8LB. Tel: (0733) 64200.**
Five day camel safari in the Thar Desert of India as part of tour of Rajasthan. 21 days November-February. Prices from £690 plus air travel to India.

# Cave Studying

**SOCIETE SPELEOLOGIQUE DE WALLONIE**
**Rue du Magnolia 20, B-4000, Liège, Belgium. Tel: (+32) 41-657482.**
Non-profit making organisation.
Society founded in 1954.
Holidays for 1,000 arranged annually.
Cave studying in Southern Belgium. 10 days in August. Camp accommodation. Scientific study of caves (known as speleology), for people interested in their formation and structure. Youth hostel accommodation available in Ardennes all year round.
Ages: 15-35 years.
Bookings through: Société Spéléologique de Wallonie, Rue Jules Verne 10, B-4900 Liège, Angleur, Belgium. Tel: (+32) 41-657482.

# Falconry

**BRITISH SCHOOL OF FALCONRY**
**Stelling Minnis, Canterbury, Kent CT4 6AQ. Tel: (0227 87) 575.**
Proprietors: Stephen and Emma Ford.
In business since 1981.
Courses for 100 arranged annually.
Falconry courses for 6 days February-July.
Beginners course flying a common buzzard and Advanced courses with a Harris Hawk. Prices from £130 (non-residential) and £180 including accommodation and meals. "The only professional school in the world specialising purely in teaching falconry". Minimum age: 12 years.

## SEE THE BRITAIN NO-ONE ELSE SEES

Six days camping in Rural Wales and Prehistoric England.
This will be nothing like your last bus tour!
Fare £89 inclusive

**BLUE HEDGEHOG TRAVEL**
**3 Strode Road, London SW6 6BL**
**01-381 2296**

# Special Tours and Expeditions

**BLUE HEDGEHOG TRAVEL**
**3 Strode Road, London SW6 6BL. Tel: 01-381 2296.**
Proprietors: R H W Smith, J P Gunningham.
In business since 1984.
Holidays for 300 arranged annually.
Tours from London on the Blue Hedgehog bus. A wide variety of activities including hiking, pony trekking and visiting ancient monuments. Tents, sleeping mats and blankets provided. Price around £70 (includes transport and entrance fees) plus £10 food kitty. 6 day trips (Sunday to Friday), April-October.
Minimum age (unaccompanied): 14.
"We specialise in the little-known and unusual away from the normal tourist attractions. We don't get caught in traffic jams!"

**BRATHAY EXPLORATION GROUP**
**Brathay Hall, Ambleside, Cumbria LA22 0HN. Tel: (0966) 33042.**
Ski-trek across winter wilderness of mountain Sweden, living in tents and snowholes or igloos, climbing peaks and traversing valleys.

Climb and explore a remote part of Europe's largest ice-cap (in Iceland) and assess potential for future scientific studies.

Backpacking and whitewater rafting in SW United States, studying landforms and geology and examining impact of American Indian and settlers cultures.

Carry out field studies projects with a group of young Chinese in the massive Longsheng forest and in Zhangjajie, South China.
Prices from about £635.
Ages: 16-23 years.

**DERBYSHIRE ACTION HOLIDAYS**
**Kirby House, Main Street, Winster, Matlock, Derbyshire DE4 2DH. Tel: (062988) 716.**

Expeditions arranged throughout the world include cross country skiing in Austria and Canada and hiking in Spain and Yugoslavia.

**ERSKINE EXPEDITIONS**
**14 Inverleith Place, Edinburgh EH3 5PZ, Scotland. Tel: 031-552 2673.**
Dog sledging in Greenland and reindeer safaris in Finland for small groups. 2 or 3 weeks in March and April.
No experience needed.
Ages: 16-60 years.

**FIELD STUDIES COUNCIL**
**Overseas Expeditions, Flatford Mill Field Centre, East Bergholt, Colchester CO7 6UL. Tel: (0206) 298283.**
Field studies aiming to make original investigations in bio/geological aspects of Iceland. Also general history and landscape studies of Brittany and the natural history of the Scilly Isles.
Further details from: Miss Ros Evans, Flatford Mill Field Centre.

**IKARUS EXPEDITION GmbH**
**Fasenenweg 1, 6240 Konigstein, West Germany. Tel: (+49) 6174-7017.**
Directors: Dr Horst and Ursula Kitzki.
In business since 1979.
Expeditions of between six and 35 days in small groups. Over 400 departures annually: to Asia (Nepal, Tibet, China, India, Sri Lanka, Pakistan), central Africa, the Americas and the South Pacific. Prices in range DM1990-DM15,990 including air travel from Frankfurt.

**PEREGRINE HOLIDAYS**
**Town and Gown Travel, 40/41 South Parade, Summertown, Oxford OX2 7JP. Tel: (0865) 511341.**
Special interest tours including botany, ornithology, archaeology and wildlife to Greece and its islands, Italy, France, Spain, Sicily, North and South America, Turkey, Tunisia, Israel, Zaire, Rwanda, Galapagos, India, Nepal, Malaysia, Seychelles, Gambia and Tanzania. All tours are accompanied by a lecturer and administrator. Prices range from £395 for 12 days to £700 for 2 weeks. Long haul holidays from £1,800 to £2,200.

Can also arrange individual itineraries to most countries.

## REGENT HOLIDAYS
**13 Small Street, Bristol BS1 1DE. Tel: (0272) 211711.**
Directors: N Cairns, A Lloyd, N Taylor.
In business since 1970.
Member of ABTA, IATA.
Special interest holidays to unusual parts of the world. Rambling, fishing, geology, ornithology and cycling in Iceland, Greenland, Cuba, China and North Korea. Approved Albturist operator for holidays to Albania.
"The chance to visit unusual places with the benefit of an experienced guide."
Most holidays are unsuitable for children.

## SACU TOURS
**Society for Anglo-Chinese Understanding 152 Camden High Street, London NW1 0NE. Tel: 01-482 4292.**
SACU is a friendship organisation attempting to increase awareness and understanding of China. It organises special tours for societies, colleges and youth clubs as well as general tours. They also specialise in organising tours to meet the requirements of other groups. Special interest tours for 1986 include Chinese Cookery, Language Course in Beijing and Harbin, Women's Tour and Publishing Tour.

## SOBEK EXPEDITIONS, INC.
**One Sobek Tower, Angels Camp, CA 95222, USA. Tel: (+1) 209-736 4524.**
Expeditions originating in Santiago, Chile to Antarctica. Exact itinerary depends upon weather, but plans include King George Island, an elephant seal colony, a penguin rookery, research bases and Deception Island or Paradise Bay. Two weeks in November/December for around $4,500 plus air fare to Santiago.

## SOCIETY EXPEDITIONS
**723 Broadway East, Seattle, WA 98102, USA. Tel: (+1) 206-16-35.**
Cultural tours and adventure cruises to unusual destinations, for example cruising to Antarctica (16-35 days, from around $5,000 plus air fare to South America,

November-January) visiting Mongolia, the Galapagos and the Amazon. Guided by expert naturalists, historians or anthropologists.
Minimum age: 16 years.

## SPECIAL ODYSSEYS
**PO Box 37, Medina, WA 98039, USA. Tel: (+1) 206-455 1960.**
A 'swift but serious' expedition to both the true and magnetic North Poles. Originating at Resolute Bay, Canada; 8 days for around $7,000.
"After an advenure like this, it's all downhill."

## THOMAS COOK LTD HOLIDAYS — MARLBORO ADVENTURE TRAVEL
**Thorpe Wood, PO Box 36, Peterborough, Cambs. PE3 8LB. Tel: (0733) 63200.**
Husky sledging in Lapland. 15 days February-April. Chalet accommodation. Participants learn cross-country ski techniques and how to handle Siberian huskies. Price from £1,150 including travel from London.
Minimum age: 17 years.

## TWICKENHAM TRAVEL
**33 Notting Hill Gate, London W11 3JQ. Tel: 01-221 7278.**
Special interest tours in Iceland including birdwatching, geology, horse riding, photography and trout fishing. Three-day package for participants in the Reykjavik marathon. Holidays to Greenland also arranged.

## WEXAS
**45 Brompton Road, Knightsbridge, London SW3 1DE. Tel: 01-589 0500/3315.**
Overland train journeys using sleepers and good hotels via Russia, Mongolia and China to Hong Kong. 24 days May-September. Price £1,680 including flight home from Hong Kong.
Membership required.

## WILD & SCENIC EXPEDITIONS
**PO Box 460, Dept V, Flagstaff, AZ 86002 USA. Tel: (+1) 602-774-7343.**
Directors: Patrick and Susan Conley.
In business since 1977.

River rafting and you-row-it sportyakking down the major whitewater rivers of the western United States, 1-13 days, May-October. Overland vehicle tours into National Parks of the western United States, 1-8 days, May-October. Horseback trail rides or wagon train rides for groups, Grand Canyon area, 2-4 days, May-October. All camping equipment and meals provided. No experience necessary. Prices average $85-100 per person per day. All ages.

# Space

### SOCIETY EXPEDITIONS
**723 Broadway East, Seattle, WA 98102,**

**USA. Tel: (+1) 206-324 9400.**
Provisional reservations accepted for trips to space, orbiting about 300 miles above Earth. Society Expeditions plans to celebrate the 500th anniversary of Columbus' discovery of America with the first passenger expedition to space, departing on October 12, 1992. It is expected that this will use a 32-passenger module in the cargo bay of the NASA space shuttle, but other technological methods are being considered. Price estimated at around $1,000,000 (including full board) — but may be considerably lower; no cash deposits are being accepted at present. A physical examination and some special training will be required.
"It will be a shirtsleeve environment, just like sitting in an airplane."

*Husky Sledging*

# Index of Companies and Organisations

Advertisers are shown in **bold**

The first entry for each organisation (indicated by the first page reference) includes more details than subsequent entries.